PRAISE FOR
PLEASE UNSUBSCRIBE, THANKS!

"An extraordinary book. Simultaneously hilarious and deadly serious, *Please Unsubscribe, Thanks!* connects the dots to show how our time and attention got hijacked—and offers brilliant practical advice for seizing this unusual moment in history to build the saner, more joyful and meaningful lives that too often feel just out of reach."

—Oliver Burkeman, *New York Times* bestselling author of *Four Thousand Weeks*

"A potent slice of social commentary and strategic advice on re-claiming valuable time and personal joy. . . . Gambuto's enthusiastic delivery and practical self-help tactics will remind readers that significant internal work is necessary to clear out the clutter, making room for beneficial relationships in real life and online. Witty and passionately written, the book shows that 'there actually is time to process your life' once you eliminate seductive inbox offers, opt-in links, premium memberships, and toxic 'people subscriptions.' It all starts with the 'deeply gratifying' process of cutting the subscription cord and being wholly present for renewal with oneself and communion with others."

—*Kirkus Reviews*

"These years have left so many of us reeling and wondering: Where do we go from here? In *Please Unsubscribe, Thanks!*, Julio Vincent Gambuto offers answers. And energy. And hope. He recognizes the gravitas that this transformative time in the world demands and he approaches it with empathy and humor and practical solutions to help us cut out the bullshit and be happier, healthier, and more purposeful going forward. I need this book in my life and so do you."

—Sarah Knight, *New York Times* bestselling author of *The Life-Changing Magic of Not Giving a F*ck*

"What Marie Kondo did to your closet, Julio Vincent Gambuto will do to every other part of your life—and to your heart. You will be transformed. Joy and fulfillment await you on the other end. *Please Unsubscribe, Thanks!* will make you question why you didn't unsubscribe earlier."

—Ali Wenzke, author of *The Art of Happy Moving*

"Julio Vincent Gambuto is a necessary and urgent voice for our turbulent times. His essay *Prepare for The Ultimate Gaslighting* was a clarion call for change: individual and collective. I first read it during those dark, early days of the pandemic when the prospect of a return to normalcy seemed both dim and distant. I've read it several times since; it is more relevant now than ever, as we are starting the slow, strange return to 'normal'. . . . His prose is a rare bird indeed, combining intellectual rigor with th common sense of the Staten Island that we both grew up on. Julio has something to say and knows how to say it."

—Eddie Joyce, author of *Small Mercies*

Please
Unsubscribe,
Thanks!

Please Unsubscribe, Thanks!

How to Take Back Our Time, Attention, and Purpose in a Relentless World

Julio Vincent Gambuto

Avid Reader Press

New York   London   Toronto   Sydney   New Delhi

AVID READER PRESS
An Imprint of Simon & Schuster, LLC
1230 Avenue of the Americas
New York, NY 10020

First Avid Reader Press trade paperback edition July 2024

AVID READER PRESS and colophon are trademarks of Simon & Schuster, LLC

Simon & Schuster: Celebrating 100 Years of Publishing in 2024

For information about special discounts for bulk purchases,
please contact Simon & Schuster Special Sales
at 1-866-506-1949 or business@simonandschuster.com.

The Simon & Schuster Speakers Bureau can bring authors to your live event.
For more information or to book an event, contact the
Simon & Schuster Speakers Bureau at 1-866-248-3049 or
visit our website at www.simonspeakers.com.

Interior design by Ruth Lee-Mui

Manufactured in the United States of America

1   3   5   7   9   10   8   6   4   2

Library of Congress Cataloging-in-Publication Data has been applied for.

ISBN 978-1-6680-0954-3
ISBN 978-1-6680-0955-0 (pbk)
ISBN 978-1-6680-0956-7 (ebook)

For Peter, Lisa, Alan, and Andrew

You wouldn't believe what's been going on down here.

Contents

Welcome

Welcome to the 2020s. That's the message I beamed from my laptop to the flat screen on the wall. A digital decoration to welcome the new decade. On the morning of January 1, 2020, my friends and I gathered in my compact New York City apartment for brunch—fruit, champagne, hard-boiled eggs for the clean eaters and fluffy pancakes for those who wanted to push off any resolutions that didn't permit syrup. (The gays can be very particular.) I'm a nerd, with nerd friends, so conversation soon centered on whether 2020 was by definition the last year of the teens or the first year of the '20s. As you can imagine, it was a spirited debate. Either way, we could feel deep in our bones that a new chapter was beginning in the world. We expected flapper dresses and endless parties, "the future," full steam ahead. We toasted to that exactly: the future.

In truth, I had run out of steam by the time I raised my Crate & Barrel long-stem champagne flute. I had spent the last four years shuttling very enthusiastically between Los Angeles and New York, living the coveted bicoastal lifestyle that every up-and-coming film-and-television producer obnoxiously drops into conversation (and books, apparently) in the chic eateries of both WeHo and SoHo. It was all very high-flying, as I ping-ponged on United Airlines. I bought a memory-foam travel pillow. I asked Santa Claus (me) for a Samsonite hard-top spinner suitcase in "brushed black." I signed up for CLEAR; they scanned my eyeballs. Month after month, I was mastering the airline miles game like my nephews were mastering Fortnite. My quest was made possible by real planes and rental cars and the universal American belief that *you go where the work is.* Like my nephews, I wanted to win. At twenty-two years old, when I first subscribed to this fantasy life, it was the epitome of winning. It was all very romantic. At forty-two, it was all very exhausting.

Then the world stopped. And life fell off a steep cliff.

Pretty soon, like billions around the world, I was bathing my produce in antiviral wash, leaving packages in the corner to decontaminate, and avoiding the breath of other humans. You remember. You were there. You saw the madness that followed. We all did. Plainly put, it was a shitshow—one that killed more than a million people in the United States.

We are all sick of talking about the pandemic. I get it. There is still so much to learn from it, though—profound lessons that apply directly to the world right now. This book isn't about the pandemic, but it will be a very helpful reference point. So, I will call it by a new name in these pages: *the circus.* That's a completely arbitrary choice. We could call it *the crisis*, *the microwave*, or *the blue flamingo.* I just don't want you to have to bear the weight of "the pandemic" every time you read the word. Circuses are full of fun and acts that amaze. That should lighten the mood enough. They are also full of moments that you might call completely batshit crazy. That should keep us close enough to the truth of what it was.

It is now years after the circus brought the world to a screeching halt. Are we firmly on the other side? That's a hard question to answer when we can still see its effects—tiny and tectonic—almost everywhere. What I know for sure is that we are all wondering just how solid the ground we stand on really is. And we're looking ahead at the remainder of this decade and this century with much clearer eyes. *Hmm, this is not the future we were promised.* At the very least, this is not the future we all thought we were working so hard to create. This is a weird, alternate timeline where volatility and chaos reign, the extremes have the mic, the cynics are winning, and the robots are taking over. Um, what the fuck is this?*

This book is about breaking up. It's about breaking out. It's about shedding, shredding, and severing the ties and tethers that keep *this* version of the future alive, strong, and seemingly indomitable, so we can build a future—for ourselves, our loved ones, and our nation—that we are truly proud of, one that gets us out of bed filled with energy instead of fear, one that honors our common humanity instead of one that empowers the shameless assholes around us to continue to be their worst selves. It is time to stop feeling bad about wanting better and saying so. Very loudly.

These years—from that January morning to the circus to now—have revealed a powerful truth that will forever change us, if we would just let it: *all of this is a choice.* Look, I get it. It feels horrible if we stop and truly take that on. It feels like shit to accept the idea that all of us, together, as a whole, created the mess around us. It's easier to just say "they" did it. Insert your version of "they." But trapped at home, streets silent, the world at a standstill, we learned from the circus that society as we know it is just the direct outcome of all the choices we make when we leave our houses or turn on our screens. And of all the choices our leaders make *for us.* When we stop making the same choices over and over, it all transforms. Instantly. We saw it with our own eyes. If we can acknowledge this and own it, we can know our own power and choose a new and better future individually and collectively.

I refused, for decades, to "choose a new and better future" for myself because I completely believed that my running and going and flying

---

* I don't mean to offend. I'll be sparing with my use of profanity. These are extreme times in the world, and sometimes these words serve to express the fury so many of us feel.

and sprinting was how I would achieve happiness. *Look at me! I'm successful!* Like I said, I'm a nerd. I was raised to achieve, as if happiness were a degree I could earn, a trophy, an award. That was the trap I was caught in, one that ensnared me (or, that I chose into) a very long time ago. That was my personal "infinite loop"—a concept I will spend a lot of time unpacking for us in this book. That loop was an automated cycle of stress and anxiety, a constant need for praise and validation. It was a never-ending treadmill that found me, at forty-two, at that New Year's brunch, surrounded by friends but lonely, clinking champagne glasses but still ashamed of being a working-class kid, merry and gay but never really proud. I was, in a word, unhappy.

But the circus kicked my ass. Like, kicked it. It was horrific. I was trapped in my apartment solo for six months. Friends fled the city in droves. Family stayed in lockdown an hour away. I had no salary to speak of. Checks bounced daily. Five family friends died. Eighteen of us in my immediate family (I'm Italian American; eighteen is just our inner circle) got Original COVID all on the same day, Christmas 2020. My stepfather was alone in the hospital on a breathing tube for weeks. I was on bed rest for six weeks, fighting intense lethargy. The man who is now my fiancé lost his brother; his brother died at forty, within five days of getting the virus. Punch, punch, punch, punch.

Around me New York City was reckoning with catastrophe at an unfathomable scale. At the height of the first wave of the circus, New York was losing a thousand people a day. We love being the center of the universe. Not this time. It was excruciating. Five weeks in, we had lost the equivalent of three 9/11s. The grand total would eventually come to fourteen. (What a horrific practice to use 9/11 as a multiplier.) For months, you could hear only ambulances in the streets. Until those same streets were flooded with protestors, riots, and workers rushing to board up the Prada store. Manhattan became unrecognizable, something out of *Mad Max*. Grocery stores resembled war zones; uniformed guards manned the entrances. Subway doors opened to empty platforms at Times Square. Cars, cabs, and commuters disappeared. Desolate and depressed, the city that never sleeps finally slept.

Look, it's not a suffering contest. The whole world had it bad. I'm just sharing my experience so you understand my point of view. The circus was a *worldwide* disaster, but there was a certain intensity here, created by the sheer concentration of despair, that did some very bizarre things to us all. It was impossible to avoid being forever changed by it.

It took the circus coming to town to open my eyes. It took the world coming to a full stop to wake me up. But, hey, I'll take it. It's just how it all happened.

It's also how I found my way to you and to this page.

A month into the crisis, nightfall couldn't come fast enough in my shoebox apartment. As soon as the dishes were clean from dinner (uh, *dish*), I climbed into bed, letting the darkness of the moment come over me, weighing me right into the pillow, like a heavy hand that wouldn't leave my back, and I surrendered to the weight of it all.

The next morning, I would wake up and have those three or four happy seconds of total amnesia before the thought would download, flood in, and hit me: *this shit is still going on.* Masks. Social distancing. Zoom birthday parties. Google is reporting 33,578 American deaths (a high number at that time; imagine that). Ugh. Vertical. Coffee. Inbox.

And there it sat. An email from my favorite retailer.

Sale!

It hit me at the right place at the right time in precisely the wrong way. Only weeks before, this particular men's preppy clothier was one of the legions of brands who would politely militarize their email subscriber lists to explain to the whole country what they were doing to minimize the impending health crisis. And to teach us all how to wash our hands. Soap. Water. Left. Right.

But now, like a switch that flicked from on to off, the emails were back to business as usual; the only marker of time in them was the style of sweater you could buy for 40 percent off.

A sweater sale? Is this a joke? There is no toilet paper on the island of Manhattan. I can't wipe my ass, but you want me to click and order a $300 cashmere cable-knit turtleneck? Oh, shipping is free, you say? Any other day, I probably would have just deleted the email, but today was different. Today, the email sparked pure rage. I needed caffeine and a keyboard.

What emerged after my morning brew was a piece of writing of which I am immensely proud: "Prepare for the Ultimate Gaslighting," a two-thousand-word essay that I posted to Medium on Friday, April 10, 2020. In forty-eight hours, that essay went around the world. To date, it has had over 21 million readers in ninety-eight countries. Perhaps you were one of them. I send my gratitude to all those who read it and shared it. Yes, I am thrilled with its reach, but more important, I am proud of its message: *maybe this crisis is an opportunity for all of us to think deeply about what we actually want in our lives.* It was a unique opportunity I never intended on having: to say *that*, at that moment, to that many people.

Going viral froze me in my tracks. I was floored, then humbled, then very heartened, then totally disturbed. When millions read something you wrote over yogurt and granola—alone, angry, and despondent in your apartment—the experience is oddly spiritual. My perspective has not been the same since.

What heartened me was that I wasn't the only one who was questioning how our system was responding to the tragedy. I wasn't the only one horrified by the abusive inequities that had been laid bare. I wasn't the only one concerned that all the manipulation around us was about to get worse. Way worse. And I wasn't the only one who wanted and needed a change. A big one. Thousands got in touch with messages of support and thanks. A few found my email address so they could tell me to go fuck myself. (You win some, you lose some. Life goes on.) But most reached out with a discreet confession, some version of: "I am secretly grateful for the deep breath. I needed it. This is not working."

Throughout that weekend and all through the months of the Great Pause that followed, one singular thought kept rising to the fore: something is deeply wrong with how we're living if we were *that relieved* when it all stopped. Our way of life is in trouble. Because I am human—a self-centered human—I made it about me. *My life* is in trouble.

So, I decided to clean house. I am immunocompromised. I wasn't leaving my apartment or taking down my KN95 until there was enough data to prove I would survive. I had time on my hands. I was suddenly hyperaware of the gaslighting that my own essay had warned about, and one of the major theaters where "The Great American Return to Normal" was bound to play out was my laptop screen. So, I attacked my inbox, unsubscribing from brands, companies, gurus, influencers, groups, associations, committees, political campaigns, loyalty programs, monthly curated clothing boxes that automatically debited my checking account and sent me plaid dress shirts I didn't need to iron or tuck into my pants, and anyone and anything that fed my inbox their junk all day long. Click. Good-bye.

Three words came rushing back to me. More than a decade earlier, I had dissolved a domestic partnership with my boyfriend of five years. There was love but no longevity. For months after I left our five-hundred-square-foot apartment, I was unmoored. Shattered. Broken. So, I threw myself into my work. I sent out an e-blast (a relatively new word at the time) to a large list of family, friends, and contacts about a project I was launching. My ex-partner, whom I had kept on the list, sent a quick and short reply: *"Please unsubscribe, thanks!"*

I was gutted. I knew him well, and what he meant by the pithy request was this: "I am done with your bullshit. The relationship is over. I no longer want to be tethered to you. It just isn't healthy for me. It will continue to make me miserable." I thought that signing the paperwork at the Office of the City Clerk formally ended our relationship. Nope. These three words proved way more powerful. It was really over.

Now, 2020, stuck inside, as systems around me were failing, as my personal inbox kept filling, I realized that I, too, was tired of being tethered. I needed to break up, for real, with nearly everything. Click by click. *Please unsubscribe, thanks!*

First, I unsubscribed from what I will call "surface subscriptions" or surface bullshit. Feeling so good, I expanded well beyond screen and paper. I decided to unsubscribe from "people subscriptions" and the bullshit the toxic ones were bringing into my life, pulling away from or ending certain friendships and working relationships. Lastly, and much deeper, I began unsubscribing from my own personal bullshit, my "underlying subscriptions," certain ideas, beliefs, and notions I had about myself—some of which I had subscribed to my whole life, some that formed the very foundation of my identity and of who I was at work, with my family, with my friends, and in the world. Turns out, when you take the never-ending noise off your screen and you take some very time-consuming people out of the mix, there actually is time to process your life. And feel it. And question it. And change it.

While each of these three steps was progressively harder than the one before, I found myself happier and happier. I was onto something. I hadn't come undone; I had become *unburdened*. I was freeing myself from years of pressure under which I had begun to cave. I knew there was a joyful, peaceful, calm (even fun) guy buried underneath it all. I just needed to dig him out of a life of slow quicksand—a life that I had subscribed to for decades.

What started as a series of simple mouse movements kicked off a shitstorm (yes, that's different from a shitshow; two highly technical terms)—a beautiful shitstorm—that has called into question every part of who I am. The seemingly meaningless clicks were the first step to reclaiming my life and living it on my own terms, honoring my authentic voice instead of hiding it. It was also the beginning of looking at the world more distinctly through the lens of "we." Those three words, emailed a decade prior and once so stinging to hear, became the anthem and the mantra of the most important year of my life. And so, they are the title of this book.

This book is about that process, the journey I have been on since I decided to unsubscribe. I will call this process "unsubscription." Parts of it were conscious. I knew from my marketing and branding background what was happening on my screens and in my inbox and checkbook. That's the expertise I will share with you. Other parts of it were unconscious and could be named and identified only as I looked back. As a storyteller and moviemaker, I understood what was happening in my brain and heart. Those are the reflections I will share.

My project here is to create a framework for all of us to "unsubscribe" so we can truly renew our lives and create happy, meaningful, satisfying futures. It is also my radical plea—from one citizen to another—for us to put aside what divides us and work together to collectively unsubscribe, so we can build an equally meaningful future for our nation.

My unsubscription has been agonizing, fun, at moments devastating, but deeply gratifying. Now, not only do I have a clean inbox, but I also go to bed knowing the real difference between what I *need* and what I *want*. My work is ten times more fulfilling. My phone is quieter. My calendar only houses commitments that bring me joy or money. I have time for my loved ones—for their birthdays and their special moments. I have found romantic love and partnership after ten years of being single. I have a warm, kind, and comfortable home life for the first time as an adult. And what seemed a distant dream at that New Year's brunch—a family of my own—is now in the works.

Lest you think the picture I paint is too rosy, know this: I am still unsubscribing every day. This process is an ongoing practice, one that comes with constant mental and emotional goblins. The deeper you go, the more changes you make, the harder it can get. Sometimes it's like the best yoga class of your life. And sometimes it's a frustrating game of Whac-A-Mole. The first order of business is letting go of the need to "do" this process "the right way." Unsubscribing requires us to be wrong over and over and over. It asks us to stop needing to win all the time. It begs us to welcome failure in and have a coffee or cocktail with it.

A few important notes. First, I see the irony in my story. I could not have reached you with this book about unsubscribing—there would be no book—had I not been subscribed online to Facebook, Medium, and the J. Crew newsletter in the first place. This book's publisher could not have reached you to introduce you to this book—nor to me—without so many of the digital tools that I will critique. As you will see, this is a complicated conversation.

Next, I want to acknowledge that not everyone had the luxury I had of being solo during the circus. Don't get me wrong; it was isolating and distressing on so many levels. Like Tom Hanks called that volleyball "Wilson," I now call the mid-century modern lamp in my living room "Larry" (he who lit up the room when shit got dark). In the end my responsibility day to day was to myself, alone. Those with families, children, aging parents, and jobs that didn't offer the option of working from home—they all had a very different experience. Yes, that is a *lot* of people. Perhaps that was you. You and I may have little in common on paper. But you and I are both human beings who ultimately just want to be happy. And who want to live in a society that functions well. Like you, I am a citizen. I am a consumer. I am a customer. I am a patient. I am a voter. I am a subscriber. I, too, want to fucking scream when I call Verizon's customer service line.

As we discuss all things "we," please know that this book is not designed to be "a political book," at least in the ways that we have defined *political* in recent years in America: hyper-partisan, fabric-tearing, and blood-shedding. I will not be able to hide on which side of the political aisle I dance, nor do I wish to. But let's face it: we're all exhausted. Let me assure you, if you are a human alive right now, I am in your camp. If you want a better country and world to come out of the chaos of these years, I am aligned with you. If you are tired of the noise and sick of the bullshit we are all forced to confront, process, and manage every day, I am in your "tribe."

And that tribe is global. This book is not just for those of us here in the States. The American way of life, its economic system, its con-sumerist obsession, its democratic ideals, even Ross, Rachel, Chan-dler, Monica, Joey, and Phoebe are impossible to escape in much of the rest of the world. And so, I hope that our international friends know that there are well-meaning Americans asking important ques-tions to try to make change in our country and in the way of life that we export. I also hope that our international friends may take from this book our unabashed American confidence. We can change our lives and our country if we muster the personal and political will to do so. You may not like how loud we are at the Louvre, but we are a bold people who know how to get what we want. We are also a good people. Our system needs massive improvement.

This book is a mix of "how-to" process, social commentary, history, economics, philosophy, and practical and tactical strategies for indi-vidual and collective happiness. So, before we dive in, I want you to know where that all mixes, for me. My sense is that those all overlap in similar ways for many of us.

I grew up in the boroughs of New York City, the son of a school bus driver and a secretary, on Staten Island. Back in the '90s, on the borough's South Shore, collars were blue, politics were red, and the people were white, mostly Italian and Jewish. My parents were the children of immigrants. We had no money. We grew up on credit cards, macaroni, and love.

Mom and Dad worked tirelessly at multiple jobs to make ends meet in our eighteen-foot redwood condo. My father shuttled daily from his full-time gig (the bus) to his part-time one (as an Italian bread baker) to his third one (this one changed frequently). After commuting, working, and commuting again, my mother would lug her boss's heavy Smith Corona out of the trunk of her Pontiac and into the house so she could do overtime work at the kitchen table after dinner. But the mounting economic pressure of the '80s and '90s was too much. Three kids in braces broke the bank. After four small businesses, a crushing bankruptcy, a son's coming-out, a terrifying cancer scare, and more operatic domestic disputes than I care to remember (all stories for another time), the house of cards folded, along with their marriage. My grandfather came here from a dairy-farming town in Italy in 1946. Our family's life was supposed to be the American Dream. By 1997, it was an American Nightmare.

What got me (and all of us) through and to the other side was a ceaseless focus on "the future." The future was when it would all be okay, when it would all be "worth it." In the future, I would be happy. And safe. Oh, and rich. I didn't know at the time that *that's* what was driving me, but I was a child of the Clinton years. Becoming a millionaire was the goal—it was the success—especially when your parents went to battle nightly over the checkbook.

Despite the challenges of that time—and with the help and

support of a team of family, teachers, mentors, and friends—I was a late-'70s WIC baby (the Special Supplemental Nutrition Program for Women, Infants, and Children) who made my way to Harvard, where I was educated with the *über*-rich—tuxedoes, polos, and all. (I still can't golf.) My life now looks nothing like the life my sisters and I had growing up.

That social mobility has been a privilege. It has given me the opportunity to see life at each end of a very wide America. Plainly put, it ain't all pretty. I have experienced the darkness of wealth, how it carves out a space to do good in the world but asks you to beg for it, how it gives but hoards, how it turns up its nose inevitably when it's forced to consider those who have not, how it simply cannot—and sometimes *will not*—fathom the everyday needs and desires of the everyman.

I have also seen its grace and its generosity, its ability to think big, act with full vigor, and deliver. I have seen its vision and untiring energy. I have known well its kindness and unyielding support. I have learned from the wealthy that with great privilege comes great responsibility. Also: that the word *summer* is a verb.

At the other end of the economic spectrum, I have seen the ebullient charm of immigrants and working people, as well as their roughest edges, how they wish to include, elevate, celebrate but will rob you and themselves of great pride should you "forget where you came from." I have seen their grit, their determination, and their sweat firsthand. I have known well their boundless love, the open arms of their endless support and faith, and their selfless dedication to community, to a social network that is meant to offer strength without asking for a penny in return.

I have also seen their fear, their hope, and their longing for more, for respect and a simple seat at the table.

From custodians to congressmen and back, in all the communities

I have had the privilege of being part and at all the dinner tables I have sat, there are good actors and bad, "the good eggs" and "the rotten ones."

I am also gay, which adds an entirely different lens to my point of view.

At my highest high, I earned my master's and raised capital to start an independent film company, a dream come true. At my lowest low, just two years later, I had $2.17 in my personal bank account when the circus effectively pulled the rug out from under me. This roller coaster has been nauseating. I've spent thirty years trying to win. I'm done. There has got to be a better way.

I take the time and space here to share all that with you so you have fuller context for much of what I will say in this book about how the experiences of our lives predispose us and fuel our willingness to subscribe to specific ideas, people, and systems big and small. I also share it with you because I know there are far more of you who suffer through economic strife than our nation and its public conversation acknowledges. What most at the very top do not understand is that economic turmoil eventually becomes emotional suffering, physical pain, and spiritual anguish. Our families and our homes are each precious ecosystems of opinions and ideas, but also of emotions, expectations, dreams, and dollars. It is all related.

I have spent my entire life preparing for the future. Now it's here. Raise your champagne glass. Holy shit, it is not what I expected. I have used these last years to feel the pain of that delta—between expectation and experience—to mourn, to forgive, and to figure out how I can still have a happy and satisfying life with the remaining time I have on this planet. The answer I have come to is this: I must unsubscribe from anything and everything that is standing in the way of my happiness. Happiness, I have learned, is not that much of a pursuit. When you take the constant quest for it away, sometimes it's just there waiting. Perhaps we can transform our country, too, by staying off the treadmill, not getting back on. The treadmill goes nowhere. It is a game that cannot be won. The answer is not to run faster. It is to unplug the machine.

Here's why I unsubscribed, what that really means, what it all looked like, and how you can do it, too. If you want, please do join me.

Welcome to the 2020s. We're playing a whole new game now.

Introduction
Relentless

There's a reason "America runs on Dunkin'." It's because we're all fucking exhausted. If you're like me, life before the circus* was relentless. In fact, that's the word I would use when a colleague or friend wanted to meet up. "I wish I could this week," I would say, "but my schedule is relentless." If an email went unanswered or if I missed a text, my always anxious apology included a mention of my "relentless calendar." It worked well. It was guilt-free. I hate lying, and saying "Unfortunately, I'm not available" is a barefaced lie. I am available; I am just overwhelmed. I'm tired. And I haven't eaten lunch in three days. So, I blamed my schedule, and it never bothered anyone. It was universally understood. Why? Because as Americans, we have this in common: we're all busy. Busy, busy, busy. "Trust me, I get it" is how most people would reply.

After all, our lives have been relentless for a long time. If we're not running from a plane or a train to an Uber, we're fielding calls from a commuter bus or trying to figure out how to log on to the wifi on the subway (it never works) or texting at dinner while our kids fight for our attention. We give them an iPad to keep them occupied while we answer Instagram messages for our Etsy side gig while the Roomba cleans the floor. The stakes seem increasingly higher and higher for every business meeting, deal, conversation, and deadline. We think nothing of scheduling an in-person meeting

---

* I am going to use the word "circus" in place of "pandemic." Just in case you skipped the preface. Don't worry, I do it all the time.

across town, in "the city," or in Chicago when we live in New York or Atlanta. We pride ourselves on our United miles, our platinum flight status, our Starwood points, our ability to overcome the silly boundaries of time and space.

Our weekends are a rat race all their own as we dash from brunch to brunch or shuttle our kids from field to field, from one highly recommended college-prep pursuit to the next. Our kids are on the hamster wheel with us, learning to rush and go and hustle and shove a "nutrition" bar down so they don't miss the bus. Our communities are merely places we moved to, where bigger houses were built with nicer countertops. We're no longer *of* them. We seem to be just living *in* them.

And that's just for the privileged. For those who can't fly, drive, and Lyft from commitment to commitment, they walk, run, bike, and bus. Their relentlessness is a sprint from one job to the next. It is a limitless line of angry customers, backed-up food delivery orders, and building maintenance emergencies—the nonstop needs of an entitled public that demands to be served, fed, driven, fixed, watered, and waxed. Their day offers so little time for basic human needs that it is easier to pee in a bottle in a truck than to take a proper break.

Something is wrong here.

The relentlessness is, of course, driven by an economy that is always moving, forced to be constantly growing, ever-expanding—one that is rapidly and exponentially dividing us into only two classes of people in the United States: the rich and the not-rich. (Dare we say it, *the poor*.) The caffeinated go-go-go benefits the former and abuses the latter; the middle is dwindling fast. Somewhere along the way, the system that lifted millions out of poverty and into the comfortable reclining sectional sofas of the American middle-class suburbs is now the very system that is driving us all mad. We haven't made any of this sustainable. Instead, we have supercharged it all.

Make no mistake, we are paying a heavy price. In the United States, our levels of happiness and leisure time have fallen. (Surprisingly, those are actually measurable.) So has our life expectancy. Our standing in the world goes up and down like an erratic stock. Our *stocks* go up and down like an erratic stock. We love to tout that we're number one, but the data show otherwise. We may have an Alexa in every home (uh, middle-class home), like a proverbial chicken in every pot, but our lives seem to be less fulfilling, our schedules are busier, our families are struggling, and we are working more for less—way less relative to those in most C suites.

Our communities and our country are bearing the brunt of it all—incessant mass shootings (they returned immediately after the height of the circus), skyrocketing levels of depression and mental illness, a nationwide drug epidemic fueled in part by our own pharmaceutical industry, ever-rising racial disunity and discord, and a government and health care system that can neither absorb nor respond well to extended emergency. Security, stability, that which we want or need, always feel just slightly out of reach, so we just keep reaching.

As a nation—and even at our own family dinner tables—we are bitterly divided. We talk of civil war with disturbing ease. We now have states that serve as sanctuaries from other *states*. In some places in this "home of the brave," it is dangerous to behave in any way outside the strictest norms. Yes, it's always been that way to some extent, but I think we can all admit that this is not America in its finest form. It is so bad that no presidential election or political leader can carry the weight of the immense work we have ahead of ourselves as a society to heal, to figure out how to cooperate, to create meaningful progress together. And to protect and renew our greatest resource: the very planet we all inhabit. It is suffering greatly, and we seem to just be sleepwalking toward its demise, half measure by half measure.

These ideas have become laughable, derided as overly earnest—a true measure of just how far off course we really are. In the background, a twenty-four-hour news cycle rages on, as voracious in its search for drama as we are in our hunger for it. *Get the popcorn*, we joke on social media, *shit is about to go down*. Social media itself has eroded our interpersonal boundaries, making each of us painfully accessible, open, public, instantly trackable, ever findable. Private life is dead; our own courts are ensuring that. Our cable bill is rising, even though we cut the cord. (How does that work? Brilliantly if you're not the consumer.) The price of a cocktail in a major metro area is ludicrous; you need to drink at least three to make you forget the bill you're about to pay. College costs are so outrageous that many in the middle class feel both too rich and too poor to send their kids. And very few of us can afford to buy a home in the very cities in which we grew up.

All of this madness spins on top of a great modern lie: you and I—loving, good, well-meaning humans—we are only worth our follower count, our credit score, and our bank balance. That is our only value.

Yet it is blasphemous, even downright un-American, to ever stop and ask the question on everyone's mind: *Is this really the best way to live?* Worse, underneath it all is a powerful current of low-level but insidious fear, a fear we have gotten perfectly comfortable carrying around and making socially acceptable. No one wants to step off the speeding treadmill and live a simpler life because we're all terribly afraid of being left behind. I know I am. I'm petrified. What will I tell my parents, who have invested so much in me emotionally and financially? My friends from college, who all seem to be winning at life post by post and Christmas card by Christmas card? More important, my younger self—that nerdy, gay class president who wanted and yearned to be *successful*, to make the world proud?

Daily, we play a massive game of chicken—"you go first." And we power through it on Lexapro. (At least I did for the longest time.) We see the writing on the wall: the economic divide is no longer a crack; it's a chasm, and we can only live and breathe on one side of it. There's a reason the popular Silicon Valley joke is "HFBP"—Have Fun Being Poor. How disgusting. And if we stop for just a second to breathe, to take stock, to step away, or to question any of it, we are somehow ungrateful, even wasteful. If I do one thing right in these pages, it is my greatest hope that I can help us all create a space to do just that: step away and question.

What happened to the promise of the twentieth century? This is where it was all headed? *Here*? We worked tirelessly to become the most powerful nation in the history of the world so 2 percent of us could have trust funds and the rest could work round-the-clock? We won world wars and stormed the beaches of Normandy so we could gift the world Facetune? So we could stare blankly at the refrigerator at Whole Foods parsing the difference between cage-free, free-range, pasture-raised, farm-raised, and omega-3-vitamin-enhanced eggs? *I just want an egg! An egg! We all just want fucking eggs!* There are three hundred shootings a month in Chicago, and 38 million people live below the poverty line in this country, and we're asking voice-controlled AI assistants what types of eggs are the best? We have lost our minds.

How on earth did we get here? What do we do about it?

Let's take those conversations one at a time.

PART ONE

Subscribed

Or, How We Got to This Relentless Place

One
A Horse on Speed

This is a tale of two horses. I'm not an equestrian. I just love metaphors. Let me explain.

The narrative we repeat in America, over and over, at every Fourth of July barbecue and in every school pageant, is a simple but powerful one: We, the people, having been overtaxed and underrepresented in the British empire, banded together, rose up, expelled the British, and created a land of opportunity and promise. Why we did it reveals a tension that exists in our country to this day. *We were overtaxed* is an economic reason. We were tired of sending the king so much of our money. *We were underrepresented* is a political reason. We had no mechanism to change how the cash flowed. In fact, our Declaration of Independence listed a litany of reasons, on paper, that we were separating from the despotic king. And, of course, "We" refers to the white ruling class—a small group of British men who recruited (and forced) an entire class of laborers to the new world.

Politically, we became American citizens when we declared "We, the people." Those founding documents established us as a new and unique political community. Our political system was always intended to be revolutionary. We would govern ourselves. No king. *What?* And we would do it through (representative) democracy. We relished the possibility of building a new nation from the ground up, one in which representation, equality, and egalitarianism were paramount. That is, after all, why the streets of New York City were numbered, not named: so that no one person was considered more important than the rest. Our political system was founded on the premise of the collective *we*.

Economically, America was not as revolutionary, at first. We took English capitalism—which had developed over centuries—and applied it to our fledgling economy. (In some ways, we married it to a revived feudalism, our plantations resembling the medieval system of lords, serfs, and peasants more so than anything one might call "free.") The same year we declared our independence, Adam Smith, Scottish economist and philosopher, published *The Wealth of Nations*, the seminal text that would become the playbook for free-market capitalism, exhaustively referred to—from then till now—as a bible-like blueprint for American success.

This is where things get tricky. The exponential growth of our nation came at great cost to generations of indigenous peoples, enslaved peoples, and laborers. To cover up our sins, we created a powerful mythology (a really good story) that valorized our new legends—cowboys, pioneers, governors, even gangsters—many of whom taught us that our most problematic behaviors and business practices were justified in the righteous "pursuit of happiness" (guaranteed by our founding documents), which in turn created and fueled a unique brand of *American capitalism*, one based on rugged individualism. The development of that ethos forever bound tragedy with success, pain with money, growth with loss. This new American individualism would be the real revolution. The stage was set for our economic system to develop as an expression of the individual *me*.

Flash forward two hundred fifty years, and we have become a nation—arguably an empire—of 335 million people (citizens and nationals), in fifty states and commonwealths, a federal district, and five major territories. On the eve of the American Revolution, it is estimated that colonial America was home to only 2.5 million people, including men, women, children, and enslaved peoples (yep, that's all). Now, that's the number of people that Walmart alone employs. As societies go, we have grown fast. It is estimated that for nearly two hundred years, we doubled in size every quarter-century. Lightning fast.

Along the way, America has given itself and the world not only the framework for the modern republic, but the cotton gin, the airplane, the automobile, the telephone, the MRI machine, the Post-it, microwaveable popcorn, dental floss, the weed wacker, Wite-Out, and White Claw. We created the very machines that are responsible for just how fast our lives move now, and then linked them all together and called the grand project "the Internet." (I'm forty-four; I still capitalize Internet.)

From Liberty Bell to Taco Bell, a system driven by the *pursuit of happiness* has given us significant advances in human progress. It is important to admit, though, that what made our founders happy was not necessarily the same thing that made the masses who came here happy. We can each define happiness for ourselves, but what is common is the freedom in America to pursue it.

For some, the *pursuit of happiness* was an escape from an oppressive regime. For others, America had food when home had famine. For others, they came for those storied streets paved with gold. Millions of American families—mine included—exist today because one, two, or several of their ancestors came from lands afar where their economic potential was limited.

My own grandfather, Giulio, arrived with little more than a thousand Italian *lira* in his pocket. What did Giulio really want? Yes, maybe he wanted a car or a swimming pool, but he certainly didn't want $350 Yeezys, a $1,500 Apple Watch Hermès, or a $106K Range Rover. Countless immigrants came to the States because their native countries were often devastated or in ruin. "Gold" to them was a job and a shot at a peaceful life. It was not a 417-foot pleasure-vessel super-yacht. (Is there something wrong with a

417-foot pleasure-vessel super-yacht? When your company is not paying a fair share of taxes, your workers are striking, and you're asking to dismantle a historic landmark, it is hard to make the argument that there isn't. There's a reason the Dutch planned on pelting eggs at the Bezos boat if the Amazon chairman succeeded in taking down a beloved Rotterdam bridge to get his mega-yacht through.)

It was the ability to earn a living that drew Grandpa Giulio. He came for a chance to have a job and a family and build some semblance of a legacy in this world, because he believed, overtly or not, that earning a living would bring him *satisfaction*, family would bring him *joy*, and a legacy would bring him *meaning*. Being a citizen of the United States meant he could have it all.

I'm not a psychiatrist, but I am a moviemaker, trained in narrative and emotion. I can tell you this: every character—every person in this world—does what they do so that it will make them feel something: accomplished, respected, wanted. Ultimately, loved. Whenever I feel I don't have as much as I want, I remember Grandpa Giulio, and I wonder what he would think of my life. I have more than he could ever conceive was possible. And I live in a one-bedroom apartment.

We can debate the finer details of these arguments all day long, but what is clear is that America has given generations of newcomers (those, of course, who came freely) an opportunity to honor both *me* and *we*. In theory, that is the promise of America: one can pursue their individual desires while contributing to and benefiting from the collective whole.

The tension between our political role—with a focus on that *collective*—and our economic role—with a focus on the *individual*—plays out in our lives every day. *Do I act in my best interests or in those of my community? Do I use every resource I have to make sure my kid gets ahead or do I play a fairer game? How can I get what I want without being a complete asshole to everyone around me?*

It's like a competition between two horses racing around a track—one thoroughbred named We and another called Me. The competition is fierce. And in twenty-first-century America (what I will call "modern" America) it seems Me horse is ahead, and by a great distance.

Why? Rampant consumerism. It seems our *pursuit of happiness* has turned capitalism into a ferocious beast we can no longer control. And we have exported that beast to countless nations around the world. *Wait, why is the worldwide pursuit of human happiness a problem?* It's not, in theory, but as I am about to argue, it is the exploitation of that pursuit—by very wealthy and powerful forces—that is not only creating the relentlessness of modern life but also threatening human existence on the planet. The United States makes up 5 percent of the world's population, yet we now use 25 percent of Earth's resources and create *half* of the world's solid waste.

When did we become such voracious consumers? Most would agree it started happening after World War II, as our new position as an international powerhouse opened the window for our system to go into serious overdrive. We started producing more and more as production and technology advanced, and Madison Avenue brilliantly sold the benefits of "more" to our (primarily white) families, as they rushed out to settle the great American suburbs one Electrolux vacuum at a time. The "Mad Men" of the ad business equated consumerism with happiness (much more on that later), and the Me horse broke away from the We horse by some significant lengths. The We horse tried to catch up in the '60s and '70s—flower power was, by nature, anticonsumerist—but the '80s brought us "Greed is Good," and Reagan's America was not interested in dulling any of the roar of need, need, need, buy, buy, buy.

Capitalism had built the middle class. Consumerism was its fuel.

Socialism was now a foreign evil, associated with the worst actors of World War II. What we tend to gloss over is that there was serious debate before the 1940s about what elements of socialism might best be incorporated into our system to more evenly distribute our growing national wealth. Those conversations, which birthed social security, major public-works projects, and crucial antitrust and bank regulations, were in direct response not only to the stock market crash of 1929 and the Great Depression but to the wild wealth inequality of the Gilded Age (late 1800s), when capitalism was working well for a very small elite class. The railroad magnates were called "robber barons" for a reason: Americans felt the riches of the time were being stolen from We to enrich Me. Sound familiar? But as war broke out, that conversation about socialism died.

By the 1980s, anything that wasn't red-white-and-blue capitalist was for commies and pinkos. The promise? *Don't worry. The benefits of all this capitalist prosperity will trickle down to everyone.* (They did not.) The upward climb of the white American middle class continued right through the '90s, the decade of American millionaire-making, and by the end of the last century, our biggest problems—at least, on the surface—were Y2K and a stained dress.

Yes, I skipped a lot, but you get the point.

Then, just a year after the turn of the millennium, it all morphed. Terror came to our doorstep. Our American bubble forever popped. And in the debris of it all, our leaders told us that our patriotic duty was *to shop.* Less than a week after New York City lost thousands of its citizens—the majority of whom were first in the line of duty—then-mayor Rudy Giuliani held a press conference, during which he implored Americans to "Come here and spend money. Go to a restaurant, a play. You actually might have a better chance at getting tickets to *The Producers* now," jokingly referring to the absurd popularity of the Mel Brooks musical before the attacks. Three weeks later, President George W. Bush echoed that message, telling the American people, "We cannot let the terrorists achieve the objective of frightening our nation to the point where we don't conduct business, where people don't shop."

Yes, these speeches were meant to be encouraging, uplifting. They were meant to help us move past our fear. (Some might argue the full speeches were meant to inspire fear.) The intent was for us to get back to living our usual day-to-day. But what did these messages communicate about our values? In the face of the worst national tragedy many alive had ever seen—the only warlike attack on American soil since Pearl Harbor, an attack that had intentionally targeted two buildings representative of our economic power—we were being told that if we wanted to defeat the terrorists, we had to go out and consume. Being *consumers* would save us. Solace was not to be found in prolonging the incredible acts of citizenship that arose in response to the attacks. It was to be found at the cash register.

Without knowing it, we learned a dangerous collective emotional lesson: when we are most hurting and feel most broken, comfort and healing come from products. (To add insult to injury, years later, at the site of the 9/11 attacks, New York City would build a memorial and underground museum alongside a 350,000-square-foot Westfield shopping mall. Yes, a mall.)

There have been many moments in the history of America when we exalted our economy over all else as that which will heal us, but this one was the most dramatic, at least from my generation's vantage point. It set the course for all that has come. Because it happened at a critical juncture: the very moment that the Internet took over the world.

· · · ·

It is now a scary cycle at play in the twenty-first-century Internet-driven economy: satisfying our emotional needs is only a click away; we then need to make more money so we can click and buy more things; we click and buy more things to make it all easier because we're overwhelmed by the pressure we feel to make more money to click and buy more things. We post pictures of those things, and everyone else sees them and wants to click and buy them. Then they click and post pictures of their things. And then, because we all clicked and bought more things, we all need more space to put all those things. So we click and buy bigger houses. And those houses cost more. So we need more money. So we work harder. So we click and buy more things to make it easier. And then we click and post about how #blessed we are. Because having more shit to post about is somehow a blessing from God. Yes, I am aware that I sound like a George Carlin act. Funny how little has changed since Carlin released *A Place for My Stuff* in 1981.

This rampant consumerism is not your father's regular ol' consumerism. It is fueled by digital systems that now transfer information, messages, money, and goods and services at warp speed. That *speed* has been sold to us as sexy—who doesn't want a new toy immediately?—but it is driving us apart, fast. In fact, economists now pin much blame for our society's stark inequality on our tech. In effect, it is technology, when applied to capitalism, that is supercharging our post-9/11 consumption and reversing some of the most important gains of the twentieth century. Click by click, we are undoing a strong middle class. We are undoing a more equitable distribution of the nation's wealth. We are returning to the extreme social and economic stratification of more than a century ago. The more we buy, the worse it seems to get.

Speed is our first problem. Advanced digital technology—and "fintech" (financial technology)—has made it possible for the market to move at a faster pace than actual human interaction. And because money is now numbers on a digital screen and not actual cold, hard, physical cash—nor a check that requires a stamp, an envelope, and a trip to the post office—money moves *up* the economic ladder almost instantaneously. To be fair, technology has always hastened production and money has always moved *up* the ladder. Now, though, it happens with the ease of a click and the speed of blazing-fast Xfinity 10G. Anything we need or want, whatever it is that we desire *right now*, is available to us. We can transact and "get it" in less time than it takes to fully think about it.

But—and the *but* is a big one—money coming *down* that same ladder takes its sweet time. Have you ever tried to get a refund from, say, Citibank or eBay or Name.com? Haha. Have fun. You bought what you bought in nine seconds, but you'll be issued a refund in three to five business days, if you're lucky. Or, your refund will come as store credit or a gift card, to guarantee your business, but you'll forget you have it. You might even be sent a refund check in the mail, that your bank will then take a week to ten days to cash. (It's the 2020s, and American banks still need ten days to clear a check, as if it were 1972.) Have you ever submitted an invoice to a large company for freelance or vendor services rendered and waited "net 60" or "net 90" to get paid? The institutions and systems that dominate our economy have no need to give you money with the same speed that they make it or take it. And there are few protections in place in our public policy to protect consumers and balance those scales. Scale these practices up, to 335 plus million people, and what we've got is advanced digital technology being wielded against consumers (most of the citizens of our country).

It's not just America's brands. When you owe the IRS tax money, it comes immediately out of your check. But when the government gives you money, you, dear citizen, have to wait and be patient with the posted processing times. During the circus, stimulus checks from the United States Treasury took nearly two months to make their way from Washington. Granted, it was a national emergency (and one man insisted on having his signature printed on every one of them), but, come on, they already have our checking account numbers. By the winter of 2022, two *years* later, the Small Business Administration was still processing emergency funds for small-business owners. In May of that year, it abruptly closed its EIDL loan program, its leadership testified to Congress that it had successfully done its job (false), and the agency shut out millions of small-business owners all over the country from critical relief.* You know who wasn't shut out? America's major brands.

That's just the day-to-day home economics of it all. Let's widen our lens. If wages don't increase at the same rate that prices do— and these post-circus years have shown us clearly that they do *not*— money goes up faster than it goes down. You don't have to be an economist to see it. The price of eggs went up 60 percent in one year. My salary did not. Did yours? If the largest earners pay the smallest tax rates, and the smallest earners pay the largest tax rates, um, again, something is wrong. When too much money goes up the ladder and not enough comes down (or moves around), we have a major problem at our kitchen tables as we try to balance our checkbooks.

All of this is driving the economic and political divide wider and wider. On one side are the wealthy and powerful—on both flanks of the political aisle—well versed in leveraging technology to their benefit, as they do with our financial and legal systems. And on the other side, the rest of us are drowning in debt, ever-mounting

---

* I know this because I am one of the millions of small-business owners whose application sat in a queue for fourteen months, only to be told that "funding has been exhausted." It's not just the funding. It's us. We're exhausted by the constant bullshit.

paperwork, and painful personal shame that even though we work hard we cannot seem to get ahead.

This is the opposite of trickle-down economics—the fantasy that a robust consumer economy would benefit the common good. I will call it "click-up economics." Click-up economics supercharges our consumer spending by making our transactions easy, fast, and seamless. It satiates our desires immediately. It sends cash *up* the economic ladder, *fast*. It creates all sorts of success at the top, while squeezing wages at almost every other level. It relies on strong stories that can spread quickly through hyper-connected social circles. (We'll discuss that next. It's not a mistake Instagram Stories are named as such.) And it uses the power of concentrated capital not only to hike prices but to exert disproportionate control over our political system to *keep* capital concentrated and not distributed in any way that most would consider fair and just.

We are only twenty years into click-up economics. Can we not admit that we might need to refine how this all works? We seem to have simply accepted that this is forever our way of life.

I should be clear here: I do not believe the answer to America's modern ills lies in changing our economic system wholesale. Capitalism is a system well worth defending, improving, even reinventing for the twenty-first century. There is a beautiful baby that would die should we throw out the dreckish bathwater. Instead, I believe it is our brand of capitalism that must change—the version, practice, and execution of it—that is what is not working for millions of people. So many millions that it hurts the heart. Capitalism can be a meaningful system in this century if—and only if—we force it to evolve, along the way acknowledging its massive mistakes, reevaluating its purpose, remaking its structures and forms, and rethinking the meaning, place, and value of labor and consumers.

You can call that "socialism" if you want, but that's too easy an out. There is much to learn from other societies that employ successful social programs to benefit their citizens or that treat food, health, community, work, even sex wildly differently than we do. It is our responsibility to explore how those techniques and policies can improve our way of life and create more equitable outcomes for *we, the people*. Obsessing about the label serves everyone but us. We need to refine our system so that it rewards hard work and incentivizes success, creates wealth, and shares that prosperity with all of those who contribute to its creation. All without destroying the vibrancy of our collective spaces, our human dignity, and the planet. Yeah, that's a tall order. But that is the task at hand. This is a new time. It will require new ways.

Love or loathe capitalism, what is clear is that click-up economics is *not* capitalism as we have known it. Click-up economics relies not only on speed. It relies on an abandonment of limits. That is our second major problem.

Back in the analog days, when transactions (and labor) occurred in real-live human time, at real-live human speed, between real-live humans, our economy could only move as fast as human limits allowed. Humans require shelter, sleep, food, love, and they need to attend their kids' poetry recitals, go to temple, and iron their clothes for work. Stores had to close for the night. Humans need sleep. Newspapers had only a certain amount of space to print stories. Humans can only hold so much paper in their hands. Wallets showcased about five small family photos encased in protective plastic.

Yes, money still moved up the ladder. Producers made products for less than they sold them for, in order to make a profit. Workers made wages by selling their labor to make the products. (We can argue all day long about whether selling your labor is even kosher or not. Many great super-left thinkers argue that accepting even this element of capitalism is problematic. Put that aside for a second.) Workers put in their hours, goods were produced and sold, and we could climb the socioeconomic ladder by working hard and long, making smart decisions with the money left over after we paid for our essentials, occasionally augmenting our income with the odd side gig. The human brain could still fathom the amount of money at the top and understand the steps it would take to climb.

Even though technology changed the game phase by phase (the Industrial Revolution was, after all, a technological revolution), producers could only make profit in the time that it took to complete production. It was the same on the consumer end. We could consume products and services only in the time it took to complete the transaction and extract the emotional value the sale brought to our life. Because we took time to go buy something or waited for weeks for it to be delivered, we relished it. We were selective. We made choices after careful consideration. We had to choose which five photos to sit on.

Both producing and consuming were tied to limits.

Even as limits expanded, they didn't *break*. Consider the shopping cart. A man named Sylvan Goldman, owner of the Humpty Dumpty supermarket chain in Oklahoma, invented the shopping cart one night in 1936. Supermarkets themselves were new (a way to make shopping for varied goods faster) and Goldman wondered how customers might carry more of what Humpty Dumpty was selling. If customers were limited to the basket they could physically hold in their hands, they could only buy what fit inside. The heavier the basket, the fuller it got, the less inclined the customer was to put more in.

Goldman's big *Aha!* came one night in his office. It was a eureka moment that would forever change American commerce. He realized that if he took two office folding chairs, changed the height of their seats (one high, one low), and added wheels, shoppers could employ the wheel—Big Tech from 4000 BC—to carry the weight of a much larger basket. Customer purchases were, of course, now limited to the size of this new "shopping cart," but it beat the hell out of relying on weak little human forearms.

Limits, even as they changed—and in the case of Goldman expanded—kept a pre-Internet system in check. The system had its problems (most definitely), but it at least functioned well enough for us to lift people out of poverty, expand access to opportunity, and export ideas that liberated peoples and hearts. You cannot deny the successes of American capitalism, even if you believe we now exist in a wholly different stage of it or that this new century demands something very different.

Those limits also gave us the real-live human time to hold people accountable should they break the commitments of any given transaction. You could call out lies. You could confront a smarmy salesman. You could ask for a raise because you knew the actual owner of your company. You could see, quite literally, whether the company was doing well or not. And you could effectively beat the bullshit. Or at least beat it back. Trust in the system and faith in one another were (generally) abundant. Yes, exploitation was rampant before fairer labor laws were established, and, yes, we argued and disagreed very forcefully, but a functioning relationship existed among producers and consumers. Working hard made sense. A choice had value. The more expensive houses across the road were only one or two "notches" nicer than ours.

Click-up economics, on the other hand, is a wildly different animal. It does nothing in real-live human time, except purchasing; and with subscriptions and automation—which we are about to discuss in great detail—that step is eliminated, taken out of our human hands, so that it can be disconnected from our petty human limits. It operates on robot time, machine time, algorithm time. *Automated time.* When transactions are made in automated time, at instant speed, our economy moves faster than real-live humans can move.

As the entire economy plunged into automated time two decades ago, this faster shopping required some changes to Goldman's chairs on wheels. Goldman's dial-up counterpart was an e-commerce pioneer named Stephan Schambach, who invented the online shopping cart. Which has no limit. It's a basket with no bottom. If you held a basket in your hands that had no bottom, you might call it "broken." And because you can fill this endless basket online, stores never close. Likewise, newspapers broke through their limits. They now have endless pages. Same with that wallet. You no longer need to choose which photos to sit on. You can carry every photo you have ever taken since 2004, and you can share them and send them because you have unlimited data.

Click-up economics has made the world just that: *unlimited*. If you want to see just how this has all truly warped us, walk into a Verizon store and ask the salesperson if they have unlimited data plans. They will light up like they have discovered the fountain of youth and are offering you a sip. Click-up economics has sold us a very sexy story: unlimited equals good. It means "the future." It means an endless supply of everything we want.

Because click-up economics feeds—and feeds off—an unlimited digital world, the core event of the economy, the holy handshake, *the transaction*, is no longer tied to a human limit. Transactions now happen automatically, instantaneously, sometimes *simultaneously*, often while we are doing something *else*. Two can happen at once. Or three or four or five. We are, in effect, consuming in our sleep, sometimes literally. We don't need to make choices when we can have everything and anything with the ease of a click.

And that creates a frightening imbalance between producers and consumers. That imbalance is throwing a very precious ecosystem— not to mention our actual environmental ecosystem—out of whack. Because the transaction uses a robot to consummate the transaction (if you will allow me the sex metaphor), the imbalance grows and grows. And the more tasks that can be automated, from production to customer service to the actual purchase transaction, the more profit producers make. Money moves up the ladder faster and faster. As more producers, companies, and brands consolidate, a process that itself is made faster by digital tools (along with lax antitrust laws and enforcement), the imbalance gets worse and worse.

Workers, on the other hand can only labor as fast as their real-live human bodies allow. We—anyone not already wealthy—can no longer climb the socioeconomic ladder by working harder and longer, because the math falls apart. The money left over after we pay for essentials just isn't enough as the price of essentials skyrockets. You can't regulate or control those prices because that's *evil socialism*. And the list of what we consider *to be essential* grows and grows, as we get more and more conditioned not only to need things that we do not, in fact, need but to *require* luxury. In many cases, it is not *we* who require it but our systems that do. You *need* a smartphone to get test results. Or to transfer money if you're in a bind. You *need* a car to get to that job interview. Or to get your kids to school. You *need* health insurance to be admitted to a health care facility so you don't, ya know, die.

Where does that leave us? The ladder we are all meant to climb is now absurdly tall—in fact, it now has 214 billion steps on it (that's how much money the world's richest man has: $214 billion). By comparison, in 2000, that ladder had 60 billion steps. In 1990, it had 16 billion. In 1970, 6 billion. And when this idea of America was birthed, in 1776, it had 42,000 steps (4 million if you adjust for inflation). The wealthiest man in the colonies was Peter Manigault, merchant, lawyer, and banker. Manigault was only £33,000 richer than the poorest American. This is why the progressives are always ranting about increasing wages. A ladder that has more and more steps cannot be climbed if you only take a step or two a day. When you cannot even see the top or fathom its height, it gets harder and harder. I am continually awestruck at how much an actual *billion* is. If you started to count to a billion right now, how long do you think it would take? Look away from this page and take a guess. It would take you thirty years. To count to 214 billion? Over eight thousand years. A new billionaire was created nearly every day during the circus.

You and I both know what this all feels like. And it doesn't feel good. This growing imbalance hits everyday Americans—and our checkbooks—like a fucking bomb.

Click-up economics moves lightning fast. And it relies on broken limits. When we say "capitalism is broken," the breaking is *the point*. Few at the top want to fix it, because it is the brokenness that most benefits them. Where in all of this does the government fit? You know, the very entity meant to safeguard us? Regulations, antitrust policies, and consumer protections all generally grew more robust as Americans consumed more and more. But when trickle-down economics took over in the '80s, the prevailing thought was that government should stay *out* of the market. So, we "deregulated." We took some of the most important rules away.

Look, I have thrown about three baseballs in my life, but I do understand this: you cannot play a game of baseball without rules. How would anyone know where to run? What constitutes a foul? An error? How would men in striped uniforms and caps know *where* to even throw the ball? A market needs regulations. They define the rules of the game. Without them, there are no shared agreements. And there is no umpire to stop one team from clobbering the other with a baseball bat. Don't get lost in the metaphor. The point is this: the government has failed to do its part to design effective policy to deal with the devastating effects click-up economics is having on the American majority. The speed and scale of it all means the government cannot keep up. Regulations are few. Antitrust litigation in an age of mass consolidation is slow. And consumer protections are a joke.

This new alien breed created when you merge capitalism with advanced digital tools is painful, unless you are the direct beneficiary. When the more progressive among us advocate for "human-centered capitalism," we must reckon with the speed of our economic trans- actions. And our relationship to limits. We cannot create anything more human centered until we deal with the limits of real-live hu- mans in real-live human time—or at least until we all live, breathe, work, and exist in the same *type* of time. Everything else is just ro- bots making the rich richer.

After all, how can you win a game you can't even play? Some of our people don't know how to download a picture or open an email attachment. Others can't deposit a check by phone. We have moved our entire economy online seemingly overnight and never gave the majority the tools they need to fully benefit from it. We didn't forget to do so. It has simply never been advantageous to the most power- ful people to empower the most people.

Not only do 200 million Americans not own (or even under- stand) stocks—a primary instrument of capitalism—but a quarter of the population (80 million people) does not have access to broad- band. We can lie to ourselves and say that 84 percent of Americans are digitally literate because they know how to turn on a computer, but do they know how to use a computer to *make* money as well as they know how to use it to *spend* money? I think we can all agree the answer is no.

Click-up economics intensifies if the answer is no. And those at the top know this. They know that in their hands they have this magic tool that can generate disgusting amounts of wealth, and they have a very limited window to make as much money as humanly possible before everyone else figures out how to leverage that magic, too. Tim Ferriss tried to help us learn how, teaching us the digital tools that could give us each a "4-Hour Workweek," but all of modernity shouldn't rely on one obsessive digital nomad to democratize that knowledge. *But we have Etsy and Apple Geniuses.* That's not a responsible answer.

The worst effect of click-up economics is that it has handed our society over to some very big forces. Who are they? The jockeys of Me horse. You can slice them all a few different ways, but for our purposes here, there are the five: Big Tech, Big Brands, Big Banks, Big Media, and, yes, the Big Parties (the political ones). (I'm including Big Pharma and Big Agriculture under Big Brands.) They are each the descendants of thousands of smaller companies, businesses, and ventures that we—and our parents and grandparents—knew well in the twentieth century. Back then, their products and services were sold to us as helpful. They could solve our problems and make our lives easier, cooler, *better.* We learned to trust them. We grew loyal to them. They became as familiar and comforting as apple pie.

So, as click-up economics took over, we didn't really notice the massive changes underway. We were just excited we could bank online, shop on our phones, and never pay for news. Their logos modernized, maybe the fonts and brand colors tweaked, but behind the scenes everything was changing. And changing fast. They were consolidating, monopolizing, wiping out their competition, buying up the smaller shops that dared to challenge their industries with new ideas, playing musical chairs with their executives (some of whom we are learning are not the geniuses we thought they were), mastering tax avoidance, rewriting their contracts to exploit digital systems in their favor (thereby screwing artists, craftspeople, vendors, workers, even doctors royally), and creating new efficiencies to make more and more profit. All under the same banners we already trusted and knew well.

These Big Forces got so big because the Internet gave them the tools to *scale* (to reach millions and billions of customers) and the *speed* to do it quickly; the government gave them a clear and unobstructed path. Meanwhile, the Internet was connecting us all, fusing our social circles into one big, tightly connected circle, what I will call the "Supercommunity." Here's what happened: those with the capital and foresight to monetize our social connectedness stood to gain significantly. The more they spoke to (and sold to) the Supercommunity, the larger they grew. The Big Forces were always governing the landscape, but the Internet gave them a unique opportunity to balloon. Massively.

Now, these businesses are larger than some nations. Wells Fargo now services 70 million customers. That's more than the population of France. Same with Best Buy. Apple products go to one billion people around the world. That's one eighth of the world's population. Anthem Health Care: 49.5 million. CVS: 44 million. (HBO) Max: 50 million. That's the population of Ukraine or of Sweden, Serbia, and Australia *combined*.

(This is also why so many of us now feel that it is no longer "okay" to be regular run-of-the-mill successful. That's not enough. *We* are not enough. We have to build brands. Empires. We can't just run a shop. We must take over the world.)

Not only are these companies large, but they are also consolidated. In many industries, only about five or six companies control the majority of market share. That means only about five or six companies make most of the money. This is monopoly capitalism. And we're right back to the age of the robber barons. The lower the competition, the lower the fight for our every dollar—so prices *rise* instead of drop. In entertainment, it's Disney, Paramount, Sony, Universal, and Warner Brothers Discovery. Together, they hold 81 percent of the market. In pharmaceuticals, it's Roche, Novartis, AbbVie, Johnson & Johnson, Merck, Pfizer, and Bristol-Meyers-Squibb. In groceries and food, it's Nestlé, PepsiCo, Coca-Cola,

General Mills, Kellogg's, Associated British Foods, Mondelez, Mars, Danone, and Unilever. Same thing in clothes, energy, cable, and the like. We now have four major airline carriers; in 1980, we had twelve. Wall Street has five major banks. That's it. In any given market in any given industry, we have very few choices. We *think* we have this incredible multitude of options, but we don't.

Their systems have become so large, so sophisticated, and so powerful that their cooperation—and interconnected motives— have created a monster we no longer seem to be able to control: the staggering NOISE of modern life.

No one really designed it all this way from scratch. It's a very strange alchemy of misguided incentives and a superpowered digital world that has monetized our hyper-connectedness. It's not necessarily some evil cabal. I don't imagine that there is an elite group maliciously plotting against the American consumer. Yes, for sure, some are designing business models that exploit and abuse. Most certainly. But mostly I imagine executives who socialize in a small bubble, who value their power, and who are following a tradition of constant upward mobility, staying fully subscribed and loyal to the idea that *my business must constantly grow*. I think it's important to recognize that they are making decisions that do not serve the public nor the greater good, but without being in the room with them I cannot tell you if those decisions are purposefully malicious. It all comes down to problematic choices and flawed designs that are then scaled to a mind-blowing proportion. We are scaling whatever flaws in moral judgment are built into these systems. And our government is doing too little about it.

That is how we got to this very strange place in America. That's my diagnosis. Marry a complicated and chaotic economic and political history, pivotal collective traumatic moments, massive changes to the rules of the game, and the explosion of the Internet, and you get

a warped new system. Me horse is now on speed, galloping and galloping. Left in the dust, We horse can barely breathe.

Before we look at how these Big Forces work seamlessly together,
we have to understand the key to this brave new world. That key
emerged sometime around 2010. That's when the Big Forces figured
out a way to use tech to keep that galloping going. Endlessly. That's
when a cute little quirk of late-stage capitalism became the holy grail
of click-up economics.

Two

The Infinite Loop

In modern America, we wear many, many hats. We're residents, renters, mortgage holders, and constituents, customers, browsers, patrons, end users, and clients. We're viewers, watchers, spectators, witnesses, fans, and passengers, congregants, voters, followers, believers, supporters, employees, teammates, staff, associates. The list goes on; you get it. Above all else, though, we have become something else, something new. Click-up economics has effected a profound identity transformation in American society—one we are eagerly exporting around the globe. We have become *subscribers*. That cute little quirk? Subscriptions.

Ever signed up for an email list to get 15 percent off your first purchase? (Of course, you have; you're breathing.) You're a subscriber, just like I am. Amazon Prime member? You're a subscriber. Still trying to figure out how to link your Disney+ account with your Hulu account? You're a (*very* annoyed) subscriber. In the last of the analog days, we used to think about this word—"subscribing"—solely in the context of magazine or newspaper subscriptions. In the '80s and '90s, car companies played with subscriptions in the form of car leases. In exchange for loyalty to a brand, we could upgrade our car model every few years—and drive a much more expensive car than we could really afford. Then, the invention of the Internet and the trusty digital shopping cart—plus the purchase, banking, and digital and physical production and delivery systems that connect to them and support them—took the concept to a stunning new level. Case in point: Netflix.

You don't become Netflix without speed, a lack of limits, or subscriptions. Before it had 221.8 million subscribers, before its stock price was $345 per share and it delivered over 17,000 titles digitally all over the world, with a revenue of $7.71 billion (and paid $0 in taxes in 2020; its latest filings were 13 percent), Netflix was the 1997 brainchild of a Central California carpool. As the story goes, Reed Hastings, one of the company's founders, got angry that he was charged a $40 late fee at a Blockbuster store for being past due returning a VHS copy of *Apollo 13*. He and his partners tested mailing, via USPS, this new thing called a "DVD." It arrived perfectly safe and without a scratch, so they launched the first DVD rental and sales site on the World Wide Web, with only thirty employees and 925 movies. I can hear the dial-up noise now.

Fast-forward twenty-four years, and nearly every startup around the country wants to be the Netflix of whatever it is that they offer. Why? Subscriptions. Now, you can subscribe to monthly boxes of pre-worn, high-end runway fashions that are delivered to your door, to monthly science and craft projects for the kids that just arrive at your house while a small charge sneaks into your checking account, or to monthly flowers, chocolates, popcorn, shoes, cosmetics, coffee, wine, and printer inks and toner. If you own a luxury car, your heated seats are now a subscription. Thanks to car-share apps, the actual *car* is a subscription. You can even subscribe to recurring cannabis boxes (weekly weed) or monthly letters from dead people. Yes, you can get a box of clues from late 1920s New Orleans, apparently transcribed by psychics, that "help you unravel a larger, sinister mystery"—your own escape-room experience delivered to your home. Anyone who sells anything in the modern economy wants you to not only buy it but buy it regularly, consistently, monthly; and they will happily automatically charge your credit card. Welcome to the madness of the modern world.

It is getting increasingly difficult to simply buy something and walk away, i.e., to just be a *customer*. Everyone wants to be in touch. Everyone wants your email. They not only want it, they demand it. They require it. You cannot leave the register with your new Nike kicks without turning over your personal data. We now trade valuable information for access to what used to simply be available in the free market.

And thanks to a sister movement in business that goes by the nickname SaaS (software as a service), even computer software that you used to buy just *once* now sits on the cloud and you pay monthly to use it. Your laptop is now not just a personal computing machine. It is a magic portal to an endless marketplace as soon as it turns on the wifi—which, of course, it is programmed to do automatically. This is all a far cry from the magazine subscription to *Sports Illustrated* or *Seventeen* you got as a kid in 1988. This is the whole world delivered to your doorstep or your screen—on repeat.

The subscription model is the fastest-growing business model in America, the "modern" way of doing business for countless companies, brands, and organizations around the country. The average US consumer now has subscriptions to five retail brands and twelve media platforms. For Millennials specifically, that number jumps from twelve to seventeen. Research shows that almost half of us have forgotten that we're still paying for a subscription we no longer use, and nearly a third underestimate just how much we spend on subscriptions by $100 to $199 each month. That amounts to thousands of dollars per year. Um, *per person*. Amazon alone has 153 million subscribers. Our individual forgetfulness and underestimation are scaling to be *a lot* of money for 417-foot pleasure yachts.

Let me be fair. Subscription is not a new concept. I am highlighting it because it has become the dominant paradigm of twenty-first-century consumerism, and I believe the Big Forces of click-up economics are using subscriptions to manipulate markets, trap consumers, and enrich their bottom lines at the cost of employees and consumers. But, yes, we have been signing and agreeing to contracts for centuries. In America, the founders *signed* our nation's founding documents for a reason: contracts and agreements run societies. Literally, *subscribe* means "to sign under." Signatures are how we bind our commitments and promises—which, funny enough, an entire generation of kids cannot pen or read, because they aren't taught cursive in our digital world. (I digress; I love cursive. And pens. And paper. I imagine you're not shocked.) These contracts are so ubiquitous we don't even notice them anymore. Even a receipt, too, is a legal contract. You promise to pay for a good or service. You sign. You are committed.

Do we commit freely? Yes. Contracts reflect free will and our ability to make agreements for ourselves. But some are negotiable and some are not. More and more, they are *not*, as they are written by the Big Forces. There is no consumer lobby negotiating these terms. They are dictated. These subscriptions set the tone (and many of the terms) of countless transactions for millions of people here at home and for billions of people around the world. They have, in effect, become our *public policy*. If imbalance and inequity are built into these subscriptions, we are spreading imbalance and inequity. If a lack of fairness and justice is built in, we spread that. If we absolve companies of responsibility to and respect for consumers, we spread that. With great speed. At great scale.

These subscription agreements then become the templates for small businesses, nonprofits, schools, even government—all of whom take their cues from big business. They also set the tone, more and more, for how we interact with each other socially.

If the Big Forces can get us to click Subscribe (or Agree), we enter into a contract with them, and they can get to know each of us intimately, they can measure and predict our behavior, swap and sell our information. They can update the terms of that agreement, as they dictate them, by simply emailing us from a noreply@ email address. They can craft agreements of any nature, bury the details in endless legalese, and no one is the wiser. Is it intentional deception? Sometimes. Mostly, it is an effort to make big businesses more *efficient* (more information about you and your behavior means less money spent to market to you) so they can take less risk, *scalable* so they can apply one rule or practice to millions, and financially *sustainable* so they can continue to return the same level of profits to shareholders and not have to ride the waves of moody consumers.

The subscription model is not meant to be nefarious, but it does distinctly benefit one side of the economic equation: the side writing the agreement. The side that already has power and money. (And a vested interest in maintaining the status quo.) As a producer or provider of goods or services, I don't need to be standing in front of you and swipe your credit card, verify your signature, and say "thank you" with my human lips. Instead, I can just store your information and continue to use it, and you'll get a thank-you note generated and sent by a computer. And with contact information for every subscriber, I can now annoy the shit out of you until you buy something.

And so, we commit every single day—with a nod, a signature, a checkmark, a simple "yes" or a "like." We are in a constant state of subscribing, ever contracting, making agreements and promising. We are, after all, a "culture of yes"—a dangerous meme that has convinced us all that endless possibility breeds happiness. *Yes, sure, I agree, let's do it, uh-huh, sign me up, sounds good, carpe the diem, say yes to the dress.* We cannot stop agreeing to shit we don't want to do or consuming bullshit we don't need. Very often, assent and endorsement come when we simply fail to say no and stop ourselves from participating in the momentum around us. The momentum is strong, on purpose.

It's a lot harder to say no when you don't need to take the minute to sign a document with a pen. Subscriptions in an analog world relied on your John Hancock, scrawled in ink on a piece of paper. But subscriptions in a digital world do not, and so they shift the gear and move the whole affair of contracting—a foundational act of a civil society—into uncontrollable overdrive. The number of contracts between each of us has been driven up exponentially in the digital world, all in the name of a healthy economy, all in the name of convenience and ease. Now, when we do say yes and sign on, we often don't even read the agreement. Most of the time we click Agree, we don't even know what we are subscribing to. Who has the time to read a thirty-page contract just to open yet another "loyalty" account?

The subscription model emerged after the turn of the millennium. It was nurtured by business schools, reinforced by constant competition, and formalized by books like *Subscribed*, by Taiwanese entrepreneur Tien Tzuo, and *The Forever Transaction*, by business guru Robbie Kellman Baxter. Books like these have become modern business bibles around the country.

"Today successful companies start with the customer," Tzuo says. "They recognize that customers spend their time across many channels, and wherever those customers are, that's where they should be meeting their customers' needs. And the more information you can learn about the customer, the better you can serve their needs, and the more valuable the relationship becomes. That's digital transformation: from linear transactional channels to a circular, dynamic relationship with your subscriber."

What is this "dynamic relationship" that Tzuo praises? Let's look at an example. Instead of you going into a local hardware store, buying a plunger, and leaving—a singular transaction that made you a onetime "customer"—you can now establish a "relationship" with Home Depot by signing up for a "Home Depot Subscription." For no money or membership fee, you can "Put your to-do list on autopilot and get 5% off repeat purchases." (Yes, that is a direct quote from their website.) As a subscriber, you will constantly be fed the brand's message, its value proposition (why it's so great and why you *need* it when you really don't), its products, and its daily digital detritus (my new favorite word for *crap*). In turn, you will give the brand your time, your attention, space on your screen, room in everyday conversation, a special place in your brain (orange = home improvement), and, of course, your CVV code—on a consistent and predictable basis.

But, most destructively, you are now subscribed to a long list of ideas like (1) *your to-do list is never-ending, as home improvement is not an act, it is an ongoing practice, a lifestyle, an identity*—one that, incidentally, takes you out of your community (and breaks you away from your personal relationship with the local hardware store owner and employees) and keeps you inside your house constantly redoing the fucking bathroom; (2) *having new tools, supplies, and gadgets that arrive in a box will make you as happy as you used to be on Christmas morning when you were a kid*—i.e., happiness is a wrapped surprise; it is not the joy of knowing the hardware store owner and his children; and, taking the logical next step, (3) *a home-equity loan to do the larger home improvements is an investment in your future, because selling the house and doing it all over again with another fixer-upper will make you rich.*

You see how subscriptions work? You never actually leave the store, or the mindset of the brand. Home Depot is not just a seller of plungers. It is an ever-present part of your life. And a main character in the American story.

The Big Forces need the subscription model. To stay as big as they are, they require mass subscription. Subscriptions are no longer a fun way to get Jamba Juice points. They are now the main event of our commercial system, a cornerstone of modern commerce, a way to keep incredibly large numbers of consumers relentlessly consuming.

Subscribing is now the *holy grail* of click-up economics—a fully automated subscription society in which money moves reliably, predictably, and Google-Fiber fast monthly, weekly, daily, second by second up the economic ladder. It is seamless. It is frictionless. It has no more pain points. It has been in the making for decades, but there was never a way to truly automate consumer behavior. Now there is. It is now fully possible because of sophisticated tech and how very addicted we all are to it. What's happening? Our money is being sucked up and out of our wallets and bank accounts. It is being sucked out of our towns and Main Streets. Out of our public systems and shared spaces. Automatically. On repeat. We now live in a powerful subscription society with thousands upon thousands of brands that seek—blatantly—to put your life on autopilot.

On autopilot, we are caught in an infinite loop. "The infinite loop" is the point. In computer programming, an infinite loop is a sequence of instructions that just continue endlessly, until some sort of external intervention occurs. In behavioral science, that's called a "feedback loop." Big Tech understood they were the same. And that if they merged them, the results would be explosive. Because in that loop with us is our money.

The infinite loop is the very graphic (see figure 1) at the heart of endless Keynote and PowerPoint presentations from Silicon Valley to Burbank to Chicago to Dallas to New York. In conference rooms and Zoom rooms all over the country, business teams work nonstop to find the best ways to easily get us *in* the loop—to get us to *subscribe*—and the most effective ways to never let us out. Or at least to make it really, really hard to break free.

The infinity symbol, also known as "the lazy eight," was first used in mathematics in the seventeenth century, to represent a lack of limits. Before that, though, it could be found in a number of traditions, a representation of the cycle of life. The ancient symbol, the ouroboros, depicts a serpent or dragon eating its own tail. In modern iconography, the symbol is dangerously close to the icon for a lock or chain—which is exactly what it feels like for consumers: we are locked in, chained to, tethered.

FIGURE 1
The Infinity Symbol

It is no wonder that the new logo for Meta is an infinity loop shaped like an *M*, or that the address of the Apple campus is 1 Infinite Loop, Cupertino. The infinite loop has taken over capitalism. That loop is what's making modern American life relentless. It is all designed to be never-ending. To be unlimited. To never let up. It is equally unsurprising that Jeff Bezos originally wanted to name Amazon something different: Relentless.com. For millennia, history's greatest thinkers have explored the concept of the infinite loop. But it took American capitalism to find a way to employ it to make money. Relentless and unlimited profits.

The infinite loop relies on behavioral automation. Let me clarify what that means. There are two types of automation that have come into our vocabulary in the twenty-first century. One is the type that former presidential candidate Andrew Yang, for example, discusses in his book *The War on Normal People,** which warns us all that ro-

---

* For what it's worth, I'm not advocating for or against the Yang Gang, a third party, Asian American candidates, ties, open collars, the politics of the New York mayoral race, ranked-choice voting, or universal basic income; I am simply clarifying Yang's version of automation.

bots, which can in most cases complete labor tasks better and with more efficiency than humans, will replace large swaths of the American workforce—very large swaths—and likewise, that the mental work of non-manual-labor roles will also be replaced by artificial intelligence. AI is scaring the shit out of school systems, engineers, creatives, and even lawyers. Since the Industrial Revolution, technology has been replacing workers, but few in power minded so much. Now AI is coming for the handsomely paid and highly educated, and alarm bells are ringing. The nature of work and labor will change in ways that will wildly transform and challenge society as we know it.

For the purpose of our discussion, let's call this type of automation "labor automation." (That's not Yang's phrase; it's mine.) Labor automation uses machines to put *labor* on autopilot, thereby replacing the need for humans in the manufacturing of goods or services (or art or sentences). It's the initial step toward a larger, wider, far more destructive type of automation. Let's call it "behavior automation."

Behavior automation uses machines to put our *behaviors* on autopilot—what we do, what we buy, where we go, to whom we talk, how we move through our lives and through the world and marketplace. *Like habits?* Well, like habits to which you are contractually obligated. Or habits that the digital ecosystem around us will not let us break. Are we in control of our bodies and minds and fingers and hearts? Yes. But we are ceaselessly prodded, prompted, and poked to behave in specific ways by automated systems. What does that look like? Pure noise. It's endless messages. Emails. Texts. Notifications. Alarms. Beeps. Buzzes. Dings. Rings. Pings. Pavlovian bells.

At this point in the 2020s, the infinite loop has been shamelessly exploited to put America on autopilot. Sure, we can now work from home, work from the road, even from the beach (those are life-changing opportunities, ones I take advantage of often), but we can now also consume products, spend our ever-dwindling paychecks, and use and abuse the planet's limited resources with the same ease. Automatically. On repeat.

(Worse, dark forces have weaponized that automation to trap us all in fucked-up cycles of disinformation. We'll get to storytelling in the next chapter.)

What does behavioral automation look like day to day? It looks like life on a loop. Take the example of a certain high-end luxury gym and health club that operates in a number of major US cities—you know, the one that charges over $200 per month to access just one of their locations (it's more if you want an all-access pass, and even more than that if you want one of the really exclusive specialty clubs). In late March 2020, as those cities shut down, the company announced that they were generously freezing all memberships until it was deemed safe to return. I would love to believe that the reason for the freeze was a concern for public and personal health, the very thing the brand sells. Or perhaps an awareness of the great economic shift hitting members and their checkbooks. Maybe someone somewhere in the corporate ladder expressed these concerns. It seems far more likely that what the gym feared most was a rush of cancellations, which would have driven their profits and cash flow into the ground.

To avoid that, the company quickly launched an online virtual fitness platform it had been developing, to make sure its brand remained an integral part of the daily routines and identities of its subscribers. (Without it, after all, people might discover that you can do push-ups in your own house or that running in the park is actually free. And there are trees. *People might associate fitness with trees!* Members might awaken to the reality that they spend hundreds of dollars every month to lift heavy things around pretty people and moisturize with high-end face products.) At no point could you cancel. Memberships were frozen. Members were told there was no mechanism to cancel until the crisis was over and everything was back to normal. Once it was deemed safe for health clubs to open again, the brand didn't even have to ask you to re-submit your credit card information. It just started charging your card again.

That example is one of the many that demonstrate a funda-mental truth of click-up economics: automated subscriptions allow brands to lock you into agreements that do not always serve you, nor allow you as the customer to be responsive to the actual moment you are living in. They believe that they are "automating customer happiness," but in fact many are automating restrictive business practices. Their massive scale has allowed Big Brands to grow and grow, returning more and more to shareholders, but getting further and further away from delivering an honorable customer experience.

When I say "honorable," I mean fair, balanced, respectful, re-sponsive, honest, just. Instead, most modern customer service is a minefield of robots, tangled phone trees, useless online FAQs, and emailing into a black hole—all meant to exhaust you and send you away. Help is seemingly limitless, yet we feel less and less helped. Gone is the intention to truly assist, support, or make right, because with such enormous customer bases, any one given customer rela-tionship means nothing. And when you scream and go full Karen on them, you are just part of the noise—a noise that continues to serve them well—and just gets you called out.

Very importantly, it is not just our economic transactions. It is our social ones, too. The infinite loop also automates our consumption of people. The concept of subscription has jumped from a business practice to a cultural one. We now *consume* our friends, colleagues, coworkers, gurus, influencers, celebrities, athletes, YouTube content creators, and sixth cousins. Social media, after all, is simply a feed of our subscriptions to other humans. You may not even remember where, when, or how you met someone, but they are in your feed. The choice to dub these "feeds" was a stroke of marketing genius. The metaphor suggests that we are meant to ruminate over and digest everything that comes down our trough. We see each other's lives, updates, thoughts in real time, whether our friends are in fact selling something or just offering a consistent emotional experience from their *personal brand* for us to consume and react to. *This person makes me happy; they always share funny memes. This person justifies my anger at the world; they always post about how dumb people are. This person represents my fantasy life; man, I wish I was in Italy right now, too. And had those muscles.*

The term *on brand* is now completely ubiquitous in our pop culture—meant to evaluate whether something you say or do is consistent with the image you project. It was once the case that our personal and professional identities could be kept somewhat separate, that what we did never quite blurred with who we were. Even celebrities who were able to monetize their identities were able to do so based only on the strength and relevance of their talents and careers. In the age of social media, people are famous for just *existing* and can attract and lead microcommunities made visible through the vast interconnectedness of the Internet. People can build entire careers overnight and out of their own version of "content." Business lives and personal lives have gotten so enmeshed that the common user now must specifically note in their social media posts what is an "ad" that they are being paid to post and what is their actual, real life.

As these platforms get more robust, we are trained, encouraged, even *expected* to commodify ourselves, to turn our daily lives into digestible bites of content, mistakenly believing we are the sellers— the "creators"—when, in fact, we are the unwitting product. What is unique about this moment in history is the rate at which we are being asked to commodify ourselves, by turning ourselves and our lives into digital profile pics, avatars, memes, photos, and videos. At this point, we're doing this all semi-consciously.

The problem with subscribing to *people* is the same as monthly recurring subscriptions: you never actually get away from them either. You are trapped in the infinite loop with them. And they are caught in their own infinite loops and keep giving us more and more of whatever emotions they inspire. Worse, they reinforce the values that got us to subscribe to those monthly recurring subscriptions (to candy, to lingerie, to Roblox) in the first place. Our digital social networks have become an *integral* element of click-up economics—a way for the Big Forces to scale their (often problematic) storytelling and to impose their values on millions and billions.

We then consume a massive volume of messages that mess with our underlying beliefs about ourselves, other people, and the greater world. Because we are *still* subscribed to the social feed of the popular girl from high school (thirty years later), we still believe we are too unattractive for a boyfriend, so we stay subscribed to Nutrisystem. Sure, that pressure existed before Instagram, but now it's piled on daily, in full color, with bountiful photo and video evidence of how popular she still is(!), activating our insecurities at eight on a Sunday morning while we're still in bed, propelling us to click on the Nutrisystem ad that *just so happens* to pop up at that very moment.

These automated, dynamic subscriptions to people work the same way. The fuller our day is with pings and rings and reminders and notifications and messages, gently and not so gently steering us to participate in this digital Supercommunity, the less time, energy, and focus we have for our families, our partners, our actual friends, or the community of humans physically around us.

The infinite loop keeps us on autopilot in our lives, and addicted to consumption of all kinds.* Automated, our lives are now a relentless race against supercomputers and the power they harness and yield. Man's great battle against the machine won't happen in the streets like apocalyptic scenes from movies propose. It is already happening on each of our screens, every single day.

And it's exhausting. We are "wiped out" and "have no time" because our bodies, minds, and hearts are living in real-live human time, but we are stuck in a world where all these subscriptions are running at the speed of light. As a result, we have no downtime to process, wait, anticipate, digest, reflect, regret, or even feel a damn thing. We are feeling so much that we are feeling nothing. It's confusing to the soul.

This is why we all felt that the circus had changed our perception of time itself. A year felt like five, three weeks ago felt like two years ago; it wasn't a "pandemic year," we joked, it was a "pandemic decade." (If only we'd known that might prove to be true, in one sense or another.) That sensation was not a figment of our imagination. Click-up economics has physically changed us, not only making our money move fast but forcing us to think, talk, walk, and respond faster. The go-go-go is being caused by the speed at which we transact and by the speed at which we interact. And it all moves instantaneously if it's automated. That temporal displacement we felt in 2020 was the result of an automated world coming to a crashing

---

* I do not use the word *addicted* lightly or unintentionally. The Big Forces have used powerful insights into basic human psychology to hook us.

halt. Our human bodies were unceremoniously flung out of the infinite loop, suddenly forced to process, wait, anticipate, digest, reflect, regret, and *feel*. Then our lives were jolted back into real-live human time while our work went into super-drive automated time. It was a jerky process.

None of this serves us. But it serves the Big Forces. Very well.

Three
One Big Collaboration

The Big Forces work together seamlessly to keep this automated system in tact. And their motives and incentives are aligned *just* enough to feed one another. Let's take a look at each force and see how it contributes. As this book progresses, this discussion will prove very helpful when we explore *what to do* about all of this.

First, Big Tech. Big Tech is the ringleader of all the Big Forces. It created the digital ecosystem in which click-up economics functions and in which all modern people breathe. Think I am being hyperbolic? Take an iPad away from a four-year-old and watch them have a meltdown the likes of which you have never seen in your life. I have seen kids go into physical convulsions. Big Tech did this. And every time we click on an app, a message, a page, a picture, a product, a post, a story, or a video, we give the entire system more power. As of this writing, the Apple App Store has 1.96 million apps available for download. The Google Play Store has 2.87 million apps. The average American has more than eighty apps on their phone. Yes, eighty. Where we put our *clicks* matters. Big Tech understands this all too well. It is high time we understand it, too.

Open your inbox. Or *inboxes*. Look at your emails. How many of these branded newsletters, special offers, or reminders do you remember signing up for? How often do they come? How many escaped your spam folder? How many wiggled their way through your junk filter? How often do you delete? How often do you click?

We think it doesn't matter because click-up economics has taken

our day-to-day lives and reduced them to a collection of micro behaviors. We watch micro stories. We have micro conversations. Our
checking account has micro charges. It's all been made tiny and
small, so that it feels insignificant.

But it all adds up. And it adds up fast. Before we know it, one
click becomes two. Five. Ten. And each of those clicks is tracked,
monitored, and measured in a process broadly called "engagement."
Once we are engaged, we are fed even more. Maybe you know this;
it's possible you don't; it bears explanation. Your engagement gives
companies major currency in business, in the culture, and in the
world. Companies will not only buy, sell, or share this data, but they
will use their "reach" (how many followers they have, how many
customers are subscribed, how many users engage with their products and *how* they engage) as the metrics to broker partnerships,
sell their services, negotiate better deals, manipulate markets, and
increase profits.

Look at Google. Not only are more than 3.5 billion Google
searches conducted worldwide each minute, but there are 2.5 quintillion bytes of data created each day, even more because of the "Internet of things"—all the processors and sensors and hidden little
robots in our lives, homes, cars, factories, offices, and cities. (What's
a quintillion? Um, I would have to Google to find out how many
actual zeroes that is; it's eighteen.) With just our searches alone, we
give Google's parent company, Alphabet, the power to determine the
future of the Internet, public policy (it has its own political action
committee), advertising, media, hiring practices, and the answers to
any number of larger cultural and social questions. Big Data gives
Big Power, and we're the ones doing the giving.

I'm not saying we should never use tech again. I'm using it right
now to type this page. I am saying that we have to wake up from
the fantasy that *tech is amazing always everywhere*. Turns out, living
in an episode of *Black Mirror* is not actually what we want. Many

of the business practices Silicon Valley has employed to take over the world are highly problematic. Lawsuits around the globe are being brought against Big Tech companies for planned obsolescence, for example, which is not only classist but arguably illegal. Whistleblowers are coming forward to warn of the grave dangers to the mental health and social development of our kids and teenagers and to our long-term economic life and social stability. The Federal Bureau of Investigation—yes, the FBI—has warned Americans that TikTok can track our every move and that the app, owned by a Chinese billionaire, may be a threat to our national security. In the winter of 2023, the entire country freaked out about spy balloons floating over Alaska, but 80 million of us scrolled through TikTok. Some of us learned about the balloons *on* TikTok. The threat to national security is not just up in the air.

(It is worthy of note that in May 2023, Geoffrey Hinton, considered "the godfather of AI," quit his post at Google to warn the nation about the dangers of artificial intelligences. While he did credit Google for acting responsibly, he admitted that it is "not inconceivable" that AI could wipe out humanity. Yes, humanity.)

We are beginning to hold tech leadership accountable for the dangers these products have brought into our laptops, homes, and families. The reckoning has begun. And it is muddy and complex. It requires sweeping policy changes from governments all over the world. And it requires committed and unbiased leadership, which is extremely hard to come by when our politicians and policymakers are using the very same products and services of Big Tech to reach people, distribute their messaging, and secure votes.

We may not be able to turn the clock back—many of us wouldn't want to—but we can find specific ways to use tech to better our lives and to solve specific problems. We can unsubscribe from *how* Big Tech has thus far conditioned us to use its products, how often, where, and why.

• • •

If Big Tech hadn't evolved to this highly sophisticated point, Big Brands wouldn't be able to stay so big and extend so far, engaging with all of us everywhere outside of a traditional brick-and-mortar storefront. Big Tech found a way to transform our clicks into money for the Big Brands. (The online shopping cart wasn't integral to the launch of the World Wide Web.) And money is power. So, just as it is important to understand how every click matters, it is equally important to understand just how much every *dollar* matters.

We love to use this funny word in America: *socioeconomics*. Socio-economics is where and how economics and social factors overlap. It's how we get away with never saying "class." We pride ourselves on not having classes in America, when we most certainly do. We have just disguised our classes using a highly sophisticated system of brands. The American brand system, perfected over a century of rampant consumerism, is how we reinstituted the English class system on this side of the pond.

Brands rely on the art and science of *branding*. Branding is powerful. Branding can take one corporation and spin it in front of you as five different ones. It can take Walmart and morph it into Bonobos. It can take Wrigley and morph it into Skittles. It can take a Honda and morph it into an Acura. Branding practices (and US corporation law) allow the Big Brands to be shapeshifters who appear to us in any form that we like so we just click and buy something. Branding used to be an art, in many ways a creative concern (design, colors, logo). Now it is more of a science, one that plays on our greatest hopes and fears. Using Big Data from Big Tech, market-ers can analyze not only the tried-and-true *old stuff* like consumer demographics (where you live, how old you are, if you're single or married), but they can now analyze and use very robust consumer *psychographics*.

Psychographics are wild. They can tell marketers what your personal relationship is to—and how you respond to messages about—success, failure, growth, power, social standing, fear. The list goes on. FOMO, fear of missing out, is not a term that just magically appeared in our lexicon. It is the product of a system now designed to exploit human psychology. If you deeply fear missing out, you will spend whatever it takes to never miss out on all that is cool in the Supercommunity. Psychographics present massive moral and ethical issues that the Big Brands are completely ignoring. I have known, been around, and worked with (and for) marketers for a long time, and not a single one has ever expressed even a minute concern about using psychographics. A massive amount of data about your emotional state—and mine—is being jockeyed daily to make the Big Brands money. Our insecurities about ourselves, our relationships, and the world are being exploited for profit. Blatantly.

More and more, we are becoming aware of just how Big Data is being weaponized against us in these ways. Thanks to good journalism, risky whistleblowing, and (some) oversight, we are understanding how, with ever-increasing precision and detail, the Big Forces are hunting us down daily based on our past behaviors. And then using messages to exploit our unique personal weaknesses. *You bought three Harry Styles t-shirts online last week in preteen sizes, and you live in Manalapan, NJ, so you must be a housewife. Your Facebook profile lists no job, so you must be a stay-at-home mom. Your pictures posted at 1:15 p.m. confirm that. And you used the word "safe" twice last week. So, you must want to protect your children. Here's an ad for a high-end security system. Here's one for tracking chips you can put in their sneakers. They make great Christmas stocking stuffers. And here's an email from a woman running for state senate in Nevada who advocates for armed security guards at schools. Because every New Jersey mom thinks and acts the exact same way and they all somehow hate the Nevada Dems. Click here to "chip in" some money. We got your email from the national Republican Party who got it from your credit card company who got it from your Life360 subscription.*

What? Fuck off. Seriously.

In her book *The Age of Surveillance Capitalism*, Harvard professor and social psychologist Shoshana Zuboff calls this exactly what it is: surveillance. We are being watched. All the time. Everywhere. Zuboff explains that the entire digital ecosystem is replete with "trackers," small pieces of code embedded in websites and apps that collect our every move online. She warns that "Even the most innocent-seeming applications such as weather, flashlights, ride sharing, and dating apps are 'infested' with dozens of tracking programs that rely on increasingly bizarre, aggressive, and illegible tactics to collect massive amounts of behavioral surplus ultimately directed at ad targeting."

I have known the power of branding well in my own life. A quick story: As a kid, I was obsessed—truly—with the Polo logo. We couldn't afford Polo, and that's all that the richest kids at school wore. One of them, William, was even asked by Polo to be a model for a spring campaign one year. A model. He was gorgeous. Little by little, I associated that tiny horse on William's chest with everything his family had and my family did not: a house on the hill, ski vacations, a Mercedes (with a car phone!), tennis courts in his backyard, even walk-in closets. I wanted, more than anything, to grow up and be the kind of man who could walk into a Polo store and buy whatever he wanted. That horse was my gateway into an entire wardrobe and lifestyle that told the world I was on my way up, economically and socially mobile, somehow better than my roots. That little horse signified all my personal aspirations, my goals, my dreams. It also reinforced the deep personal shame I had about growing up without money.

That's a crippling amount of pressure to take on. And to put on a kid. And a tiny horse. But brands do it because they know that they have the power to exploit our most intimate feelings about ourselves for their own economic gain. In the '90s, when I was in awe of William, the business intelligence was just beginning to be gathered. Now, flush with Big Data from Big Tech, Big Brands can serve me the exact message about Polo—and power and class—that they know I will respond to. (Go watch *The Social Dilemma*. It brilliantly illustrates how this all works.)

Now, look, I'm not advocating for a brandless world where we all wear the same gray jumpsuit or linen tunic. I am advocating for frank and open conversation, with ourselves and with our youngest people, about how we make meaning of such a branded world. Like media literacy, which has quickly become required learning in a society saturated with media, brand literacy is a counterpoint to such extreme brand consumption. Now that we no longer go to the mall and the mall comes to us, we need new tools to process the onslaught. Sadly, most of our schools are ill prepared to teach such twenty-first-century lessons. So, we must do it in every way we can.

Education, awareness, and any true awakening does not serve the Big Forces. Nor does our taking a breath to step away from all of this. Because in that breath we might realize that we don't need all the shit they are selling us. Our constant engagement with the tools of Big Tech allows for *constant connectedness* so that brand messages (what the brand wants you to understand about how their products and services can make your life "better") have a smooth digital highway to travel instantaneously and find us. The tighter the society's digital bonds, the more glued together the Supercommunity is, the faster these messages travel.

This is *key*. Because if these messages fall on deaf ears—or are thwarted by such silly things as geographic distance or personal boundaries—a brand has to then spend more money to reach you, and that affects their bottom line. If consumers stay *always on*, always in touch, connected tightly, constantly engaged and interacting, then we can be exposed constantly to this messaging. And our laptop, our phone, our browser, our home, our ears, our eyes, our heart, and ultimately our wallet stays open.

Reimagining the American economy starts by redefining our relationship (individually and collectively, through public policy) with the Big Brands—from food, clothing, and pharmaceuticals to home improvement, consumer electronics, and transportation. It requires us to redefine our relationship with our money—how we spend, where we spend, when we spend, *why* we spend. More fundamentally, it begs us to reevaluate our needs and wants. And our relationship to desire. Maybe it is okay to not get everything we want *right now*. Maybe it's time to live within our means. Maybe it is time to spend with strategy, to stabilize our households, to grow our savings, and to get financially fit. We must rethink every dollar that leaves our wallet. We learned even before the circus that half of the American population would have trouble paying an unexpected $400 expense, and that 19 percent would not be able to pay it at all. As the circus waned, research showed that high-income Americans were beginning to save again, but low-income Americans were not saving as much. Perhaps it is because we simply do not have the money left over after paying for essentials—that which we need, the very products inflation hit the hardest.

It is time to break up with the Big Brands, or at the very least it is time for some serious conversation about their business practices. I refuse to be gaslit into thinking that any of this is normal, that this is simply *the free market being the free market*. That is akin to saying *boys will be boys*. And we all know that that just doesn't cut it anymore. We can have no true equity in our society until we properly balance the scales between brands, businesses, capital, and workers and consumers. The subscription model does not give us more equity. It gives us less.

It is time to see the Big Brands for what they are: impersonal investment vehicles for one stratum of our society. (Yes, apparently *stratum* is the singular of *strata*. Huh.)

None of this works without the funding, investment, services, tools, and support of the Big Banks. The Big Banks shower the Big Brands and Big Tech with capital to grow, grow, grow. The money held by large banks and financial institutions—which is *our* money—is funding this entire engine, the endless, relentless hamster wheel of modern life. Somehow, because our leaders subscribed us all to the notion that *the major banks are too big to fail* in 2008—undercutting one of the primary premises of the free market—these banks have gained even more power as click-up economics has taken over. (As my mother always says, "What doesn't kill you makes you stronger.") Some of the players may have changed positions, but their stronghold on American consumer life is even tighter. We bailed them out after years of customer abuse and predatory behavior—nasty practices that tanked our housing market and then our entire economy before it sent a destructive ripple throughout the economies of the world. And not a single executive went to jail. Instead, they got bonuses. And a blueprint. When the next national disaster struck, they were all right there, ready for their next windfall.

During the circus, instead of simply sending emergency funding to our nation's employers directly (the loans were "forgiven" anyway), the US government used private banks to process $670 billion in aid from the Paycheck Protection Program. In turn, the banks took *$13 billion* in fees. The top four—JPMorgan Chase, Bank of America, Wells Fargo, and Citigroup—now hold and manage over $9 trillion in assets. (For context, the federal budget for the 2023 fiscal year was $5.8 trillion.) These are not banks. Nations. Empires.

On the investment end, click-up economics has allowed money to "work" for wealthy people in new ways that would have been unrecognizable to bankers a hundred years ago. Even to bankers twenty-five years ago. Their wealth grows, while on the consumer end, not much happens at all. According to the FDIC (Federal Deposit Insurance Corporation), the national average interest rate on savings accounts is now .08 percent. In 1984, the average rate on a five-year CD peaked at nearly 12 percent. In 1990, it was closer to 4 percent or 5 percent. JPMorgan Chase made $43.8 billion in 2021, and its CEO took home $34.5 million, but for every $1,000 you had in your saving account, you got 80 cents, which likely disappeared in your checking account in order to pay for one fee or another. Consumers paid $11 billion in overdraft fees in 2019, before the circus, down from $17 billion in 2018, before it went back up to more than $12 billion during the circus. Imagine that: as 40 million Americans were rendered jobless, the Big Banks still took an average of $24 for every overdraft, some as high as $36. With 64 percent of Americans living paycheck to paycheck, banks still profit by taking money from people—the majority of consumers—who literally do not have any.

Because your major household transactions are now a slew of micro ones, your chances of paying these fees are much higher than they used to be. If, say, in 1990 your check for the cable company bounced, you would pay a $5 fee. Now, if what you call your "cable" is made up of Netflix, Hulu, Apple TV, and Paramount+, and those transactions can't be funded by the money in your checking account, you'll pay an extra $96 to $144 in overdraft fees. As James Baldwin said, "Anyone who has ever struggled with poverty knows how extremely expensive it is to be poor." In click-up economics, it is extremely expensive to not be rich, which is why we don't even pretend anymore that that is *not* the goal.

The wealthy, of course, all have their hands in the pot to collect their share of your every transaction, thanks to the financial technology tools created by the Big Banks and Big Tech. Consider any of your $5.99 recurring subscription purchases. That transaction has four (more like six) parties involved in its processing: the consumer (me and you), the merchant (whomever we are paying), the issuing institution of your credit card, the acquiring institution, the online gateway (the tech company that provides the actual window we type our card details into), and our credit card company. This is commonly referred to as the "four-party scheme." And what a scheme it is. The deal is the same when you order takeout from a platform like Seamless, DoorDash, Instacart, Caviar (all of which, by the way, add another party to the party). What you are actually doing is shooting money up the ladder, one late, cold pizza at a time. Click. Up. If you walk down and pay the restaurant cash, five other parties would lose out on money. Is it any wonder that speedy fifteen-minute delivery services abound and that there is a deluge of marketing for them nearly everywhere you turn?

Worse for consumers, reversing charges or getting refunds is an exhausting and seemingly impossible process, thanks to automated customer-service systems (that often require us to provide information to talk to a human—information we need a human to help us locate in the *first place*), helpline phone numbers buried deep behind seven clicks in a website, obnoxious phone trees, and an army of customer-service reps who just plain do not give a fuck. (And let's be real, why should they? They're getting paid $12 an hour to deal with pure outrage all day long while their boss makes millions. Wouldn't you be as "over it" as they all seem to be?)

In modern America, the Big Banks work for the wealthy. And any effort to rewrite their rules provokes a legion of lawyers and lobbyists to exert powerful influence on our politics. Consumers have less and less power because the dollars they have at our nation's Big Banks—in our consumer checking accounts and savings accounts—are not there to be protected. They are there to be taken, fee by fee, on repeat, automatically.

Big Banks have no intention of making *you or me* richer. They are doing so much more for people who already have wealth than they are for you and me. Doors are being opened—flung open!—for those at the top and closed—slammed!—on those in the middle and at the bottom. Consider your personal savings again (if you have personal savings; most Americans do not). You are keeping your savings at a bank that is paying you that .08 percent interest. That bank is then using your money—and mine and everyone else's—to purchase treasury bonds from the US government that currently yield 4 percent interest. They are literally taking your money, making money off it, and not cutting you in on the deal. Because they have no intention of helping you. They intend on exploiting you. As my father would say, that is "highway fucking robbery." My father and I don't often agree on much, but perhaps this is where we can come together, red and blue. We are all being equally screwed by those at the very top.

We may defend our personal privacy, as quickly as that is disappearing in this new age, and praise all that is private in a prosperous America, but money—currency—is a *public instrument*. It is meant to flow and move around and change hands and touch everyone. It is the blood that runs through our collective body, delivering that which nourishes each of us. If that blood is mostly stored in one place—if it is locked up by the Big Banks to enrich one tier of society—it cannot nourish the rest. If it is solely stored in the brain, the heart will slow. The liver will break down. The kidneys will suffer. Eventually, though, so will the brain. It is all connected. *We* are all connected.

Which brings us to Big Media. Together with Big Tech, Big Brands, and the Big Banks, Big Media creates and amplifies the stories that make this all "normal." And it's constantly making louder the noise that our voices are all drowning in. Big Media dictates the focus of our attention, what we watch and listen to, what we support and what we are outraged by. And that statement is not a matter of philosophy or opinion. We know that Big Tech has found a way to quantify, track, measure, monitor, and report where we put our attention. Click-up economics has commodified our attention fully. Attention is money, and money is attention. This is why we are seeing the media and politics converge, why Washington is becoming Hollywood, and Hollywood is becoming Washington, why we are witnessing and living through a new age of bizarre leaders who seem more like carnival folk, and why we ourselves feel less and less powerful. In the relentlessness of American life, the noise ensures that our attention is everywhere but on the things that matter. It is not on our physical and mental health. It is not on our neighbors and communities. It is always somewhere else.

For most of us, our eyes are constantly on the television, or on our iPad, or on our phone. The content on these devices all used to be created, supplied, curated, and monitored by completely different industries—all of which have merged, combined, and *congealed* into one massive, interconnected, and *demanding* media world. Big Media then joined forces with Big Tech and the Big Brands. That collaboration serves Big Media because Big Media has endless channels, pages, and streams to fill with content. It serves the Big Brands because they want to flood the Supercommunity with bite-sized stories or "branded content" that sells and sells and sells.

This all adds up to endless noise for the consumer. It is everywhere. And it's constant. If we want the noise to stop, we first have to recognize our role in it. In her book *How to Do Nothing: Resisting the Attention Economy*, author, artist, and educator Jenny Odell reminds us that everything we watch or listen to is a choice. "My experience" (by which she means her life experience), she says, "is what I agree to attend to. Only those items which I notice shape my mind. Without selective interest, experience is in utter chaos." With our daily "acts of attention," she continues, "we decide who to hear, who to see, and who in our world has agency. In this way, attention forms the ground not just for love, but for ethics."

Perhaps our scattered and indiscriminate focus is why we find our ethics and our relationships in such deep crisis. Our choosing to watch, listen to, click, follow, like, or "love" takes attention away from what we actually love and gives unethical players more and more power—whether they be celebrities, athletes, musicians, social media stars, media personalities, or politicians. That makes them reliant on us for attention, and so their behaviors get more extreme, which in turn provokes more engagement. Even if we are just there to "watch the train wreck," we are feeding the genie. We may not be able to put the genie back in the bottle, but we can stop feeding it so freely and so generously. It is time to starve that fucker.

This has a real impact on our personal and global outlooks. Imagine for a moment that you saw an actual train wreck. You would be shocked, frozen, maybe even captivated. Now imagine if someone had the power to wreck trains in front of you all day long. Your shock, your fixed focus, your attention would just be sustained until it was your new normal. Eventually, you would be completely desensitized—your absorption of what you were seeing on autopilot. At some point you would start to believe that the world is just full of train wrecks. That is, sometimes, how it feels to exist in the age of Big Media. I feel that way. We are all frozen. Captivated. Captured. Trapped. On repeat. In the loop.

Who exactly creates that noise? That is well worth defining, especially considering that the media has come under constant fire, the free press has been called "the enemy of the people," and the structures, forms, and actual companies are constantly morphing. For the purposes of our discussion, Big Media is made up of three industries: social media, the news or "the press," and entertainment (film, television, and music).*

Wait, is social media—Facebook, Instagram, Twitter, LinkedIn, TikTok—Big Tech or Big Media? Yes. It's both. These platforms were created, simply, to connect friends and family and to help us build community online. Unfortunately, nothing stays simple (or small) for long when the already wealthy can make money from it; our constant need for growth ensures that. In the years since their creation, as the traditional media started to report on tweets and elevate them to "news," social media platforms have become the Wild West of free speech and personal expression, a fertile space for influencing massive groups of people and impacting cultural and political behaviors. And so "the media" has embraced, mixed with, and become entwined with social media.

As we have seen, this is not healthy for society. The data scientist Frances Haugen, also known as "the Facebook whistleblower," testified in front of Congress in 2022. "I believe," she said, "that Facebook's products harm children, stoke division, and weaken our democracy." She was the first, to be followed by former executives from the other major social media platforms, each warning that not all is right in the fantasyland Big Tech has created.

Platforms are built to be bottomless, endless, seemingly *infinite*. You can never run out of things to look at, and much of what you're looking at is what the platform has curated for you based on what you have already spent time with in the past. Welcome back to the

---

* You and I both know that the lines between all of these are blurry. How a company develops a story (development), produces it (content production), and distributes it (distribution) all take many modern forms, from iPhones to movie theaters to branded content that mixes traditional film/TV/video with brands, to podcasts to gaming to interactive media experiences—all of which contain original music or sampled music. The larger Big Media gets, the more ubiquitous its messaging gets.

loop. Your past determines your future, so that you are predictable. That bears repeating: your past determines your future, so that you are predictable. The loop deepens your worldview, purposefully reinforcing it so that the Big Brands and Big Media (and the Big Parties) can target you easily, cheaply, and keep you engaged. Soak, rinse, repeat.

Consumers are not the only ones getting shafted. Anyone who is not a Big Player is, too. Very strong myths float around our society about just how great the digital revolution has been for the various media sectors, or how we have all somehow benefitted from twenty-four hours a day of constant content. But ask a news anchor how it feels to report everything a politician tweets as if it's a nuclear event or to call mass shootings their "beat." Ask a magazine publisher how great it's been to have to move their entire business from print to digital just to keep up with that news cycle. Or a television showrunner or musician or photographer what it's like to no longer own their own content, to have to split a profit pie into minuscule portions—mere pennies—because one of the Big Media corporations rewrote contracts for the entire industry to make sure that they benefited the most.

In their book, *Chokepoint Capitalism*, author Cory Doctorow and author and attorney Rebecca Giblin detail that very exploitation of the creative industries. They define chokepoint capitalism as a system in which "a multinational monopolist (or cartel) locks up audiences inside a system that they control, and uses that control to gouge artists, creating toll booths between creators and their audiences." Both chokepoint capitalism and surveillance capitalism are key features of click-up economics. And they're not bugs. They are features.

What does this have to do with subscriptions? Subscriber-based products, services, and networks are changing our economics. There is a consolidation of money and power never before seen in all these spaces. Consolidated power not only writes subscriber agreements but it also writes the very contracts that dictate the terms of how all their products and services get made and executed—and who profits. The infinite loop we're all trapped in is a very curated place, and its systems and *subscriptions* are being refined daily by the Big Forces and the armies of highly educated and highly paid attorneys who pen these contracts.

It is all enough to drive a person—and a society—absolutely mad. If we want change, we must transform our relationship with Big Tech, Big Brands, the Big Banks, and Big Media. We must call for our leaders to enact public policy that defines the ground rules for this massive collaboration of the Big Forces. And we must demand that our government reckon with the gross inequities of click-up economics. The only way to do that is for the rules of the game to be written and enforced by someone—anyone—not directly benefiting.

Therein lies the rub. The Big Parties are in bed with all the Big Forces. Let's look one by one:

THE BIG PARTIES × BIG BRANDS collaboration serves both very well. The Big Brands now "sort" into one political column or the other (as author, *New York Times* columnist, and podcaster Ezra Klein might say), either to further a corporate mission, to win the public-relations race, or simply for profit. The Big Parties use this sorting as a shorthand to mine data and learn voter behavior, as it is based on consumer behavior more and more. Case in point: Pride Oreo cookies. Really, we're doing *this* now? Oreo puts the rainbow flag on their packaging and positions itself as a liberal brand. They make more money in June for Pride month. And the political messages of the Big Parties are reinforced through, um, gay cookies on every shelf in every grocery store. Take it from your gay writer, I have zero interest in Mondelez International exploiting my sexuality so they can sell more sugar. Don't tell me that it spreads awareness and helps queer kids. Let's stop using queer kids as a front for corporate bullshit.

THE BIG PARTIES × BIG TECH collaboration benefits both, too. Big Tech benefits from weak policies about data collection, sharing, usage, and sales. In turn, the Big Parties use Big Data to target voters. It is now completely commonplace to get fund-raising appeals from politicians in every state, to get text messages that put the onus on *us* to reply with STOP if we want to unsubscribe, and to get incessant phone calls—recorded and live—from major campaigns, from a politician, a state party, the national party, a PAC, and a local field office. Yes, some of our boldest public servants are calling Big Tech to task. As a citizen, let me say this: it is not happening fast enough. More politicians must put aside their own interests and act for the American people.

THE BIG PARTIES × THE BIG BANKS are equally collaborative. The Big Banks are deeply invested in maintaining the status quo and their outsized role in our daily lives. The status quo serves the parties because many of their candidates are bankrolled by wealthy clients and the banks themselves. It has become trite to call for an end to *Citizens United*—the 2010 court ruling that guaranteed that corporations and wealthy donors could spend unlimited funds on our elections (again, unlimited can be dangerous)—but the ruling upended campaign finance and has enabled the current mess. We can no longer excuse the right because they are traditionally known as the party of big business. And we can no longer excuse the left because they somehow have the moral wherewithal to keep undue influence at bay. (As we unsubscribe, we would be wise to unsubscribe from any candidate who takes corporate money. "We need money, so we'll take it from wherever it comes. It doesn't affect my thinking"—that common refrain from our politicos—is no longer acceptable.)

This last collaboration is probably the most dangerous: **BIG PAR-TIES × BIG MEDIA**. The Big Parties exploit the Big Media to tell their stories, reinforce the underlying beliefs of their parties, and spread all kinds of toxic messaging. In one of my all-time favorite books, *Winning the Story Wars: Why Those Who Tell—and Live—the Best Stories Will Rule the Future*, author Jonah Sachs explains the power of narrative-making for storytellers, creatives, businesses, brands, and public figures. He recommends that readers "orient your entire brand toward storytelling by defining and defending a powerful moral of your story in every communication." Sachs intends his work to help empower truth tellers and to advocate for empowerment marketing that can help a society mature and embrace citizenship, but these tactics have been weaponized by bad actors, who now use the storytelling craft's most powerful tools to persuade, manipulate, even gaslight the public.

All of which makes unsubscribing a highly political act—not one divided between red and blue but one divided between those who exploit this new economy and those of us who are tired of the utter bullshit that it brings into our lives.

Four

The Heart of It All

In America, we love to gut criticisms of our system by chalking up its problems to being "just business." If it is "just business," then it is not personal, it is not intended to harm anyone, and it is not imbued with silly things like feelings. That is a very easy, flippant way to excuse us from doing the hard work to improve our system or even discussing the implicit moral questions that it raises. It absolves us of having to structure policies that protect against consumer abuses or fix the larger structural inequities that have developed over time like plaque develops on a tooth or cholesterol clogs the arteries. The next time someone casually says, "It's just business," take a deep breath, and tell them, "But it's not." Business is highly emotional. And it is emotion, after all, that glues the Supercommunity together. The Big Forces need the Supercommunity, so they rely on and seek to manipulate that emotion. Plainly put, they abuse that emotion.

Do I mean abuse, like *abuse*? I do. "Abuse" is the use of something for an ill purpose. Remember, we revolted against the king because of his "abuse" of power. That's not a word we are unfamiliar with in America. Let's not all clutch our pearls. If we all claim to be loyal to our constitution, we must wake up to how power is being used and abused by the Big Forces.

We are addicted to consumption because it allows us to feel one half of the wide array of human emotions—the "good ones"—with less and less risk of encountering and having to feel the "bad ones." Click-up economics helps us "get" good feelings fast and use our tech, like a pacifier, to calm ourselves quickly when we can't get what we want. Perhaps we have focused away from people and on products more and more over this last century because products promise us clean and positive emotional experiences without the murk and complication of other humans. Humanity is messy. It is full of loss, discomfort, displeasure, disappointment, disapproval, disgust; the list goes on.

Marketers understand this, so much so that emotion is the very core of the advertising industry and of its main tenet: people buy based on positive emotion (e.g., *Doritos will make you feel as cool as cool ranch*) or fear of negative emotion (e.g., *Allstate car insurance will save you from the agony of a lawsuit*).

The latest iPhone makes you feel smart, modern, ahead of the curve—cool, even. You command attention. You are loved. In the same way, a new Lexus makes you feel powerful, successful, triumphant. These emotional promises are wrapped up in the car company's invitation to you to "Experience Amazing." (I think I can have amazing experiences without a Lexus, but I digress.) Dove body wash will make you feel refreshed, new, clean, and—dare I say it—virginal. As peaceful and tranquil as a dove. Even Citi Bike, here in New York City, a service that took the European model of bicycles for the masses on every corner and commercialized it, promises that its riders will feel "accomplished" when they tackle biking in such a dynamic city. By no means do I except myself here. Before I unsubscribed, staying at expensive hotels (that I could not actually afford) made me feel special, better than my peers, successful. My MoMA watch (from the Museum of Modern Art) made me feel modern and cool. Ordering from Seamless made me feel powerful, like a king commanding to be fed!

Brands pay teams of creative professionals millions of dollars to connect products with positive emotions through *stories*, which are then exploited in photography, graphic design, and video, across both physical and digital platforms. And to make sure that these stories are landing as intended, the Big Forces spend big money to poll, survey, and focus-group consumers. Emotionally aroused consumers buy. Bored consumers don't. That's why sex sells, and it always has. More sales means a company is successful. A successful company makes stockholders happy. Again, emotion.

Emotion has great power. And the Big Brands wield this power brilliantly. You know this in your own experience. Williams-Sonoma sends you constant messages that remind you that you should be cooking with very high-end cookware. *You don't cook enough. You don't even bake! That means that you don't love your kids. You are an awful person.* You feel guilty, so you buy. Individual infinite loop. Big Tech sends constant messages that you are not engaging enough with the modern world. *You have an obligation to every human you have ever met.* You feel old, obsolete, and selfish, rude. So, you engage. Individual infinite loop. Same with the Big Banks. *Everyone else has more money than you do.* Same with the Big Media. *Everyone else is watching season 74 of* Hot Tub Sex Party. The Big Parties, too. *If you don't have an opinion about Donald Trump Jr.'s ex-wife's latest post, you are not an engaged citizen. You are not a patriot. You are not a loyal American. You are a piece of shit.* And on and on.

It's all one big Emotion Engine, sending millions and billions from every screen in our lives to the bank accounts of the nation's largest stockholders.

Is there something wrong with being a stockholder? Of course not. But let's remember that it is the wealthiest 10 percent of American households who now own 89 percent of all US stocks. The top 1 percent of Americans own 54 percent of individually held stocks. And I'm not talking about your friend who is technically "in the 1 percent" because she and her husband make a combined salary of $541,612 in Pennsylvania (the threshold is different in every state). I am talking about the top 1 percent of *wealth*, not *income*. That means your friend has to own $11 million plus in investments (or assets) to "get into" the top 1 percent.

A lot of us behave like the 1 percent because we fantasize about being in the 1 percent—or even the 0.1 percent—when, in fact, we have much more in common economically with, say, the rail workers who almost went on strike in 2022. Or those Amazon drivers who were forced to urinate in a Snapple bottle. Or Starbucks baristas who are subjected to over two hundred labor violations in the workplace. We are *all* concerned about our retirement. We are *all* concerned about the price of our dream home. We are *all* concerned about what shot our kids have at experiencing the same standard of living we have been able to "achieve" over the last fifty years in America. Our general lack of empathy toward the plight of these people is the result of a brilliant story sold to us that our participation in click-up economics—as consumers—somehow makes us all digital capitalists. We are not. There are about two thousand people or families in that group. The rest of us work for them. Is there something wrong with working for them? No. But let's be clear about how this all works. I want to vacation in Turks and Caicos, too, but that doesn't mean Kroger workers are my enemy. They never will be.

Just like investors, we, the consumers, want to feel good and take fewer risks. Which is why a national system of brands works so well in the United States. We're a large country, nearly three thousand miles wide. We have a system of roadways, trains, and planes to connect fifty very different states—and all the various cultures that live in them—into one union. That union would be far less cohesive if, when you traveled, you felt like you were in a different country every time you crossed a state border. Brands provide a consistent experience that's dependable for consumers. We know when we walk into a 7-Eleven that the coffee will taste the same in New York, Idaho, or Arizona. Our experience is predictable. And we like that. Same with Target, Best Buy, Jeep, Disney, and Google. If the experience were different in every state, we would have to risk food tasting bad, clothes not fitting, cars being less comfortable, and banks operating differently. These things make us feel those five *d* words: discomfort, displeasure, disappointment, disapproval, and disgust. And we don't like that.

Is it any wonder that the cultural meme "Karen" is so pervasive? Karen is a privileged white woman who complains to the manager because she has had to suffer the indignity of one or many of those five *d* words. Karen is America, and America is Karen. I propose that there are two Karens: Karen—with a *K*—asks for the manager because she feels something negative. *She is not supposed to feel bad things!* Worse, she is being forced to confront a reality of the world that differs from her curated bubble. She yells at the manager because she is entitled to get what she wants when she wants it.

Caren—with a *C*—asks for the manager because she is exasperated. The manager is the only human face she is permitted to interact with—the frontline soldier of a system designed to exploit, abuse, and screw her. She has empathy for the manager, knowing the manager is getting screwed way harder by the corporation than she is, but she has *nowhere else to turn*. She must speak up and ask and hope that the message works its way up the chain of command.

I love Caren. Karen gets pretty annoying. The Big Forces love that we all hate Karen, because our collective shaming sends a powerful message to Caren: do not speak up against the system.

Wait, what's wrong with trying to eliminate feeling bad? Nothing, in theory. Why shouldn't we work together to eliminate human suffering of any kind? Wouldn't life be better for all of us if we found a way to eliminate negative experiences? The problem is that we are not eliminating them. We are overlooking them, closing our eyes to them, medicating them away, or simply shifting them to other people: foreign workers and our own working class. The inconvenient truth is that you can't eliminate feeling bad, no matter how sexy the sales pitch is. Someone somewhere will feel it. Is there a difference between feeling bad, suffering, and experiencing pain? Yes. But we're all connected, parts of one large system. We must realize that when we sit in conference rooms working to eliminate *friction*, *seams*, and *pain points* from consumer experiences, that someone is going to feel that friction. Someone is going to feel that seam. Someone is going to feel that pain.

Our globalized economy, as currently designed and supported by both sides of the political aisle, allows Americans (and other wealthy nations), for example, to experience the pleasure of new clothing at low prices and the emotions that come along with that—joy, happiness, confidence, pride. It allows the owners and the investor class to reap financial benefit, which creates similar positive emotions, for them. And it shifts displeasure and suffering to other peoples in other lands. Yes, there is an argument to be made that globalization is a net positive for the world, a rising tide that raises all ships, and that an interconnected global economic system can lift underdeveloped countries out of poverty. But the toll it takes on working people in other lands is out of our control. So, it seems, is the toll it takes on the environment. This ultimately affects us all.

Second, the loss of jobs in our own country creates despair here at home. I have seen it in my own circles. It is that despair that working people then seek to offset, or mask, or eliminate through further consumption. That factory worker whose job is gone because we make the majority of our goods in other countries now turns to food to make them feel joy, drugs to make them feel happy, guns to make them feel safe, Facebook ranting to make them feel purposeful, and television to make them feel any number of human emotions that the characters on the screen get to feel: pride, appreciation, excitement, love. A knockoff Gucci bag helps, too.

I don't include guns to be provocative, merely to point out that when we feel unsafe, not secure, vulnerable, we have been trained to look for products that can help us offset that feeling. Gun sales skyrocketed during the circus. Is it because Americans genuinely believed that the Black Lives Matter protestors were going to bust into their houses or that a well regulated citizen's militia would be necessary? Some did. That Missouri couple who came out their front door with guns drawn certainly did. But I would wager to say that most of us simply *felt unsafe* as an invisible assailant floated from person to person in cities and towns across the country. Viral plague may be unfamiliar to us, but the *feeling* it elicited is not, and neither was the product that offered the solution.

As a result of this massive daily transfer of emotions, the Emotion Engine is making us all less and less tolerant of negative emotions and less and less adaptable, nimble, and resilient when faced with the harsh realities of what it is to be human. Deeper, you can't ever *really* eliminate feeling bad. Feeling bad is not a human flaw. It can be a beneficial human perk. Its importance goes well beyond helping us to know the difference between pleasure and pain. It helps us to see how our desire (what we want) is out of alignment with reality. We want a diamond. We got a cubic zirconia. We feel bad. The Big Forces collaborate to maintain that misalignment. Because feeling bad makes you say, "Fuck it! I'm buying the diamond! Even if I have no business spending that much money right now!" True liberation—true joy—comes from learning how to accept reality as it is. Not easy.

Click-up economics is amplifying all of these dynamics faster than we can solve the problems they create. So, no, it's not "just business." It has real-world effects on actual real-live humans, because it takes small micro abuses—those little moments when CEOs and their closest teams make moral decisions about how to wield the power of human emotion—and writes them into each of the subscriptions that hold us in the infinite loop. In effect, click-up economics automates emotional abuse.

These are strong words. I get it. I'm leaning in to make as clear a point as I can. But let's stop pretending we can't possibly understand when we see otherwise "normal" Americans acting in extreme ways. They are doing so because the system they live in is playing high-stakes poker with their very sense of self, the future of their family, and their innate human instincts to love and be loved.

The most dangerous effect of this automation is that this emotional abuse primes us to put up with more and more bullshit. In his brilliant, pocket-sized book *On Bullshit,* moral philosopher and Princeton professor Harry G. Frankfurt observes that "one of the mostly salient features of our culture is that there is so much bullshit. Everyone knows this." His analysis of bullshit—and his earnest search for the word's etymology—is not only engaging and entertaining in its academic approach to a word that we all find to be wholly unacademic, but also offers us a definition of bullshit, which he proposes to be nearly identical to *humbug,* as defined in *The Prevalence of Humbug* by Max Black. "Black suggests a number of synonyms for *humbug,* including the following: *balderdash, claptrap, hokum, drivel, buncombe, imposture,* and *quackery.*"

Frankfurt proposes that our choice to use the word *humbug*—or its equivalents—is an effort to appear more genteel. That is likely why, he might agree, President Biden calls it *malarkey,* meaning nonsense. It isn't my desire to appear genteel. This book is an exercise in authenticity. So, I am more than happy to call it in these pages what we all know it is: bullshit. The infinite loop is exhausting because it is full of this bullshit. We want lives of meaning and purpose, but this never-ending bullshit is in the way and only seems to be intensifying.

What is that bullshit? You and I know it well. Bullshit is walking into a mall and seeing a thirty-foot banner that reads "Dress like you are somebody." Bullshit is print cartridges that cost as much as the actual printer, and toner protected by three cubic feet of Styrofoam like it was the Hope Diamond. Bullshit is the pharmacy refusing to fill a prescription because the insurance company won't approve your life-saving meds on a Sunday. Bullshit is $93,000 Taylor Swift tickets. Bullshit is calling spyware "cookies." Bullshit is allowing George Santos to be seated in the Congress of the United States of America. Bullshit is the insufferable lying that underpins our politics, our banking, our media, our brands. Bullshit is endless marketing emails, texts, notifications, calls, brochures, catalogs. Bullshit is advertising as ubiquitous as air and round-the-clock media on every screen—much of which abandoned a long time ago the norms that once held it in a certain balance with truth, integrity, and goodwill. Bullshit is egregious hold times, because corporations don't want to pay for too large a customer support team to service their 76 million subscribers. *Sure, I have all day Saturday to sit on this phone so we can somehow find the one person in your mangled corporate org chart who has the power to reverse the double charge on my Visa for an umbrella I bought in the rain because the old one was so incredibly shitty that it fell apart in my hands the first time it encountered water.* Bullshit is not even having a customer service phone number. *Click here to text with Emma, our AI chatbot who can read real, actual human words and respond with utterly unrelated nonsense, like she was programmed by a Shih Tzu. Don't worry. She learns on her own. In two years, she'll be able to charge your Visa whenever you even think about umbrellas or rain or Shih Tzus.*

You get it. You've been there. Rant over. The systems of the Big Forces are now so big that all they can produce is Big Bullshit. Which is polished and served to millions. So, it must be scalable. Which makes it standardized, cleaned, and void of humanity. These systems have no soul left in them. And they do not respect the individual because the individual is completely expendable when you have more subscribers than the United Kingdom has people.

The real problem with such overwhelming bullshit is this: the bullshit must be extreme or it cannot break through its own noise. Saturation is how those in power stay in power. It requires money to break through all the noise, and the Big Forces have the capital to do that. They have the cash to fund the marketing to actually be seen and heard. And when they do break through, they must hold our attention with even more extreme bullshit, because if they relent for even a microsecond, we'll move on to the other forty-seven pings and rings that are annoying us and vying for our limited focus. The larger players get larger because they are the only ones who can afford to engage. The rest of us—consumers, local chains, Main Street shops, small-business owners, nonprofits, entrepreneurs, schools, independent artists, doctors, accountants, anyone who is not a Big Player—we are all screaming into the void. And we all just swirl and swirl and swirl, in the infinite loop. And pray for a vacation.

Tech-fueled messaging gets super dark when it starts to create unique realities for each of us to swirl and swirl in. We have always been surrounded by ads and marketing. That's not new. But click-up economics breeds extreme messaging to cut through its own clutter, which alters our relationship with truth and authenticity and generates (then amplifies) the lies, the manipulations, and constant drama in society.

There is a reason Merriam-Webster declared *gaslighting* the word of the year in 2022. Gaslighting is the intentional creation of an altered reality in order to manipulate. The term comes from a 1944 MGM film in which a husband, intent on making his wife lose her mind, raises and lowers the lights of the gas lamps around their house. He deliberately tries to convince her that she can't trust her own perception of reality. Whereas *exaggerations* and *mistruths* sit on one end of a spectrum of lies, *gaslighting* occupies the other.

Gaslighting is creating, disseminating, and defending "alternative facts." It's denying the scientific realities of both climate change and the efficacy of vaccines. It's spreading a Big Lie about election fraud. Yes, there are plenty of fine points to argue in our politics, but you cannot have a legitimate discussion that solves a problem if you can't even agree on the basic facts of a situation. Our digital ecosystem is a breeding ground for gaslighting because all of our screens can now be fully customized with targeted messaging, resulting in the creation of countless altered and warped realities. My dad and I see the world differently because we literally see different worlds.

Government is not the only perpetrator. When the circus hit, the advertising industry—a $148.8 billion message machine—suddenly stopped. Overnight. Turns out, you can't bullshit your way through a worldwide crisis, so the Big Brands pulled their ads. Very few stepped up with *Mr. Mom*–style "Tuna with a Heart" campaigns. (Google it.) Instead, they waited to flood the market with the usual nonsense in 2021 and 2022. Were there exceptions? Of course. But the gaslighting took the form so many of us felt it would. The ad industry revived the same bullshit from 2019. No mention of what we had all just been through. No care for reality or for an honest, authentic message. Just back to normal, deliberately stoking the flames of consumer desire and intentionally creating a fictional reality in which Americans were somehow ready, willing, and able to consume relentlessly again. After a million people died. *What the fuck! Are we crazy or is now not the time to buy an $80,000 Infiniti SUV?*

How is this gaslighting? By ignoring the circus and the heavy toll it took on all of us, the Big Brands once again constructed their own reality of the world—ad by ad, message by message—a curated reality in which those two to three years simply *never happened*. This collective ignorance, in which we were all just expected to pick up exactly where we left off on March 17, 2020, left (and continues to leave) no room to feel the grief or pain of the collective trauma we had all experienced. Like the wife in *Gaslight*, one starts to question: *Wait, am I crazy?*

We can argue about the distinction between manipulation and gaslighting another time. What is clear is this: Good people are exhausted by the never-ending bullshit. We are trying to live positive lives that benefit those around us. We have no problem with success or achievement or even making money. But we do have a problem with abuse—of our emotions, of our talents (we'll get to our discussion of work), of our deepest hopes and dreams. We have a problem with the theft of our time, the exploitation of our attention, and the outright denial of our very reason for being. We are not on this earth to consume endlessly. We are not here to further enrich the already rich. The bullshit creates constant conflict in our lives.

It also creates constant conflict between the people around us.

Five
The People Problem

There is great confusion in our society about the roles we play in each other's lives. Click-up economics has only fostered more confusion (and served the Big Forces at our expense). For example: if we think of our coworkers as our *family*, then our boss and colleagues feel totally empowered to use guilt and shame (proven family-style emotional tactics) to get us to work more, attend that annoying drinks gathering, show up on the weekend, or interact with unconditional love and support. That's bullshit. It's okay to just be *colleagues*. It's okay to be a *community*. It's okay to be *friends*. Not everyone has to be our family for us to care about them, root for them, and participate in their success.

Likewise, if we think of brands as people—even as our *friends*—then we're invested emotionally in their communications, and we feel bad not buying something in their store or unsubscribing from their email list, especially if "the brand" is an influencer who leverages their personal life to get you to buy utter nonsense. It's not easy to say no to purchasing that new capsule collection when it's being modeled by the influencer's adorable kids. *Buy this bag! It'll pay for my college education.*

We'll talk more about these specific social and work circles later, but for now, it's important to see that the never-ending bullshit is also coming from the humans around us. Thanks to Big Tech, we are stuck to them, too.

• • •

Big Tech understands a very subtle truth about human relationships. They are subscriptions. Sounds odd, even clinical. I get it. But, yes, every relationship in our lives is a subscription. It's a commitment, a contract, a promise. An emotional one. Whether it's our mother (hey, Mama) or someone we follow online (hey, Brené Brown), we are subscribed just like we are subscribed to Audible. If you're uncomfortable with that line of reasoning, think of it this way: our human relationships *mimic* subscriptions. Let's think about it step by step.

When I use the word *relationship*, I refer (for now) to any non-work social relationship in our lives: family, friends, spouses, partners, our neighbors, that Supermom who hunts you down at the PTA meeting to make sure you are contributing your share of the class fucking cupcakes. We may not even remember when we said it or shook on it or pressed Agree, but we did. *We subscribed.* We said yes to having these people in our life or on our screen, in whatever capacity, or else they simply wouldn't be there at all.

When we were kids, our parents—who themselves made an agreement, by having you, to be your parent—agreed with the other mothers and/or fathers that you and Little Mark would be friends. They signed you up for your first baseball league or karate lesson or Kindermusik class. They sent you to a certain school where you would be a student to a faculty of teachers—and on and on. The formation of these relationships was a process, one often guided by traditions and rituals that were ages, if not generations and centuries, old. It was a process that started by signing up. Every relationship is an agreement. Friends. Romantic partners. Business partners. Mortgage lenders. Car dealerships. Children of our own. Sometimes we intentionally diverge from how we were raised; sometimes it is simply easier to surround ourselves with the familiar dynamics that filled our younger lives.

After we sign up, at any given point, *we can re-up our subscription to people*. We can make another phone call, another date, respond to that text, join for another holiday, or attend the Labor Day barbecue year after year. What matters here is that we have a choice. We get to decide how much time we want to spend with people. For me, it became empowering to think of my relationships with even my own parents this way. Exercising that choice—actively choosing to live closer and spend more time with them in this life—created a space for me to double down and form deeper bonds with two human beings whom I respect (in different ways and for different reasons) but whom I had previously quite taken for granted.

Convincing ourselves that we can have it all, all of the time endlessly, is the fastest road to powerlessness. Joy comes from powerful decisions. We can keep our lives full of great people (and all that comes with them) as long as we make a practice of taking stock and letting go of the relationships that are consistently toxic, tit-for-tat, overly competitive, dispiriting, demoralizing, and just plain "not working."

While I think the phrase is a bit woo-woo, "conscious uncoupling"—introduced into the national lexicon in 2014 by Gwyneth Paltrow and Chris Martin as a way of explaining their modern version of divorce—is another form of this idea, rejecting the notion that major organized religions (mostly the Judeo-Christian ones) have forced upon mankind that the terms of a long-term relationship are set in stone. Religion and social custom may have wired us to cloak divorce—or separation of any kind between two people, even friends—in great guilt, shame, and pain (I saw it with my own eyes when my parents divorced), but as Paltrow and Martin tried to show us, it need not be the traumatic, dramatic, and toxic process so many of us know all too well. It can be healthy. It can be kind. It can even be loving. To know when things need to change is not failure. We can choose who gets to be in our lives and for how long. (Conversely, for some couples, the act of "renewing" their vows demonstrates the same principle. It is a declaration to themselves and to the world that they are actively choosing this relationship and taking it off autopilot.)

Finally, *relationships come with certain terms and conditions*, just like a contract. Those terms include the types of activities you engage in, where you meet, who else joins when you gather, what you talk about when you are together, who pays the bill, who initiates the renewal. They aren't usually written down. Sometimes they are, like in a prenuptial agreement or group policies for a club or such, but for the most part, they evolve over the course of the relationship as the two parties negotiate their unique dynamic.

For example: I have one friend who will not meet above Houston Street in New York City. It is *maddening*. But it is a term of our relationship that, until the circus, I had just accepted. Everyone's got their little quirks, and this would have seemed like one, except for the added fact that there is an age difference and a socioeconomic difference between us. I was always traveling to him. I felt I *had* to. (People pleaser.) The power structure seemed inescapable, until, much to his surprise and dismay, I simply booked a restaurant reservation in the Flatiron (a neighborhood twenty blocks north). (Spoiler alert: the sky, in fact, did not fall.) After much ridiculous negotiation over text, he came to understand that if he wanted me to resubscribe to our friendship, he had to accept this change. My line in the sand woke us both up to how unconsciously we had been behaving, how much we had both taken the terms and conditions of our friendship for granted.

Let's zoom in. If our human relationships are subscriptions naturally, or if they *mimic* subscriptions, it is no wonder that the architects and popularizers of the subscription economy very savvily saw a way to exploit our innate tendency to "attach" and "invest" in people (as Sigmund Freud may have described it). If they could put the people we love (or at least like) on the same screen as the Big Brands, all the Big Forces could benefit.

It's not so much the subscribing to social relationships that's the worst problem; it's the *automation* of them. We—and our humanity—have been taken out of the process entirely, so much so that a computer (and a commercial system designed around its constant use) tells us that we are *still in a relationship* with every human with whom we have ever come into contact. Automatically. Unconsciously. Forever.

Automating the renewal of thousands of social relationships— daily (they're all still there tomorrow morning)—floods our lives with more and more noise and can bog us down in a perpetual swamp of toxic tethers, i.e., more bullshit. Because the more people we know, and the more we want to interact and engage, the more opportunities there are for the Big Forces to broker that engagement. Think about it: we can only see our sister's vacation photos if we stick our eyeballs on an ad for Avis Car Rental. We can only video chat with our college roommate if we watch thirty seconds of branded content from Vrbo or purchase a recurring subscription to Zoom. We can only eat at a restaurant with a friend if we book a reservation on the app, give our email address, and answer an automated survey that will appear via text twelve minutes after we finish our London broil steak salads with Danish blue cheese. *How was it? How would you rate it? Did we do a good job? Would you be willing to post a review of your London broil steak salad with Danish blue cheese? How likely are you to eat here again?* Not very if you keep annoying the living shit out of me.

No wonder no one wants more friends anymore. Friends have to be managed. Friends clog our channels. They create more texts and emails. They need room in the calendar. Friends require *work*. That's also why those of us over forty have such trouble meeting new people. And why our single friends are struggling—very painfully—to find love in this mess. We have eliminated divergence and newness. We have killed discovery and the spark of new relationships because we are simply oversaturated. All of the bullshit is in the way.

Of course, click-up economics has given us fun tools to manage all these people—social media is, after all, a sexy spreadsheet—but pull the camera back. Is spending our time this way good for us? Does it create a more satisfying or meaningful or even joyful life?

In his book *Four Thousand Weeks*, journalist and modern sage Oliver Burkeman recalls the wisdom of history's greatest philosophers to remind us of our "finitude." (The book's titular time frame refers to the length of our life, should we live to the age of eighty.) "The average human lifespan is absurdly, terrifyingly, insultingly short," he points out in the opening pages, before going on to argue that by accepting the limit of our human lifespan and truly understanding the unchangeable truth that we will die one day—soon—we can find and create more joy in our day-to-day.

I find this to be a particularly profound way of thinking about digital social networks. Why am I spending my time and energy with every person who has ever come into my life? Why am I wasting even thirty seconds writing a "happy birthday" message to a guy I met at a bar fourteen years ago and who wouldn't even stop to say hello to me on the street? We Americans now spend, on average, more than two and a half hours *a day* on social media. We have double the number of friends online than we do off. And we use an average of twelve gigs of data every month texting. Just texting. Sure, some of that is for work, but most of it is to manage our social relationships.

The sheer volume of time and energy spent is not our only problem. The effect is more problematic. And the smack to the soul is incalculable. Seemingly overnight, our digital society has morphed our relationships from organic to coordinated, from unconditional to transactional, from fulfilling to surface deep. The surface: a screen. The people we love are reduced to text messages on our phone, group chats, email threads, and pictures in any of our photo or video feeds. They are *digital content*. They are *products*.

And they respond accordingly, branding themselves as a corporation would—with perfectly Photoshopped pictures, a unique and identifiable communication style, and consistent and reliable messaging. We then begin to evaluate these friendships based on business principles. We want ROI, return on investment. We want efficiency. The need to be efficient is a profit-making impulse, not a human need. It has seeped into our social lives. We want to get something—validation, social utility, contacts—from our friendships or they're "not worth it." (That is one cold way for a society to function, and yet I'm sure none of it shocks you.)

And not only do we consume their updates—more dangerously, we consume their emotions and emotional baggage. We watch their stories, become invested in their multi-post sagas and drama. We cheer (and envy) their successes and empathize with (or snicker at) their downfalls. At times, we begin to identify with different journeys and experiences to such an extent that it affects and alters our own outlook and mental state. Eroded are the centuries-old human social tactics and customs we developed and employed to block other people's emotions from affecting ours, or to filter them or process them properly. The gates are down, and the influx is overpowering, especially for our children and teens, who are still forming their worldview and developing the muscles and skills to process emotion. And one nerd out west wants us all to march mindlessly into the Metaverse? Nobody wants your Metaverse, dude. We're good. Please unsubscribe, thanks!

To sort through this social clusterfuck—to decipher and

untangle it all—we have developed fun methods like relationship quizzes, love languages, and relationship color wheels (I still don't get it, and I studied it for this chapter). Like modern horoscopes, these are theoretical shortcuts to help us group people, quickly size them up, and predict their behavior, so that we can decide if a person is good for us to consume (or even employ). As we do with food, we have moved away from a holistic, natural, and organic source of sustenance—instead, we're counting individual calories and making sure we balance protein and carbs in a healthy way.

And we wonder why we're lonely? It is one of the great ironies of the twenty-first century that having more and more ways to connect and communicate is breeding more and more loneliness. British psychologist and anthropologist Robin Dunbar contends that humans are cognitively able to maintain only about one hundred fifty connections at once. That's it. Our computers may be wired to manage massive social networks, but our brains and souls are not.

Pre-Friendster, we had a handful of "friends" in our life. We maintained stronger boundaries, and we could decide—actively, purposefully, intentionally—what to "take on" from our friends' opinions and beliefs and incorporate into our own worldview. People came in and out of life. They moved away. They grew in importance over time from an *acquaintance* to a *friend* to a *girlfriend* to a *best friend*. Or from a *neighbor* to a *pal* to a *drinking buddy* to a *best man*. We could not scale easily in this analog world, so instead we spent our time digging deeper. Our time—and the activities we engaged in with that time—built and maintained those friendships, relationships, and communities. These progressions fostered depth, which fought off the loneliness inherent in the human experience.

That changed when Mark took the Face Book from his Harvard dorm room and put it all online. He didn't *mean* to do this. But this deeply human process has been warped and perverted. We all now "agree" to dozens, hundreds, thousands of new relationships quickly, easily, and without much thought or ritual—sometimes literally, with the quick addition of their name into our contacts, or the click of a Follow or Add Friend button. Within the first few moments of meeting someone, we can request to follow them on social media, or know personal details about them in the seconds it takes to type their name into a search bar. From Monster and Glassdoor to Hinge and Bumble to Zoom and TikTok, we have added a middleman into nearly every relationship in our social lives, just like we have added multiple middlemen into every economic transaction in our click-up economy. We have convinced ourselves that a supercomputer's algorithm can somehow generate better results in our search for satisfaction, meaning, and happiness than we can for ourselves.

We are participants in this system, and the more we participate in it daily, the more our behavior and mindsets are affected. We start to believe that we are our follower count, and our self-worth is measured by the number of friends we have online. We have taken the humanity out of human interaction and pushed ourselves to the limit of what humans are naturally capable of creating in order to somehow achieve maximum value. (Can you imagine having *only* one hundred fifty connections on any social media site?) By making each of our social lives this public, we have offered ourselves up to endless scrutiny, judgment, and measurement. On behalf of the 107 billion people who lived before us and who had perfectly joyful, fulfilling, and meaningful lives without social media, let me be so bold as to say this: the time has come to stop. Since 2004, when Facebook launched, we have spent twenty years agreeing, signing up, and subscribing indiscriminately.

Enough already.

We are feeling the consequences across the culture. The effect of the infinite loop is stunning. During the 2016 Democratic primary campaign, mayor-turned-presidential-candidate Pete Buttigieg released a nineteen-page white paper outlining plans to combat what it called "deaths of despair," a cultural phenomenon of loneliness that had led to a noticeable spike in suicides and overdoses, through policy changes that would rebuild community and belonging in our nation. The report said:

> Yet for all the attention the opioid epidemic has rightly received, Pete understands that it is only one part of a much larger mental health and substance use disorder crisis. Last year, for every five people who died from opioid overdose, three died from overdose due to other drugs, such as methamphetamine or cocaine; five died by suicide; and nine died an alcohol-related death. Combined, these deaths have contributed to the longest sustained decline in American life expectancy since World War I. Collectively, these deaths due to drugs, alcohol, and suicide are characterized as "deaths of despair," which are often preceded by people and communities being left behind. It is parents being laid off from the job they've had for decades, and a society's inability to provide them with the opportunity to take care of their family, so they turn to alcohol to numb the pain. It is teenagers coping with childhood trauma or living in constant fear of hearing gunshots at school and needing a way to manage their anxiety and stress. It is older people whose aging friends don't stop by as often, if at all, and a society's inability to take appropriate care of its elders, even as they become lonelier and more isolated.

While Mayor Pete's White House campaign ended after some hard-fought primaries (he was later asked to become Secretary Buttigieg, serving under President Biden as Transportation Secretary), his efforts are part of a growing national conversation about mental health issues and personal relationships. In 2017, the former US Surgeon General (under President Obama), Dr. Vivek H. Murthy, published a cover story for the *Harvard Business Review* called "Work and the Loneliness Epidemic," observing that our loneliness and isolation extend into the workplace, where we spend the majority of our time. Is digitizing our human relationships alone to blame for such despair? No, but it provides a poor substitute for what matters in our day-to-day lived experience.

We've all seen it. We've all *felt* it. There is a disconnect in our communities, in our families, in our offices, and in our own daily lives, one that has begun to have undeniable impact on our emotional and social health. The truth is that the infinite loop *feels* bad. Trapped inside with both the Big Forces and the extended Supercommunity—thousands of friends and millions of people we don't even know and will never truly know, all feeding each other more and more bullshit constantly—we start to feel like every day is *Groundhog Day.* Another sale? Sure. Another wedding photo? Sure. But also another crazy fucking tweet from an insane billionaire that will render thousands jobless tomorrow. Another politician calling for us to shred the Constitution. Another stock slump. Another mass shooting. All of which sits on the same plane of reality, believability, experience. Our existence *becomes* a nightmare on repeat. Life is no longer full of joy, punctuated by bullshit. It is full of bullshit, punctuated by joy.

Well before the subscription economy, Nietzsche, the nineteenth-century German philosopher, pondered the infinite loop. He asked us to consider the ancient concept of "the eternal return." Eternal return is the belief that everything we do in this life will come back to us, over and over again. Nietzsche proposed that *if life is this eternal return, if it is an infinite loop, how might we each feel about reliving every choice we have ever made?* Interpretations of his ideas vary, and they are not always aligned with a Christian-majority American free market. Shocker. My purpose in referencing him is to ask us all to consider his question. Here's my version: If you had to live with the consequences of every click forever, how might that change where you click? What you buy and watch? Whom you spend your time with? Even further, why do we want algorithms automating our economic and social choices if we (generally) agree that humans have free will? And that free will underlies our free market? Worth thinking about.

Did I just sit next to Nietzsche and ask you to think about his question? Yes, I did. Go with it. You bought the book.

Nietzsche enjoins us to live our lives such that we *will* the eternal return of every choice we make. In other words, we want what we choose forever. Think of someone who's trying to break a bad habit or quit an addiction (to alcohol, to sugar, to social media, whatever) and says, "I'll give myself one last drink today, and then I'll quit tomorrow." That person is not truly living in the spirit of the eternal return if they wouldn't want to live forever with the choice they are making *right now*.

Now is the time to make changes. Big ones. This is just the beginning. Because if this fully automated economy and society succeeds, the loop keeps going and going. The relentlessness will never end. Your inbox will never be empty. Your phone will never stop ringing. You'll get notifications on your contact lenses and on the windshield of your car. Over and over. Your kid will dance on TikTok until their legs fall off. Then they'll get new legs. Then those will fall off. You may not even have a kid; you'll have a digital child who lives in the fediverse (I almost spelled that *fetaverse*, which is where your child only eats Greek cheese) and a robot dog who magically never shits on your carpet. Drones will land on your porch, secure your home, and send you a picture of your cheating spouse. Your checking account will become a frenzied highway with no speed limit—money out before it's ever really in. You'll have fifty thousand friends you never see, call, or hug. And it will all be easy, pleasurable, comfortable, and sexy. And it will all repeat. Endlessly.

Scaled up? The difference between the haves and the have-nots will widen and widen. I joke about what it will all look like, but it is likely—as detailed by economists, scientists, and analysts—to spiral into our society's destruction, if that spiral has not already begun.

Not only is our relentless material consumption killing the planet, using natural resources at an alarming rate, and keeping us addicted to dangerous fossil fuels, but also the footprint of our digital activity alone is enormous, contrary to the story we have sold that *all things digital are good for the environment*. Not true. They may be *less bad*, but they are not *good*. Crypto harvesting alone emits as much carbon as a small European country. The carbon footprint of all our devices (and the digital systems supporting them) accounts for more than 3.5 percent of global greenhouse emissions and is expected to *double* by 2025. For context, that 3.5 percent is similar to the percentage of emissions produced by the airline industry globally.

What is at stake here—besides the fate of society and the very Earth we live on and depend on for human survival—is our spiritual health. I don't mean that in some esoteric way. I mean, the infinite loop is replacing conscious thought and action throughout society. The infinite loop is the death of risk. It is the death of imagination. It is the death of spirituality. We cannot stay present, alive, and awake to the incredible act of living if what we do and how we do it is on constant autopilot. I don't care if you worship Jesus or follow the teachings of Buddha or idolize your spin instructor (I *revere* my dance instructor), we will never be present enough in an automated society to experience any of the things we all look to Jesus or Buddha or Tootsie (my dance instructor) for: change, love, success, health, patience, peace.

We are at a crisis point. And we cannot look away. Too much depends on us getting this right.

• • •

But wait, come on, hold on. Isn't an automated society progress? Isn't this "the future"? In two letters: no. This is not progress. Progress would mean things are getting better. Progress would mean we are experiencing more joy, more freedom, more leisure time, more opportunities to connect and experience whatever it is in the world that we each deem to be our own personal version of *happiness.** Progress would mean expanded opportunities and access to them; cheaper and better health care outcomes; rising education levels and lower tuition; less medical debt, student debt, and credit-card debt. None of that is happening. At least not for the majority. We are going backward in many ways, reverting to extreme levels of inequality, rolling back social advances, resorting to political violence, *banning books*.

We tell ourselves that we are moving forward, better than we were before. And what evidence do we offer? Well, because we can upgrade from the iPhone 12 to the iPhone 14. We got a new laptop or car or jeans, because we *stream* television now, because we have a flat-screen TV, because we can ask Alexa for the weather. Are these advances? Sure, if you mean we "advanced" from a time when we had to turn on the television to check the weather to a time when we could just yell at the air and get it. But is it progress? The future is always sold to us as a good thing—because we are supposedly making progress. All at the cost of our values. The relentless noise makes no time for us to evaluate those values. Automation assumes we have *already evaluated them* and are placing them on autopilot.

In his book *Civilized to Death*, psychologist Christopher Ryan calls this type of self-delusion Western civilization's "narrative of

---

* We can each decide for ourselves if we are getting progressively happier as these years go on. I won't pretend to know if you are happy or not. But we do know that as a society our mental health is getting worse, our free time is shrinking, and our happiness levels (as surveyed by multiple polls) just keep going down.

perpetual progress" or "NPP," a centuries-long fallacy that we have constructed to keep workers in our post-agriculture societies toeing the line. Our way of life, he argues, is *unnatural* and works to condition out of humans our natural tendency for teamwork, egalitarianism, and the social balances that maintain peace and security. In effect, we have used the NPP to justify and fortify feudalism, mercantilism, and capitalism. Even the very premise of capitalism—that *humans operate out of self-interest*—is refuted. According to Ryan, if we are not evolving toward more egalitarianism, more peace, and more security, we are not being progressive.

In 2022, Timothy Snyder, professor of history at Yale and author of *On Tyranny*, explained a similar concept on a podcast with *New York Times* columnist Ezra Klein. He calls it the politics of inevitability. "What the politics of inevitability does," he said, "is that it teaches you to narrate in such a way that the facts which seem to trouble the story of progress are disregarded. So, in the politics of inevitability, if there is huge wealth inequality as a result of unbridled capitalism, we teach ourselves to say that that is kind of a necessary cost of this overall progress. We learn this dialectal way of thinking by which what seems to be bad is actually good." That confusion between what is "bad" and what is "good" always stands to benefit the *über*-wealthy and keep the entire system in place. Confusion is their friend. The more workers and consumers are confused, the more producers can create products and services that provide clarity. *Invent the problem, then solve it* is Advertising 101.

The cost, according to Snyder, is that "You lose the habit, you never perform the mental gymnastics of stretching to figure out what a better world might actually be, because you think you're on track to that better world no matter what happens."

Okay, fine, but it can't be that bad. After all, aren't habits good? Doesn't automation help me keep good habits? Can't the infinite loop be a good thing if we automate good behaviors? These are perfectly logical questions. Repeated behaviors can serve us incredibly well, especially when we are trying to lose weight or, say, write a book, or keep a steady date night. Author James Clear has sold more than seven million copies of his habit guide *Atomic Habits* for a reason. He understands the power of habit, offering four laws to superpowering our ritual building: (1) make it obvious, (2) make it attractive, (3) make it easy, and (4) make it satisfying. In his case, building atomic habits rehabilitated him from a horrible injury.

What is paramount is the nuance here. Hello, nuance, old friend. We must decide whether what we are automating is serving us well and creating a happier us and a better world (*atomic good*) or whether it is not serving us well and creating an unhappy us and a darker world (um, possibly literally *atomic bad*).

Yes, if our personal day-to-day systems—and the larger systems in our society—are working well, then automation can potentially be a net positive, if we also make a habit of periodically reevaluating and refining. So, sure, make your morning protein shake a habit, but every few weeks or months stop, check in with yourself, and make sure this protein shake, with these specific ingredients, is making you healthier. I used to think I had automated my healthy eating by having a protein bar every day at 4:00 p.m. Then I noticed that the bar had more sugar in it than a scoop of ice cream. I hadn't automated my health. I had automated my weight gain. Even good automation requires planned periods of checking in.

On a national scale, our highly stratified economy is working very well for the wealthiest—this many people spending this much money, constantly mesmerized by the glow of their phones, clicking up billions, on autopilot—that is a pretty damn good automated system to have in place if you are benefitting directly from it. But we saw during the circus (and since) that, in fact, this economy is *not* working well for millions of us. If the system is not working, behavior automation spells disaster, because we are just destined to get more of the same. A lot more of the same. And the worst of it will get much worse.

Automation is not progress. Close your eyes and put yourself inside the loop. You try to move forward, but the road just leads you backward. Forward, then backward again. You never progress anywhere. Are you having the same experience? Yes and no. Yes, it's on a loop. But your frustration builds and builds and builds. You are stuck. And stuck feels like shit. A society that constantly feels like shit is a powder keg. Our political anger is peaking because we are collectively stuck. We are not progressing.

Allowing Big Tech to claim the infinity symbol, to make it represent "progress" and "the future," is a grave disservice to the larger society. Telling us they are leading the way, lighting the path forward, is a lie. The infinite loop is a trap. It keeps us locked in the past—doing what we have always done, repeating our consumer behaviors, circling and circling in the same social networks, reviving old conversations, "settled law," that which we thought we had *moved on from* in our personal lives, work lives, and in the national conversation. It also potentially extends the worst of the past into the future.

Bill Gates explained this concept perfectly when he said, "The first rule of any technology in business is that automation applied to an efficient operation will magnify its efficiency. The second is that automation applied to an inefficient operation will magnify its inefficiency." That's twisty, so stop and think about that. Automation magnifies even the tiniest of problems. Take a laser printer, for example: if the paper going in page after page is perfectly aligned with the gears inside, the printer will spit out a hundred pages flawlessly and in seconds. But if the paper is not aligned—if it's off by even a millimeter—one page will print with slightly skewed text, the next will catch in the gears, and the next will jam the machine and blow up your whole fucking day.

Let me be so bold as to sit next to Bill for a second, too, and draw a parallel for us here: behavior automation applied to a society that is well-functioning will magnify its wellness; behavior automation applied to a society that is ill-functioning will magnify its illness.

As the circus showed us, we are automating *a lot* of societal illness. It's happening automatically on repeat. Over and over again. And it is getting worse. We are magnifying loneliness. We are magnifying keeping up with the Joneses. We are magnifying income inequality. We are magnifying political and social strife. Greed. Impatience. Isolation. Fear. And violence. You do not get to January 6, 2021, in the United States of America because one guy wanted to hang his office mate. You get there because a massive system, the entire society, has created that moment. Yes, lock up everyone who stormed the Capitol (100 percent), prosecute and lock up *He who incited* (100 percent), but let's not miss the (uncomfortable) opportunity to fully understand our collective role in creating a moment like that, so we can truly heal and begin to undo the damage click-up economics has done to us as a nation.

Our only break, our only moment—ever—to collectively step off the spinning hamster wheel, was the circus. We were thrown out of the loop. In that year between panic and vaccine, millions of us decided that we were ready for change. We saw behind the curtain. Our eyes were open. We were awake to our personal and societal problems in a totally new way, without the usual distractions that capitalism affords, even requires. We knew we could not "go back to normal." We knew the way it was before was exhausting, inequitable, unbalanced, and unsustainable. We felt it in our bones. We had just witnessed, with our own eyes, all that click-up economics hath wrought. So many of us experienced our own version of "I am secretly grateful for the deep breath. I needed it. This is not working."

And yet, with some notable exceptions, like the Great Resignation, as soon as we could, as soon as we were shot in the arm, millions upon millions of us went right back to how we used to do things. I'm not passing judgment. We all had loved ones to see and jobs to do and mortgages and rent to pay. I am just fascinated by *how* it happened the way it did and *why*. In so many ways, it was all so much bigger than us.

A few obvious reasons present themselves. First was our human need for safety. According to psychologist Abraham Maslow's hierarchy of needs (that pyramid we saw in high school), first we seek food, water, and shelter, then we seek safety and protection. Once the grocery shelves were restocked, we sought safety. What is familiar is safe, and the longer the circus went on, the stronger the need for the familiar got. The heartbreak came when we tried to "go back" to our old lives but realized the world had changed. The circus was no blip. It was a war. The entire society had undergone a tectonic shift. At least when a war ends, you have a parade. We just had "Are you coming back to the office on Monday?" There was no clear national moment for us to cross from *unsafe* to *safe* again. So, we found safety in doing things the way they had always been done before. At least, we tried to pick up where we left off in March 2020.

Second: because the slog went on so long, many of us experienced a strong rubber-band reversion effect. We went *overboard* in our getting back to normal, because we had been made to live in such an uncomfortable limbo for so long. We doubled down on normal life the second we could. We were not only vaxed, but we're *vaxed and waxed* and ready to party. Here in New York City, one of the reasons the Omicron variant spread so quickly was that it hit during "holiday party week," the week before Christmas when employees who had been remote for over twenty-two months dared gather for a spiked eggnog. It seemed anyone who had gone to their office holiday party—or who was even on the island of Manhattan—around December 22, 2021, was in bed with COVID soon thereafter.

But there was another reason: we were subscribed. Individually and collectively.

It is time to unsubscribe.

Um, Now What?

That's how we got here. That's part one. That's a lot to process. Trust me, I get it. I have been processing through it all since March 2020. Before we move on to part two, which is what we can *do* about it all, I just want to check in. There were horses and loops and circles. There was 9/11 and Home Depot and amphetamines. There was an extended rant about bullshit. Then I equated Mom with Audible. We talked about politics, economics, emotional abuse, Bill Gates, Nietzsche. And we landed at January 6.

I hope you didn't think this book was about email overload and cute tips and tricks for cutting down on screen time. Yes, we will get to some practical and tactical strategies for how to be happy in this mess, but here's what you need to know if you really want to effect transformation in your life and in our society: Change, even individual change, is not a solo act. The canon of self-help and personal growth tells us that change is something we do in a vacuum, by ourselves, for ourselves, with ourselves. With our vision boards and sticky notes on the bathroom mirror. I love a good vision board, just like the next gay. There is more than a valid place for that. (And apparently for microdosing, too. I haven't microdosed yet, but my college roommate is trying to get me to do it.) But you can't just tell people to love themselves (or get them micro-high) and think the world is just going to magically transform.

This book proposes a different way to effect change. We cannot divorce self-improvement from collective improvement nor individual happiness from our larger systems. It is all related. Always. Because the collective always influences the personal. And the personal always affects the collective. Especially now that we are *this* connected to one another. Subscriptions, as you will see, always involve someone else, except when they involve just you—and even then, they involve someone else (whomever you promised that you were not the version of you you really want to be). Any talk of change, growth, even habit-building is well served by including a conversation about all of this. In that regard, I hope that this book is additive. It's not just about getting happy, it's about how to be happier *in this system*. Or how to change the system to effect more happiness.

Once you have had the chance to process the last chapters, let's move forward. *What do we do about all this?* Here's my proposal: First, we unsubscribe in our individual lives so we can quiet the noise and protect and restore our mental health. I will outline how to do that in the following chapters, and also how to renew our lives so they truly represent the fullest version of our humanity. Next, we work with our families, our community groups, and our larger circles to help them unsubscribe and renew. Then, we band together to demand that those who write the subscriptions for our society—the public-policy makers—unsubscribe us from all the written commitments, contracts, and promises that keep our society in the dangerous infinite loops that are magnifying and amplifying our collective illness.

Let's take those one at a time. Onward to circles and parking lots and elephants and icons and wells and bright flowers.

PART TWO

The Great Unsubscribe

Breaking Free, Step by Step by Step

Six

How to Beat the Bullshit

In that first year of the circus, most of which I spent completely solo in my apartment, I unsubscribed from every subscription—every commitment, contract, promise, or tether, both on my screen and in my life—that didn't truly make me happy. It all started with the Mute button. You know it. It's on the cover of this book. Funny enough, the reason the Mute icon is on the cover is that we don't *have* an unsubscribe icon in our culture.

I propose we create and use one. (See figure 2.) It could look like a broken chain, a loop that we escape, or a torn tether. Whichever, an unsubscribe icon is a way to balance power between ourselves and the Big Forces. It allows us to exit the infinite loop as easily as we enter it. It also communicates an integral part of the story that has been very conveniently forgotten: we have every right to step out of the infinite loop.

Back to muting. First, I muted every notification. I muted my phone. I turned it off. I posted a message to my social media that I was "on a digital detox." And I got real comfortable real quick with simply not participating. In effect, I gave myself a digital retreat. Was it lonely? Sure. Was it nerve-wracking? Definitely. I was already alone, I feared I was just going to make the terrible loneliness even worse. Immediately, I felt bad. *What if someone needs me? What if I miss an important update? What if I need to Google something? How can I survive if I don't know if it will rain at exactly 5:30 today?* The immediate guilt, shame, and panic is what keeps us in the infinite

FIGURE 2
Unsubscribe Icons

loop. So, fighting through it is necessary. It was for me. My life depended on it. All our lives do.

The quiet—the incredible quiet!—that emerged created a sacred space. I don't have any tattoos, but the only phrase I would ever permanently scrawl on my skin is this one: *It finally got quiet.* I would come to realize in that quiet that I am naturally happy—or, at least, I know *how* to be happy. It is my strongest belief that happiness is our natural state before we bury ourselves in the never-ending bullshit of the modern world.

Happiness is not actually that much of a pursuit. It is much simpler than American capitalism will admit. Happiness comes from time spent with people we love. Happiness comes from running toward hard conversations, not away from them. Happiness comes from community and contribution and citizenship. Happiness comes from quality, not quantity, from going deeper, not wider. Happiness comes from finding and experiencing the joy—and pain—of life day in and day out. The chaos of the modern world, so much of it meant to shield us from that pain, is an obstacle, not a pathway. It has been sold to us as a pathway because someone somewhere is making money off our need to take negative feelings away. Happiness comes from stopping the madness constantly swirling around us, not sustaining it.

In that sacred space, I discovered that I was just wasting all my energy on the crap that I had piled *on top of* that happiness. I had filled my life with distraction and noise and busyness and halfhearted commitments—all in the name of living life to the fullest. A full life is not necessarily a rich one. It is just a busy one. That fullness was crushing me. When I finally rid my life of all of it, I got to come out from the enormous weight of it. And I refuse to go back under. I was faux-filled, not fulfilled. (I couldn't resist.)

I digress.

The idea here is simple: unsubscribe from everything, breathe, put back into life only what you truly want in it, what will make your life more joyful, more meaningful (for you), what will make you and your children proud. That looks different for each of us. It is not my role to tell you what to put back in. We're all exhausted by "experts" telling us what to do with our lives. You do you. My intention here is to show you how to create that same sacred space so you can actively decide.

Before we get started, I want you to **CONSIDER HOW YOU WILL APPROACH THIS PROCESS** (in other words, how you will use this book). I am going to depart from history and economics and all the intellectualizing I have been doing thus far so that I can get up-close and personal and offer you practical and tactical strategies for unsubscribing. (Then, after that, we'll return to the larger questions and how they affect society at large.) I am going to give you the *extreme* version of unsubscribing, what I did when (during the circus) I (single, no kids) had weeks and months available to me to change my life. I *fully* realize that that is just not the situation most readers find themselves in. So, know this: there are levels here, and you get to choose how big a game you want to play. My one request: play a bigger game than you think you are ready for. Get uncomfortable. As the saying goes, "Life begins at the end of your comfort zone." So does unsubscription.

I hear you, *I'm not Gandhi. I cannot (and will not) give up all worldly possessions and responsibilities. These are things I have worked for, have earned, that I need to be a member of society. They keep me from going insane!* Totally fine. Look, when I read *The Life-Changing Magic of Tidying Up,* I didn't do *everything* Marie Kondo suggested. If I held every photograph I own in my hand to see if it brings me joy, I would still be holding middle school pictures from 1991 (zits, braces, a home perm—and lasers in the background). But each of the suggestions in that book were powerful because they each held the promise of change. I am giving you a full menu here, and I invite you to pick the meal you want. You can go to the extreme as I did, you can do a "light version," taking a week-end morning each week (or whenever you can block off time) to employ some of these strategies, or you can simply read this book in full and let it all wash over you, coming back to it when you feel you're ready to jump in. The everlasting gift of a book is that I will always be here.

So where do we start?

First order of business: **STOP SAYING THE WORD YES.** For the length of this process, yes is not your friend. Don't agree to do anything. Don't add anything to your calendar. Don't meet up, sign up, or put up with anything that doesn't give you more time and space. This might just be the hardest part of all.

I am a people pleaser. Maybe you are, too. For many years of my life, if you said the sky was green, I would say, "You know, it does look a little green today." I would find some speck or ray or shadow of the clearly blue sky, just to make it true. Hunter. Lime. Olive. Fern. Pick a shade. There must be some green in there. I made it my mission—in a nanosecond—to find the green. Why? Because I wanted so badly to connect with people. I wanted to belong. I wanted to be part of the group. I wanted to find common ground so badly that I would blatantly ignore my own eyes in order to agree. It was just easier. I saw zero value in disagreeing. Disagreements lead to conflict. Conflict means arguing. Arguing leads to fighting. I grew up in a house full of fighting, void of boundaries, void of harmony. I just couldn't do it. I could never muster the word no. Yes avoids the ugliness of its opposite.

America is the land of yes. Yes means opportunity. Yes means access. Yes means we are expanding—as a person, as a brand, as a force in the world. Why would you say no and cut off a possible path to all the things that you want: love, money, success, connections, new experiences? This thinking is a problem. I can no longer subscribe to the notion that *yes is the path to all I have ever wanted.* In fact, I have found that no is the road back to me. No keeps the path clear for you to protect that sacred space. No stops feeding the genie.

Next, **TAKE A FULL ACCOUNTING.** Simply stop and notice just how many subscriptions you have in your life. These are all the contracts, agreements, promises, the tethers of all kinds that you are bound to and that you continue to make and honor every day. They are determining your behavior. They control you. They dictate when you wake up, what you touch first, what you eat, where you drive, how your calendar lays out, all of it. We cannot pretend that our behavior, our habits, our day-to-day lives exist in a bubble and that if we only buy an expensive electric toothbrush, life will transform. It is vital that we understand what our subscriptions *look like* (and sound like) so we can notice them and truly reevaluate them.

It's helpful to look for your subscriptions in three general places. The first are what I will call "surface subscriptions." These surface subscriptions bring a lot of surface bullshit into our lives. Surface subscriptions are often commitments you make to the Big Forces: email newsletters, updates, monthly purchases, anything recurring that comes at you from a corporation. Next, look for the "people subscriptions"—the ones you make to all sorts of groups, from family to schools to community to work. (We'll talk about work a lot later.) People subscriptions bring a lot of people bullshit into our lives. Last, look at your "underlying subscriptions." These are, frankly, your own personal bullshit. I continue to battle my own bullshit. These are the deeply seated ideas, beliefs, and notions you have about yourself and the world around you. You may not be present to a lot of these (I wasn't), so if you want to hold off on thinking about these until later, go for it.

You can think about these three types of subscriptions as three rings of a circle. These are your subscription rings. (See figure 3.) The outer ring is full of *surface subscriptions* (figure 4). The middle ring represents your social or *people subscriptions* (figure 5). Inside (your heart and mind) or at your core are your *underlying subscriptions* (figure 6). If you're a nerd like I am, make a list of your subscriptions in each ring. Um, it'll be a long list. If a list is not your thing, by all means, skip it. Maybe just take a moment and see what comes to mind as you consider each ring. Don't let the perfect be the enemy of the good here.

What's most important is to just get present. Take an easy first accounting. Look around, start paying attention to all the commitments that beg for attention, all the little robots automatically communicating with you and the ones consistently taking your cash. Who and what is prodding you today? Who and what is pinging? What are you being notified of, reminded to do, pushed to follow through on? What and who is in your line of sight and in your space that you didn't invite in here and now?

Last prep step: allow me to show you **THE PARKING LOT**. In the parking lot, you can park a limited number of things you simply cannot part with. What do I mean? Maybe you're a longtime American Airlines AAdvantage member. You have two hundred thousand airline miles. They are precious to you. You are not willing right now to cancel your membership; that would wipe out all your miles, but you are willing to unsubscribe from the constant barrage of emails

Unsubscription Layer by layer, get rid of it all and get to you.

FIGURE 3
You As Target

FIGURE 4
Outer Ring
Surface Subscriptions

FIGURE 5
Middle Ring
People Subscriptions

FIGURE 6
Core
Underlying Subscriptions

that American sends you, and you are willing to take their app off your phone, and you are willing to take their bookmark out of your browser, etc. Let's put your AAdvantage membership in the parking lot. Commit to *no travel* while you're going through this process but keep the membership active. Unsubscribe from everything else that reminds you constantly that the membership exists and that you would be much happier jumping on a plane to London this weekend. If you get through this process and decide that that membership is important to you and you want to choose it back into your life—it brings you meaning and fulfillment—your miles will still be there. Enjoy London.

Use the parking lot sparingly. Be selective. You don't want to put all your clothing into your storage unit and convince yourself that you have tidied up your closet. You haven't. You have simply moved your clothes to a bigger closet. And now you're paying an automated recurring charge of $100 a month for storage. I give you the parking lot because jumping off a cliff is scary, and it's a lot easier if you know you at least have a parachute. You'll still get to the ground, but you will drift calmly, not plummet screaming. When I did this, I went full bore because I was so fed up (so full bore that I wound up writing a book about it). I get that you might want to do this in a different *style*.

Yes, I know this is all super uncomfortable. You are about to break many promises. But not all our promises are good for us. Or for the world. We have been raised to always honor our commitments, to bear down and suffer until we check every box. Judeo-Christian religions teach us that the breaking of covenants will send us to hell. (I was an altar boy until I was taller than the priest at my church. Catholics love to remind you of the burning fires that await you should you step out of line.) Pop culture songs bemoan the heartbreak of broken vows. Civil society says *word is bond,* that *our word is our honor.* Businesses, friendships, personal partnerships are all built on some form of mutual promise. If we don't fulfill them, we're threatened with anarchy. Even violence. Signing up, signing on, and staying committed is how we succeed, lose weight, win the championship, do right by our teammates, become and stay a respectable person.

We have an endless multitude of voices to teach us *not* to break our agreements, yet so few to teach us how to make them properly and with clear eyes. There is an important subtlety here that bears exploring. We need clear eyes to understand the *terms and conditions* of our agreements. The truth is that each of us is committed to too much we don't want to be committed to, and we got here because we agreed without ever understanding these fully. That, as they say, is where they get ya. The terms don't always allow for our humanity or our growth. They don't allow for changing conditions in our environment, in our world. That's because those seeking to get us into the loop rely on automating *more of what is happening right now.*

We wouldn't stay in an intimate relationship that had reached its breaking point, one in which abuse was normalized or violence exists. We wouldn't stay in a job that makes us truly mentally unhealthy or one in which our boss changes our place of work, salary, responsibilities, or expectations without our consent. *Consent* is a modern buzzword (for very legitimate and obvious reasons, but also) because it is an integral part of this awakening. I must understand what I am getting myself into—as much as I ever can fully—before I say yes.

Most of us are good and loving people, and we tend first to look at ourselves when we reflect on what is not working about our lives. We tend to blame the relentlessness of life on our personal failings, something we have done wrong, a flaw in our nature or nurture or soul. I have news for you: There is nothing wrong with you. You are whole, beautiful, and good. You are not overwhelmed. You are not ill prepared. You are *oversubscribed*. And the terms and conditions shifted under your feet without your consent. When and where we can't unsubscribe, it is time to change the terms and conditions of our subscription.

This is cause for celebration. Yes, I am serious. I use the word *celebration* because part of this process is the institution or reinstitution of certain ceremonies in our lives. The ceremonies you and I know well in other parts of our lives—religious, cultural—those are hundreds or thousands of years old, handed down by generations. The digital age—the last twenty-five years out of the last three hundred thousand years that humans have been on the planet—requires new ceremonies to help us bring importance and meaning to what we now do with our time and to delineate chapters of our digital lives. This is a new chapter. Time to turn the page. I salute you.

Welcome to the Great Unsubscribe.

Seven

Breaking Up with the Big Forces

The first phase of the Great Unsubscribe is focused on breaking our *surface subscriptions*—the outer ring. (See figure 7.) It is time to break up with the Big Forces. Most of our subscriptions to the Big Forces take the form of digital commitments and contracts (and, of course, paper commitments and contracts)—legally binding and not legally binding, both signed and unsigned.

Let's start with Big Tech and the Big Brands. Most of our interactions with Big Tech are on our phones, our tablets, our devices. Since a lot of these keep our engagement strong with the Big Brands, let's address them together. Big Tech and the Big Brands are taking our time and money constantly. It's time to take it all back.

Where to Begin? Our Inbox

Email is not life. Life is not email. "The inbox is nothing but a convenient organizing system for other people's agendas," says author Brendon Burchard. (I tried to say it better myself, but I simply could not.) What began as a simple landing page for electronic messages has become a battlefield for our behavior. *Can we really change our lives and the world by clicking Unsubscribe on a bunch of emails?* That's a legitimate question, and the answer is yes. In order to unsubscribe from the larger subscriptions that run our world, our community, our country, we must start with the ones that run our mornings, our

FIGURE 7
Outer Ring
Surface Subscriptions

days, our laptops, our calendars. By starting with that which is seemingly small and most immediate, we do two things: (1) we take life off autopilot, beginning to extract ourselves from the infinite loop, and (2) we give ourselves an experience of choice, of responsibility, and of personal power.

More than 300 billion emails a day are sent around the country, and nearly 40.6 billion more than usual hit our inboxes during the circus. The digital detritus that our inboxes house creates massive anxiety for each of us. It's that constant low-level anxiety we all now have—and have accepted as part of life—that sits just below the surface, that whisper that nags, "You have unread messages *somewhere*." This overload is real. The anxiety will only go away when we unsubscribe from all of the places that we know our data sits, all of the anonymous ties we have to companies, businesses, brands, organizations, groups, and institutions.

For me, this started with unsubscribing from emails from West Elm, Room & Board, Crate & Barrel, and Restoration Hardware. I have no idea where any of their products are made, how they get to my door, or how they treat their workers, vendors, employees, or the like. (Now you know they also reinforced the notion that I was a luxury-brand kind of guy. And that I like furniture porn.) No, thank you. *Please unsubscribe, thanks!* Next was *Out Traveler*, *Vanity Fair*, and *Architectural Digest*. All they seemed to do, I realized, was make me feel bad that I do not live in a gorgeously appointed four-thousand-square-foot loft and cannot jet to Mykonos in linen pants and Versace sunglasses. With a perfectly tanned eight-pack. Besides, I was already getting their printed publications in my mailbox, so why did I need to see their digital ones? And then there was Orvis. I'd bought one preppy wax jacket from them four years ago, and I was getting invited to go fly-fishing three times a week. Enough already. I also unsubscribed from AMC, Target Optical, and the Cross pens newsletter. (I love movies, glasses, and a good Cross pen, but do I really need emails from them twice a week? Come on.) I even unsubscribed from my doctor's office's email updates.*

You can do this. You can unsubscribe from all of it. On one side of the wall is click-up economics. On the other side is your sacred quiet. You won't miss any of it. I promise you. In fact, I can almost guarantee you will breathe a sigh of relief tomorrow when you open your inbox and see how little is in it. It doesn't mean you are not loved. It doesn't mean you are not an involved, dynamic, and engaged human. It just means you have taken back control over what your inbox really represents: your mind. You know where to go to get the information you need; you do not need it fed to you on autopilot. *But what if I* miss *something?* If you miss something, someone will hunt you down and tell you. The whole world has gotten really good at hunting, and at calling out our every flaw.

---

* They're not a Big Brand, but they were behaving like one. I refuse to have my relationship with my doctor reduced to a marketing email (here's a letter from the president of NYU Langone about what we're doing to better serve you), online messaging, Zoom visits, and an online chart. While some of these new practices use technology and data collection to predict illness and create better health care outcomes, some of them have buried doctors and their patients in their computers. Click-up economics has rendered our greatest healers and practitioners constantly accessible to every patient's every ache and pain, and an insatiable appetite for profit at the country's biggest hospitals and health care systems has filled their days with endless data and communications management, giving them less and less time for actual patient care. I'm good without it all. I'll call when I'm sick. The more we participate and feed this system, the less of our doctor we actually get.

When you think you're done, keep going. There is more hiding somewhere.

A good guideline is this: let your emails pile up. The week before you unsubscribe, or a few weeks (whichever works), let all your automated subscription emails pile up. Don't delete them. Deleting them leads you to believe falsely that getting rid of these digital pests is as easy as a Trash click. They are cockroaches. They keep coming back. If a pile of automated emails gets in your way, shuttle them into a folder. This lets you see truly how many you get in a week and allows you to unsubscribe all at once.

Dedicate your first day of unsubscribing to overhauling your inbox. Go to that folder, find the unsubscribe button on every email. Click and unsubscribe. I bet you will be shocked at how much time this actually takes. Yep. And it's been taking all that time from you since you subscribed. If you forgot one or missed a few, don't worry, they will find you. Beware of two things: the unsubscribe buttons on mail services like Apple Mail (they tend not to fully unsubscribe you) and online services that promise to mass unsubscribe you (many are actually data-collection services). The blatant lies of the Internet never cease to astound.

In the end, it's not just about fewer emails or texts. Daily exposure to each of these messages forces you to *consume* them. You are consuming their beliefs, their way of operating, their vision for our world. You may not click every day. You may not purchase every day. You may not even read every day. That's not the point. Pinging you daily accomplishes a vital goal of the brand's marketing strategy: it shows you their logo, which keeps their brand alive in your mind. Next, it reminds you of the brand's core DNA: its mission, its vision, and its values. And not the mission, vision, and values posted on their website. Those polished, media-ready messages are written by underpaid writers who took the gig to make ends meet and who spent weeks racking their brains trying to figure out how to make brands sound friendly, kind, and well-meaning. The brand's real mission: to make money. Their real vision: to keep making money. Their values: to do it by any means possible to show a profit to their shareholders.

Notice as you revolutionize your inbox just how much we all use email for conversations, especially now since we're all scared shitless of being sued (so we constantly want everything in writing). For me, email is best used for the transfer of large pieces of information. We all employ email differently, so you decide what you can use it best for. As you move through this process, start to set some rules for yourself about how you will use email to make your life easier, so your inbox is not just a digital dumping ground without any order or intention.

Once you've cleaned out your inbox, truly, then *consolidate your email addresses* and inboxes. A lot of us have created separate email inboxes for every project, venture, initiative, and department of our life and business. I did. Now, that's what folders are for. I keep it easy: one inbox for business, one for personal. That way, when I leave the office—even if I work from home—I just set one autoreply for business emails. All of our lives and businesses are different, so this will look different for each of us, for sure. The point: minimize, consolidate, and do it with purpose.

Next, turn your attention to those *other inboxes*, the ones on your social media platforms. (Yes, those are also inboxes. If it can receive and/or send a message, it's an inbox.) Go to your Instagram, your Facebook, your Messenger (which now works for both of those, since they're both owned by Meta), your Twitter, your Pinterest, your LinkedIn. I wish I could say this: disable them. But Big Tech has not given us the ability to do that nor to set autoreplies for them, because that would tank their engagement metrics. So for now, while you're engaging in this process, simply stop using all of them. You can always come back to them when you've made your way to the other side and identified these as valuable to your life. For now, your sacred quiet depends on eliminating the noise.

I have stopped checking them altogether. They were causing too much anxiety for me. I now only answer messages on email, and I have written that in the bio section on each of the social media platforms I use: "Please don't message me here. I don't check it. Visit my website to connect." The truth is if people really need to talk to you, they will do so in the way you ask, because that's how they'll get their message in front of you. *But if I ignore these inboxes, won't I miss out on platform-specific communications, like recruiting emails, partnership opportunities, or my best friend forwarding from that silly meme account?* Yes, you will. For now.

Getting a new email address is always an option. If you're ready for some advanced-level unsubscribing, move off your existing Big Tech email providers and set up a fresh account—or, opt out of allowing your provider to scan your emails to tailor advertising to you. (You can do this in your settings.) If you feel like you want a fresh start, there are alternative services to Google, Yahoo, AOL, etc., like Zoho Mail, Proton Mail, and Fastmail. (I know a few people who have stopped using email altogether, but I know that's not feasible for most people. If you want to try, though, more power to you.)

It is important to note here that you should confirm if you are *deleting* an email address, *disabling* it, *closing* it, etc. The language each provider uses is different. And sometimes misleading. It's important, if you do take this step, to disconnect these addresses from any of the apps and services that use them as a login, etc. You can see how this tangled web is already tough to untangle. Do your best to minimize the number of message spaces so that when you think about *messages*, you think about one place.

A tool I use often is my autoresponder. Over the course of the last twenty years, Big Tech has trained all of us to eliminate our personal boundaries, selling to us as "freedom" the ability to answer emails on the go, from the bathroom, in the car, and walking down the street. Work has become personal time; personal time has become work. Unsubscribing includes unsubscribing from this very dangerous (and completely bullshit) idea. For your business email, set an autoreply that tells your colleagues what hours you work and what a reasonable response time is for them to expect your reply. Here's some sample language, if it helps: "Thanks for your email. My virtual desk hours are 9:00 a.m. ET to 6:00 p.m. ET. I usually reply within the business day. Looking forward to connecting." If this is just an insane idea within your work environment, see chapters 10 and 11.

Same holds true and effective for personal relationships. Consider adding an autoresponder to your personal email that tells your friends, family, and acquaintances how you want to communicate. "Hey there. Thanks for your email. Big changes here. I only check personal emails a few times a week now. I'll get back to you next time I am online. Feel free to call (number below) if it is urgent." (It's never urgent.) Amend to your liking and to your personal communications specs.

Most important of all, *stop apologizing*. Remember, none of us ever signed a contract that commits us to respond to anyone in any timeframe. (Maybe you did at work; if you did, it is time to renegotiate that agreement. Have a private conversation with your boss. More on that later.) You must be the driver of this car and set the cadence yourself. You have to set the expectation. At the beginning of this century, we all just subscribed to this idea that *email requires an immediate response*. Cultural subscriptions are powerful. They spread across a culture as fast as a snarky tweet about Ted Cruz. And without knowing it or intentionally signing on, we commit to certain behaviors that do not serve us. *Please unsubscribe, thanks!*

Let's Move to Our Laptop and Our Devices

Our laptops used to be "personal computers" until the Internet turned them into portals to never-ending noise. It is time to *unsubscribe from software that requires a monthly subscription* and access to your checking account. Next, *remove autofills* on credit cards and passwords that then let your laptop automatically charge a credit card. This will be particularly challenging for professionals who use software that have moved over to the SaaS model. If you must keep the software (perhaps for work), close and delete any of the shortcut icons on, above, or below your desktop. I took mine out of the dock. When I need to use them, I know where they are: in the Applications folder. I challenged myself to keep only ten icons in my dock. Limits. My anxiety dropped as soon as I did.

Then, *unplug from cloud storage.* It is just a digital storage locker that you are keeping crap in. No more Dropbox, Google Drive, or the like—use them sparingly, if you want, to transfer large files to others, but reembrace the limits of an external hard drive. What this looks like for me is setting aside one business day per year to archive all the files from that year on my external hard drive. I save those folders until the hard drive is full, then I delete the oldest folder if I need more space. This will look different for each of us (I'm giving you the extreme version), but try as best you can to replace *storing* with *deleting* or *archiving.* We will never look at or need most of those files (just like my mother will never need the endless Tupperware containers she keeps in a box in the attic). Deleting things is okay. It's actually good for us. It helps us focus on what is important without the distraction of what is no longer relevant.

Now, look, I understand that disconnecting from the cloud can be a massive challenge. So can taking even one business day a year to archive shit. At this point, in a digital culture that constantly reinforces that *you can keep everything forever*, we have to reembrace limits. It is important to begin to create new traditions, rituals, and ceremonies that serve our mental health (and businesses). Just like April 15 is Tax Day, December 21 is Archive Day on my desk (which also happens to be the "shortest" and darkest day of the year; perfect). Right before I break for Christmas, I archive. I clean my digital and physical brain so I can relax for the holidays.

Next, it is time to *redefine our relationship with our web browser*. Get rid of Chrome or Safari and switch to Brave, Firefox, DuckDuckGo, or Tor, which allow you to set strict privacy settings and block ads, pop-ups, and annoying messages. They also block the monitoring devices that Big Tech has created to harvest your data, track your activities, and the like. Think, too, about *how* you browse, and retrain yourself. Do not subscribe to anything to simply view a webpage. Likely, what you are searching for is available somewhere else. And it will probably only take five more seconds to find it. Do not bookmark pages. Do not accept cookies. Cookies are the biggest fraud on the Internet. (They were named that way so you would *want* them. Remember how we talked earlier about marketing and positive feelings? Who doesn't want a cookie?) Cookies are the very tiny robots that track and report your behavior online. You have the opportunity, when you enter a website, to reject them. You can also clear or disable them within the browser history. To unsubscribe fully, delete your web browser entirely. *What? Are you crazy?* Well, maybe a little. You can reinstall it, if you want, at the end of this process. If that's too extreme, try this: take your web browser out of your dock for a few days. Just take notice of how often you go online.

Some other quick (possible) changes: turn off all notifications; turn off location services; make your wallpaper and browser backgrounds a single color so you can create calm as you unsubscribe; and review and set your privacy settings, if you have never done so. Make your laptop yours again by setting clear boundaries. Disconnect from shared apps and reduce how many of them are on multiple devices. Chances are, you're carrying one or two with you on a regular basis—why do you need notifications on all of them to tell you the same thing?

Finally: *make your phone a phone again*. It is time to choose only ten apps. *What?* You choose the number, but pick a number and commit to it. Create a limit. Organize around a handful of the most important apps. Or do what I did: get rid of your phone.

I know, I'm pushing *every button* here, but that's the point. There is really zero reason any of us needs a $1,000 phone that's actually a computer in our pockets. When I leave the house, I want to step away from the noise, not carry it with me. I just bought a Jitterbug (yes, I am forty-four years old and use a phone created for and marketed to senior citizens). Sure, it has special features, like a medical-alert button in case I fall, but otherwise it has very limited capability. And it was $100. It makes calls. It receives and sends texts. That is all I want, personally. That is all I need. My father, who is seventy and an actual senior citizen, thinks I have lost my mind. "How can you be a movie director without the latest iPhone?" Watch me.

If all of this seems too fast and furious, I challenge you to try this: Leave your phone at home when you go out for a coffee (fifteen minutes), or for lunch (an hour), or for a meeting or event (a few hours). Start small. See what it's like. Yes, you'll feel anxious at first. But sit with that anxiety until it fades. See what's on the other side. Funny enough, I recently checked in at a restaurant and told the host that I was there to have lunch with my friend. She asked me to text him to see where in the (large) restaurant he was sitting. I said, "Sorry. I didn't take my phone with me today." She looked at me like I was an alien from Planet Landline. "Ohmygod," she said, "you're giving me so much anxiety. No phone!" Her anxiety may have been higher, but mine was much lower. I had the best adventure out for lunch in the analog wild. Try it. Just try it.

This is all called "downteching," the act of not upgrading but downgrading, not upscaling but downscaling, not running and running in the infinite loop Big Tech has created but stepping out of it and saying, "Hey. I'm done. I'm out. You guys can all play this game with seventeen camera lenses on the back of your phone, but I will live a perfectly fulfilling life with my Jitterbug." Or, ya know, something like that.

Now, go one step further and delete or remove Messages or similar texting apps. If that's a bridge too far for you (I can hear the moms and dads laughing), change your settings so that the phone deletes any text that is more than thirty days old. That's doable, no? That way, you can start to realize how many people you really do text within any given month. You can also silence your text notifications during the day while you're working or at night while you're sleeping. Give some thought to what you want to use texting *for*. Why do you need it? Who is allowed to reach you this way? Who is not? My new ground rule is this: I don't send outgoing texts. I will respond if it is urgent, but otherwise, I treat my text messages like my inbox. When I "do email" in the morning, I also respond to texts, all at once. In my message, I now say, "I don't really text anymore. Email me or call? Would love to talk." Or, I just pick up the phone and call whoever texted me. It is time to retrain one another to stop relying on texting as conversation.

Making conversation micro, delayed, and disjointed is having terrible effects on our relationships. And it is robbing our young people of the life experience of pushing through their anxieties to talk to that cute boy or to strike up a conversation with a potential business contact or employer, or (more important) to really say what needs to be said to establish open lines of communication in our most intimate relationships, instead of hiding behind three little bubbles that pop up while the other person is typing.

A good practice here, too, is to clean out your contacts. It's all noise. Choose the people you truly want to be in touch with and delete the rest. If you treat your phone like a digital Rolodex, and you want records of all your contacts, export your contacts and print them out. Keep them in a binder on your desk. It's very old school. Do what works. But less is more. Even less is even more.

For right now, give yourself the break and the sacred space to fully process how you *want* to use your devices and their apps to better your life.

And while you're at it, set a new voicemail message, much like your autoreply, that tells your callers how often you check voicemail (if at all) and when they can expect a call back. Change your phone settings to stop tracking you and your location. Commit to touching the phone only when you leave the house, if you feel you need to take it with you for safety.

This is going to feel weird. Really weird. But I promise, it is worth it.

Next, Reclaim Our Homes

The rise of smart-home devices has turned our homes upside down. I have a friend whose home makes me extremely anxious. Every room has a television that is on, no matter if anyone is watching. Every kid has an iPad in their hand. Both she and her husband are on their phones. She markets her business on TikTok; he loves Angry Birds. Every room has a camera in it, spying on you while you eat. Every window has a wifi-enabled alarm device. And there is a wireless smart speaker in every room. Some have two. When the phone rings, the entire house lights up like the East River on the Fourth of July. It's like having dinner inside a Best Buy. The modern middle class has been seduced by so much shiny new tech that we now live in a state of constant alert. At any given moment, something can ping or ring and grab our attention, disrupting the very act of building and raising a family. Enough already.

Unplug all your smart devices and lock them up in a trunk in the garage. It may be jarring at first, but remember: these devices are only a few years old. Chances are, you lived at least a couple of decades without them. Again, *you can do this*. If you are feeling bold (go, go, go!), cut the cord by physically taking a pair of scissors and cutting the cord off all of these devices. (Funny enough, most of their cords disconnect so that they can be replaced should you have a fit of consciousness and decide to mutilate the tails of these digital pets.) Commit to *no television* right now. Check the news once in the morning and once in the evening to understand what is happening in your world, if you want. But set a strict limit for yourself. Make your home quiet. Return it to its natural state as a place of solitude, recuperation, restoration, and peace.

It's also important to get Big Brand messages out of the house by *recycling your magazines*. Some of them are just catalogs disguised as journalism. At the end of this process, you might want to welcome a few select mags back in, but for now make your space as brand-free as possible. If budget allows, donate T-shirts and other clothing items that have big, bold brand names on them. At the very least, collect them all and put them away in a storage bin. (That does not mean go out and buy new clothes. That is the opposite of my point.) Rid yourself of the constant reminder that you are the brands you buy. You are not. You're a human being who needs a shirt, and you like white T-shirts. You're not a paid marketing associate for Calvin Klein. This goes for branded shopping bags, too. Anything with a logo on it goes on the other side of your boundary. You'll soon realize just how many logos you see, touch, and consume every day. Our consumption of these logos reinforces in our brain—and in everyone's who sees them—that people come in tiers, classes, hierarchies, levels of importance, that people are high end or low end; first class, business class, or economy; worthy of luxury or not worthy of luxury.

Next, let's *stop ordering online*. For some of us, this will be *extremely difficult.* I get it. But take this time to stop buying. We don't actually need more. Take the bookmarks out of your web browser. Take the apps off your phone. Close your Amazon account. *Woah! No one messes with my Amazon account!* I hear you. I'm pushing hard for a reason. Breaking out of the infinite loop asks us—requires us, *begs* us—to reflect on our relationship with convenience. It is often the brands that have us most addicted that are exploiting us most blatantly. The sexy sell of convenience is that we will never have to make a choice—between our kids and our job, between cooking or shopping, between one commitment or the other. We get to be Superman and Superwoman. Unsubscription is about letting go of the expectation that we will ever be anything other than plain old human.

At the very least put Amazon in the parking lot.

Same for food delivery apps. Stop using Seamless and Grubhub and any other online food-delivery service that charges $12 in fees (which go directly to at least three already wealthy parties) for a $10 hamburger and has underpaid workers cycling madly through our streets risking life and limb to get us cold fries we could easily cook or pick up from the local restaurant. The relentlessness of our lives demands these conveniences, which then enables more relentlessness and traps us in a cycle.

A slower life means trips to the grocery store again, trying on clothes in a fitting room, perusing bookstores and furniture stores and shoe shops—and of course learning to wait for products and services that take more time to reach you than next-day shipping. There are plenty of cases to be made for and against online retailers. And while worker abuse and environmental abuse are grave concerns for me personally, my concern as your writer is your happiness. Rewiring ourselves to not need anything instantaneously except the bare necessities of human life can re-connect us to the joy of living. It did for me.

• • •

Now that you have cut ties with the Big Brands and Big Tech, it's time to unsubscribe from the Big Banks. The Big Banks are taking our money not safeguarding it. It's time to reclaim our cash.

Let me be clear: unsubscribing is not necessarily about collapsing a system. It's about making yourself less dependent on that system and creating clear boundaries so that system is not exploiting you. And your money. It's also about consciously reallocating our attention and resources into the parts of the system that *do* work for us.

If you're ready for a big change, go to the bank and withdraw your cash. Put it, instead, in a local community bank, a not-for-profit bank, or a credit union. But do your research first. Some community banks are owned by other banks which are then owned by funds that are then owned or operated by the Big Banks. Confused? Yep. They like it that way. The Big Banks have used the same branding processes that the Big Brands use to project safety, solidity, and strength. And to shapeshift into whatever form you like so you will open an account. We all yearn for the emotional comfort of safety, solidity, and strength—especially when it comes to our money. It's a radical position, but I went full bore on this one immediately.

When I did this, it suddenly occurred to me: *Wait, all this time I could have just not been a Wells Fargo customer?* Um, yes. The infinite loop is a fast place, purposely full of flurry and good old-fashioned hubbub so that you never take the time to consider any other way.

This is an ideal place to start. But if you can't take your money out (because, say, your credit cards are tied to the account) or you would rather keep your money where it is, consider the following strategies to reinstate control.

Unsubscribe from autopays

The promise of autopay is peace of mind. You won't have to worry about missing a payment or encounter the fees the Big Banks are charging you, or risk "bad" credit, which triggers all sorts of unpleasant emotions: shame, guilt, embarrassment, humiliation, disgrace, dishonor. Our national credit-reporting system is a mystery wrapped in a puzzle wrapped in a riddle wrapped in an enigma; it is the turducken of the financial system. Even during the circus, as unemployment rose to historic heights and an uncontrollable virus killed a million Americans, nowhere in any of our relief legislation were proposals to allow Americans to keep their credit scores as they were when the crisis hit. If you are at risk of missing payments, automation is not your friend. Stop anything that is recurring, even donations. Kick everyone out of your bank account.

This is *slow banking*. For the purposes of this process, go back to paper, go back to a weekly trip to the bank, go back to formally balancing your checkbook instead of checking your bank balances on your phone fifteen times a day. Unsubscribe from digital communications from your bank. It is your money. It is too important to manage over email and text. When it becomes part of the noise, it gets lost in the chaos of the pinging and the ringing. If you go back—even temporarily—to managing your money this way, something magical happens: you re-sensitize yourself to the value of your own money. A hundred dollars is very different when you have to go to the bank to get it, keep it in your wallet, and spend it with discretion. When it flies out of your checking account, it's not even money anymore. Try it this way for a month. See what it feels like.

Unsubscribe from your bank's overdraft program

Most consumers are automatically enrolled in their bank's overdraft program as a "courtesy." *Don't worry if you write a check you can't cash, we'll cover you!* This is a trap. They will cover you, but they will charge you an exorbitant fee to do so. Call your bank and unenroll. This will force you to know if you have the money available in your checking before you write a check. It will force you to get conscious about your funds. In 2022, Elizabeth Warren brilliantly skewered all the major bank presidents for their abuse of overdraft charges. Thank you, Mrs. Warren. The Big Banks have used overdraft "protection" to make money. A ton of it. US banks make a combined $15 billion a year on overdraft fees. Fifteen. Billion. Dollars. Eighty percent of that comes from just 9 percent of customers who just keep getting hit over and over.

Clean out your card information online

I mentioned this already, but it bears repeating. In most web browsers, you can delete your credit card information so it stops autofilling for online purchases. This will slow down your spending so you can use this process to get present to what you are actually buying, how often, and how much. Likewise, delete or empty your phone's digital wallet app. Yes, you'll feel a lot less cool (I did) when you're buying a $13 smoothie at the gym, but in the time it takes you to get your credit card out, you can actually take a beat to think: *Wait, why am I paying $13 for a smoothie?*

Now let's move to Big Media. Big Media has commodified our attention. It's time to restore our focus.

Commit to no media

Yes, there is plenty of edifying media in the world. And there is plenty of media that is not Big Media. It is just dwarfed by the Big Media. For now, go cold turkey. Stop watching and listening to movies, television, videos, podcasts, all of it. It will be horribly uncomfortable. But you will get to experience your truest nature. We'll talk about that in the later chapters. *Did a filmmaker just tell me to stop watching movies?* Yes, I did. It's temporary. And it's important.

Unsubscribe from cable

Cutting the cord is old news, and yet our cable bills are still a staple of our monthly expenses. Just because the old-school "cable box" is no longer in our house doesn't mean that we no longer have cable. The *full unsubscribe* here is to cancel wifi service, cable, all of it. You can't really bring a cocktail into rehab, can you? Best to stop the flow at the source. (The beginner's version: designate an hour an evening as "wifi-free" or "tech-free.") At the end of this process, you are likely to turn the wifi back on, but give yourself the time and space without it. You'll quickly realize just how many of your daily processes require it. It has been designed that way. Take a deep breath. If you need wifi for work, experiment with toggling your "wifi" switch to Off during your lunch break.

Unsubscribe from entertainment subscription services

Yes, it's temporary. If you are not ready for a house with no wifi, step away from all the entertainment subscription services, the news services, anything that requires an automatic monthly subscription. If you're using the parking lot, pause the services and keep the accounts active. If you're already beginning to see the danger of the parking lot, burn the bridge. Unsubscribe and cancel all the underlying accounts. Little by little, they all crept into your life and into your checking account. Watch the latest episodes of *The Handmaid's Tale* and then say good-bye to June Osborne for a little while. Elizabeth Moss is out living her life. She's not trapped in Gilead. You are entitled to live your life, too.

Downtech to one television

If you want to stay informed during this process, pull the plug on all your televisions but one. Put them in storage for now. Or recycle them. You choose how extreme you want to go. Keep one, your main one, and keep it unplugged. Nightly, plug it in to watch the six o'clock news. Then unplug and get back to life. That's what I did. With hours back in my day, suddenly, I started reading books again. Turns out, I love books. If you're looking for the *light version* here, just give yourself a limit. How many hours per week do you want to watch TV? Stick to it for four to six weeks and see how it feels.

Unsubscribe from the drama

Big Media thrives on chaos. Drama, by definition, is performing at a scale larger than life. In ancient times, you had to do this from the stage so that the very last row in the amphitheater could see and hear you. Your voice needed to be louder. Your gestures needed to be larger. Your energy needed to be more forceful. Our earliest actors and dramatists created theater to always be larger than life because of the limits of the physical stages they performed on. Our modern problem is we keep living, behaving, and performing at this scale. It is not natural. It is not real. It is not authentic. As you unsubscribe, pay attention to your own inclination toward drama. When do you respond, react, behave, and perform larger than life? We all do it. And we do it because we have been trained by decades of media that this behavior is how we capture attention. We are all part of this same ecosystem. Not only would we all be healthier if we didn't watch *The Real Housewives*, but it is important to catch ourselves when we begin to behave the way they do. Tables are meant for eating, not flipping. This can help us reset our emotional barometers so that when we see drama—from celebrities, the news, politicians—we can call out their bullshit faster and with more ease.

Lastly, it is time to step back from the Big Parties. Does that mean don't vote? Absolutely not. It means stop participating in the day-to-day, minute-by-minute red-versus-blue street fight. How do we unsubscribe from one of the biggest forces running our country? We start on our screens. Stop warring about politics online. Stop reading and responding to posts by politicians on Twitter. It is time for all of us to unsubscribe from the war between the Democrats and the Republicans—online, in our news, at our dining tables. No one's mind is changing. We are simply killing civility, tearing our social fabric, and pitting brothers against sisters. No more email lists, newsletters, and party website logins. It is time to unsubscribe from recurring donations, text alerts, and phone calls. *Please unsubscribe, thanks!*

If we want our politics to work, they must be divorced from the digital commercial system we have embedded them in. First, unsubscribe from political newsletters, event notifications, and marketing emails. In your inbox, in your home, and on your phone, unsubscribe from and cancel any and all apps, feeds, threads, and tethers. We cannot truly effect change if we continue to feed the very systems that perpetuate the never-ending bullshit. I realize that this severely handicaps our ability to get "good messages" out and to effect the type of change that we each deem to be "right." It is all coming at the cost of our mental health. It is also coming at the cost of the very change we all so earnestly seek. When we become part of the never-ending bullshit, we feed the whole of it.

Trust me, I see the irony in saying that in a book you perhaps bought online, heard about through the media, or got an email about. I have dedicated a year of my life after the publishing of this book to tour the country offline in order to rebuild my own communal muscles—those that have atrophied in each of us as click-up economics retrained us to only think of digital spaces as important and worthy of our time and attention. I am doing the best I can, too.

If you have followed all my early recommendations, this should shut out the Big Parties well, since they use the same systems as the other Big Forces, but a few additional steps follow.

Depoliticize your space

Our homes have become messaging hubs for the Big Parties. Get rid of, donate, or store away your political hats, T-shirts, banners, and household goods that speak the gospel of your politics. And take the lawn signs down. You may fully believe and support the elected officials and ideas that these goods communicate, but for now, it is important to get to a space as clean and neutral as possible. That also means stop watching the news 24/7.

Stop donating online

Political donations made online give the parties way more than your money. They give them your email, your phone number, all your contact information. That information is then shared by the Big Parties, which is why you're getting emails and texts from candidates in Oklahoma when you live in Georgia. Is there anything wrong with donating to candidates in other states? No. But let's make that our choice, not the party's. We take our personal power back—and our political power—when we stop donating online. For now, give none of your clicks, money, or time to the Big Parties. Later in this process, you can decide where to put your energy and money. In the last election cycle, I wrote checks to my three favorite candidates. You can be sure they cashed them.

Unsubscribe from the party

If you're ready to go all-in, this is an option. You can still vote in general elections, but you'll save yourself the grief of the group think. Or put your party membership in the parking lot for now, and let's reevaluate it later in this process.

Unsubscribing from the Big Forces is tough. But it places a boundary between you and them. That boundary has been systematically eroded over the last twenty years. Putting it back up is the first major step we all need to take in order to break out of the infinite loop. This process will look different for each of us, and for each of our families, but getting this far means you have considered deeply how to rebuild that boundary and have taken action to do it. Or, it is my hope, that you are at least entertaining some of these ideas and their ability to help you limit the never-ending noise. What you will quickly realize—just like I did—is that the bullshit seeps in. It seeps past the boundary. Because all the people in our lives are texting, emailing, forwarding the constant nonsense. They are not evil because they sent you a funny meme. They are as beautiful and whole as you are (well, most of them). They are just caught in the infinite loop, too.

Eight

Reevaluating Our Relationships

The next phase of the Great Unsubscribe is focused on untangling all of our social or *people subscriptions*.

This is the middle subscription ring of our circle. (See figure 8.) Let me be clear up front: I don't want us to abandon all our friends or stop talking to our families. In fact, I am advocating for the opposite: for each of us to have people in our lives who inspire us, who embrace us, who keep our candle lit, and who support our joy, and to focus on them instead of the ones who simply pop up and demand the most attention. Unsubscribing calls on us to get rid of that which stands in the way of spending time with those we truly love to be around. (And if we have not even *met them* yet, we have all the more reason to clear some seats at the table so they can come and sit.) This may be intense. Let's dive in.

Just like unsubscribing from the Big Forces begs us to reexamine what we get from each of them emotionally, rethinking our social lives requires a truthful examination of the same—a keen look at where we get praise, validation, love, acceptance, belonging, and meaning. Yes, it is a tall order. It requires a level of honesty and emotional awareness that we do not actively practice, and a certain amount of time and space that we find nearly impossible to carve out as we dart about maintaining every relationship we have ever formed in our lives. Our time outside of work is precious, and how we spend that time—and with whom—matters.

FIGURE 8
Middle Ring
People Subscriptions

We start in our calendar. Let's clear it—all of it—for at least the next four to six weeks. Tell every person you have plans with that you have to reschedule but that you'll get back to them. It is that simple. If your work commitments are also social commitments, find ways to limit them. Turn them into Zooms. Do a phone call instead. Combine them all into one big client party. The point is to change your *approach* to making plans. Stop filling up your calendar just because that is what you have always done. Do your best here. This is an imperfect process.

Of course, eliminating the commitment to see someone—or video or call or whatever—does not really unsubscribe you from them. To really unsubscribe, you must break the (emotional/friendship) contract you have in place with them, or it will stay intact and linger, adding to the low-level noise and anxiety that we all have begun to feel. I recommend that you *hold off on that for now*. This is very tricky business, with heavier implications than getting off the Macy's mailing list. People's feelings are at stake. Human people with human feelings. They deserve your best. As a first, bold step, put everyone in the parking lot. They are there, *in* your life, but you have zero commitment right now on the books to see them, talk to them, or the like. You don't want to fully unsubscribe until you are sure that it is truly the right move for you.

What you'll quickly realize is that in some of your friendships and relationships, you are always the one initiating. In others, it is always the other party. It's just good to notice this. What that means to you is up to you. But it's hard to see when you're going and going and going on autopilot.

Now, it's important to retrain yourself to understand where each person fits into your life. That middle ring of the circle? It's actually *many, many circles*. These social circles are circles of people to whom you have some sort of relationship, agreement, contract, promise, or emotional bond. Click-up economics calls them networks. And click-up economics benefits when you think of all of these circles as *the same*. They are not.

This list might be different for each of us. You can decide which buckets work best for you. And their order. But for the purpose of this book, let's use these ten social circles:

- The Supercommunity
- Community institutions, associations, and organizations
- School communities
- Extended family
- Work teams
- Friends
- Immediate family
- Romantic partners
- You

The social circles are like a dartboard, with you at the center (see figure 9). Click-up economics has collapsed every circle around you into the Supercommunity. This chapter is about reestablishing the lines between each so that we can build dimension and texture back into our social lives.

One reason we often feel so very disempowered in our lives is that this dartboard is alive with people, their needs and wants, their struggle for survival and their desires and ambitions. These circles

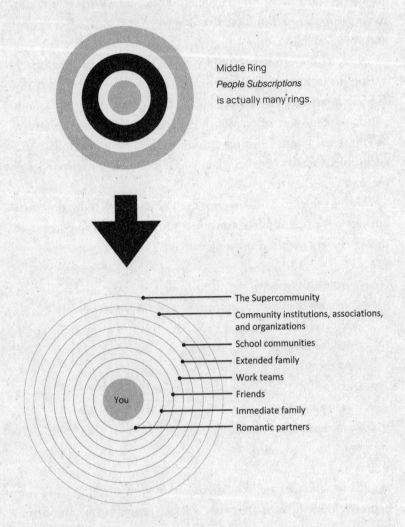

Middle Ring
People Subscriptions
is actually many rings.

The Supercommunity

Community institutions, associations, and organizations

School communities

Extended family

Work teams

Friends

Immediate family

Romantic partners

You

FIGURE 9
So Many *People Subscriptions*
(aka The Dartboard)

all push against each other all day long, fighting for power. Pressure, pressure, pressure. Most of that pressure lands on you. And makes you feel small. And the bullshit of the Big Forces—who have captured the Supercommunity and use it to inundate us with a steady stream of their bullshit—reinforces that smallness. They don't care if you're small, they have sophisticated tools to land their dart right where they want it.

This next stage of unsubscription calls on us to cut the tethers—physical, financial, emotional—to each of these social circles, temporarily, so we have the time and space to reevaluate these relationships, determine what they truly bring into our lives, and reestablish healthy boundaries. Understanding them each as clear and distinct can feel formal, perhaps too formal, but this process can help us to truly see where and how deep our emotional commitments are—and to whom.

I want to take our social circles one by one and use the rest of this chapter to show you how to unsubscribe from each. Remember, this is a *temporary* process to help us eliminate the noise. In later chapters, we'll be reengaging—resubscribing—to the circles, or the people in them, that matter most to us. Along the way, we'll explore each.

The Supercommunity

The largest, outer ring is the Supercommunity, which for most of known time included people who were unknowable to us. It includes hundreds of millions of people in the country and billions of people on the planet. Click-up economics, of course, connected everyone together and threw your mom and your best friend from third grade into the Supercommunity. No. They belong in other (perhaps closer) circles. Before the Internet, we generally didn't concern ourselves with the Supercommunity or at least we didn't have access to it. You couldn't fit these people in a room or even in a convention center. We call our role in this circle and its subsets "world citizen," "citizen," "voter," or even "reader" or "follower" or "user." This circle does not necessarily overlap extensively with our immediate geography and may or may not overlap with our lived experience. At publication of this book, there are more than five billion Internet users. While language and digital infrastructures around the world may limit our access to *everyone*, we are still connected to those five billion just by being online.

Throughout history, we have employed all sorts of practices— like representative democracy—to manage the fact that millions of us were connected under one flag despite being physically separated by thousands of miles. Now, we can access and dissect that Supercommunity into endless subsets (lovers of knitting, lovers of pure anarchy) that cut across state, national, and international lines and have an emotional connection to each of them. This ability can be used for good—coming to the rescue with money and messages of love when disaster strikes—but often our loyalties and commitments to these subsets are magnified (and commodified) by click-up economics. We are identified by our subscription to them, and once again become consumers to target. In some cases, once the habit of engaging with them is formed and automated (ah, the ever-present loop), we begin to believe that that subset is the entirety of the Supercommunity. *The world loves to knit. The world loves anarchy.* We curate a massive bubble and block out everyone else.

Why? Well, because it's a hell of a lot more obvious, attractive, easy, and satisfying to maintain our loyalty to that digital subset than it is to wade in the murky waters of the humans who are physically around us, who ask us to explain our values and debate the nuances of their application (less obvious). They come in a wide variety of unbranded packaging that is often cranky and displeasing (less attractive). They are hard to talk to (less easy) and they can disagree (less satisfying). But not online. Online, millions will come to our rescue should our worldview be challenged. They come with a built-in protocol for interacting. And a built-in distance. These digital armies can then empower us to behave in extreme ways in real life.

The limitlessness of the Supercommunity has altered how we see the world, how we interact with it, and what we expect from our experience of life. It also creates much of the noise and confusion that keeps us from focusing on the center of our dartboard. For now, I recommend coming off all social networks completely for at least a month. (Post on your preferred platforms—if you didn't completely come off them in the last chapter—that you are "taking a break" or "stepping back for a bit" or "need a digital detox." Do you *have* to post? Of course not. But it may make you feel better. I have no interest in you feeling bad.)

You will twitch. You will shake. You will go through withdrawal. Let's finally face this fact together: it is not natural to be in constant contact with millions of people. Period. We are simply not wired for it. We can choose to reconnect to the Supercommunity if we find at the end of this process that it significantly improves our life and provides deep connection and belonging. But for now, let's look elsewhere.

Community Institutions, Associations, and Organizations

The next ring inward is where you move out of the Supercommunity and become part of a crowd. These *larger circles* can include hundreds or thousands of people—we call our role within them "participant" or "member" or "neighbor"—and they can overlap heavily with our geography and lived experience. In my life, this includes my middle and high schools, my college, my graduate school, the alumni networks of all of those, the professional associations for film and television, a union for freelancers, a guild for screenwriters. Local arts groups, community organizations, faith groups, and even the PTA are included in this circle as well—basically any group that you might interact with on Facebook in "Groups" from whom you receive newsletters, magazines, updates, texts, and invitations. Together, you and all the other members are subscribed to not only their communications materials but to their values. You believe in similar things.

Take a moment and list all the community institutions, associations, and organizations to which you belong. As you review them, one by one, ask yourself: Do you get joy from contributing to it? From remaining a participant? Is this a circle you want to spend more time investing in or less time? Does it value you, your talents, and your contribution, or is it a circle that represents an older version of you from which you really want to unsubscribe? Just like every other circle, the point is not to deprive yourself of the great value that these institutions bring into your life, but to create a space where you can actively choose *if* they are bringing value in.

Once you have determined which ones should stay and which should go, it's time to address the latter. Unsubscribing from these institutions can be as simple as getting off their mailing list, unsubscribing from their email newsletters, deleting the bookmark to their website, not attending events or meetings, resigning from any leadership roles that you may hold, or simply not answering the phone when they call for money. If you have close personal relationships with specific people in those communities or with the leadership of those organizations, an email or phone call can serve you well to communicate that you are stepping back. Oftentimes it will only require a short, practical communication (though I tend to believe that doing these things publicly, to the whole group, can serve us well, too, in the right circumstance).

School Community

Anyone who has kids or who has been a student knows that the school community is its very own unique circle. I don't have kids yet (we're working on it; it's a process), but I have two sisters who have kids, and it is super clear that being part of their school community is nearly a full-time job in and of itself. I have pulled this one out from the more general "community institutions, associations, and organizations" because school can be a uniquely intense circle, one that often comes with a lot of bullshit. Families are subscribed to school letters, grade portals, homework websites, parenting guides, communications from the school board, the school district, the state, the volleyball team. There are parent groups, class leaders, team sports, academic clubs, extracurricular activities, and student organizations vying for your focus and that of your children. Subscription in this circle is strong, and the pressure is on full blast to participate and engage, and to adopt group beliefs, practices, and behaviors.

Unsubscribing from a school community will be tough if you are an active parent, but for a short time, try to create as much space as you can from the demands that this circle puts on you and from the noise its pinging and ringing creates in your day-to-day life. With the pressure to succeed ratcheted up, especially in this economy, many parents think that if they are not constantly tethered to these communications or obligations that their children will suffer emotionally, socially, academically, or intellectually. But, again, try to remember that educational systems existed for thousands of years without three dozen email updates a day. Your kids need your love. Not more prodding to be perfect and always "on." Use your voice, as a parent, to advocate for streamlined communications, realistic expectations about involvement, sustainable and family-kind scheduling. When schools adopt business practices that mimic the Big Forces, when they enthusiastically participate in the relentless swirl, all we are teaching our kids is that the only way to live—and to succeed in life—is to participate blindly and on autopilot.

You may highly disagree, but here's my point: you have the power as a member of the school community to advocate for your mental health and for that of your child and family.

Perhaps email or call the school coordinator or even head administrators. Let them know that you are engaging in an important family process to reevaluate the constant influx. You come in peace, but you need a breather. You might even use this communication as an opportunity to ask for help or to ask what the school is doing to support parents in managing the constant chaos you find yourself battling. If that approach feels too intense, perhaps attend the next PTA meeting and bring it up to other parents, many of whom are likely feeling the very same way.

If you have children of an appropriate age, call on them to manage their own schedules and responsibilities and advocate for themselves. You can drop in occasionally, but take the opportunity to step back and let the human you raised be a more self-sufficient human. And remember two things. One: you are not alone. And two: very few things in our world come with instructions. We are all making this up, especially now. When the world shut down, schools were caught by the same surprise you were and had to improvise the same way we all did. You are a valuable voice in helping them understand what is kosher in a post-circus world, what works, and what is driving you mad—and how you can help each other.

The next layer of circles on our dartboard is more *medium-sized*. These are ones in which you know everyone—or, at least, you know a smaller group within the larger whole. These circles include anywhere from one to thirty other people, generally, and we call our role in these circles "friend," "cousin," "colleague," or the like. Medium circles are our clans, tribes, kin, bonded by blood, friendship, or work. In my life, we are forty-three people in total on my mom's side, and thirty-three in total on my dad's side. When you add in my stepbrothers and stepsister, it adds five to each of those totals. We are a "clan" no matter how you slice it. Let's drill down.

Extended Family

The next important social circle is our *extended family*. This one might be one you can skip—I know some people who never see or deal with their extended family—or it might be the one you struggle most with. Depending on how you define your family, this circle may include your cousins, aunts, uncles, godparents, or even close family friends. Consider emotional and physical proximity, not just degree of relation. These are family bonds that existed before you did and exist beyond you, so they should be considered and approached carefully (think, for example, about how that third cousin you don't like isn't just *your third cousin*; she may also be your mother's favorite second cousin) (Wait, is that how that works?). For some, this is an online circle. For others, it is very much a physical one. The last few years in America have tested this circle and those in it most directly; our modern politics and conversations have made some of us question whether people in it subscribe to the same ideas that we do. We have been forced to ask ourselves if that matters to us, how much it matters, and what to do about it.

This is a good opportunity to revisit the idea I laid out before: that relationships are like subscriptions because of the terms under which we engage. Ask yourself: How often do you see the people in this circle? How often do you *want* to see them? Are these relationships meaningful enough to renew and pull closer? Or are they best kept at a distance? Where do you interact? How do you engage? Are you unsubscribing from friends or other circles to accommodate space for this one, when those others are truly more important to you? Who is best put in the parking lot and from whom is it time to truly unsubscribe? These are hard calls to make, but you can make them.

The first step is to create an initial distance—physically or digitally—from those you're considering unsubscribing from (or from the whole circle entirely), to give yourself the opportunity to choose what you want this group to look like and what role you want it to play in your day-to-day life. *But wait! I can't unsubscribe from my mother-in-law! She is my husband's mother. And she watches our kids!* I hear you, and I get it. Life is complicated, and sometimes these relationships, as hard as they might be, are necessary to keep order and sanity. It's easier to disengage from someone if the only time you're seeing them is across the table at a holiday. If you can't change your subscription (it's your husband's mother), and you can't change the fact that it is a recurring one (she babysits every Thursday), chances are you can find something within the terms that can help break you from the automated nature of it.

Let me give you an example. Before my grandmother died at the age of ninety-six, I struggled with our relationship for years. I loved her, but I found her overly opinionated, bossy, and hard to enjoy. Well into her eighties and nineties, the spark between us as grandmother and grandson had faded. In its place was a perfunctory relationship between a crabby old lady and her self-centered ambitious grandson who only called or visited when his mother guilted him into it. One day, just to shut her up (I'm being honest), I asked her how she met my grandfather (a question I had never asked). Suddenly, the eighty-five-year-old lady disappeared, and in her place was a bubbly and joyful young woman, who told me an elaborate story that took place in Brooklyn in 1943. I heard about all her other beaus, about how she fell in love with my grandfather's blue eyes, and how she refused to wear a dress to meet his mother—"I'm a modern woman! Pants! Or I don't go!" Those stories led to more stories. Those stories led to card games. Those card games helped us build a relationship we hadn't had in decades, arguably that we never had as two adults. I came to know her as Margie, not Grandma Margie.

From that moment on, I committed to myself to always start our conversations with a question about her life. That conversation always led her to eventually ask about my life in turn. As a result, we each came to accept the other for who we were as adults, instead of just continuing to exist within the same terms of my childhood—younger and elder. When I stopped sitting in my selfishness—*I have nothing to say to this woman if she can't even ask me about my life*—and spoke to her in a way that would open up a pathway to her joy and give us a place to connect, she came alive. I'm not saying that renegotiating these roles is always possible, or easy. But sometimes attitude is everything. If there are some people in the parking lot, or people that you're unsure of, switch up your approach next time you see them and see if anything changes.

(To be clear, I am not advocating for capitulating to or managing behavior to appease anyone in your life who makes you feel unsafe or unsupported. Conflicts and tensions exist on a spectrum; only you can decide where your line is. It's not your job to make everyone else feel okay. But if the relationship is important to you, changing your approach can reinvigorate the dynamic.)

If you're looking for permission, here it is: It's okay. It's okay to end relationships. It's okay to change them. It's okay to lean in even more than you ever have. You get to choose who gets a seat on your bus. You've got four thousand weeks according to our friend Oliver. With whom do you want to spend them?

Friends

While you might be able to slip out of PTA or school group membership relatively unscathed or unnoticed (if that's how you want to roll), unsubscribing from a friend circle is a much more noticeable act. Even if your communication and participation is not on a daily basis, your presence is missed if you step away. Unsubscribing requires a thoughtful and personal communication of some sort to initiate that process, and to clearly communicate the reasons for it.

At first glance, this might be really difficult. There's an old saying: "If everyone is our friend, then no one is." Chances are, when we take a step back and audit the people we call "friends," we will realize that most of them play other roles. That's because the word *friend* has mutated over the last two decades to include people who never before would be awarded the designation. Some, you'll realize, are *colleagues*. Some are *followers*. Some are *readers* or *fans*. Many are valid and valuable members of other circles, but calling everyone a *friend* and using digital platforms to be in constant contact with thousands of them, sharing everything from thoughts to jokes and photos all day long, has had some disastrous effects on the relationships that we value most in our lives. If a click brought them into your world, chances are a click can take them out.

When you begin to reevaluate this circle in earnest, it is well worth putting your actual friends—the ones with whom you have real-world, longstanding relationships with—in the parking lot so you can be thoughtful about your shared future. Run a joy test. *What do I feel when I see their name? What's my response when they call? Do I look forward to spending time with this person? Do I get excited? Am I calmed or annoyed?* (My personal test is: *Do I wake up and think "I get to see this person today!" Or do I wake up and think "Ugh, I have to see this person today."*) Your feelings are feedback. Listen to them.

We all have our ups and downs, our good days and bad days, so it's best to look for patterns over time. If this person consistently gives you a knot in your stomach, something is wrong.

If you get there, unsubscribing from the people who fail that test can be downright painful. There is a lot at stake and a lot to consider. Sometimes, a person may not bring you joy, but they haven't done anything *wrong*. You keep the relationship going out of habit or because you enjoy pleasing people (I know it well). For now, it may be best to leave the ball in their court to get in touch. And when they do, be honest and open about what you can and cannot—or do and do not want to—commit to. Sometimes people are fun to be with in a group but not solo. Sometimes a movie is a more enjoyable experience to have with them, rather than a drink or dinner. Or vice versa. One of the effects of a digital social world is that it has convinced us that every relationship ought to be "managed" or experienced *in the same way*. But human relationships are each unique. And they often go through seasons of intensity or "closeness." Their individual chemistry doesn't often conform to computer code.

In these cases, responding with "whatever you want" or "I'm game for anything" is not going to be a productive way for you to continue in the friendship. You have every right in the world to craft your friendships in a way that you truly enjoy. Otherwise, what exactly is the point? This can get messy, and you might not spontaneously say or do everything perfectly. That's okay. Come from a loving and respectful place, as best you can.

For the relationships that no longer provide a truly rewarding interaction, I have unsubscribed from gratuitous text, social media, and even email exchanges. I simply do not reply. I *respond*, but I don't reply. Instead, I pick up the phone. Sometimes a ten-minute phone call is all a relationship needs, and the quality of that conversation can indicate whether the relationship is deepening, becoming more authentic, more joyful. If it is, then maybe I do want to commit to seeing them more and putting an activity on the calendar. If it's not, maybe the next phone call is shorter. Or maybe they don't make the birthday party list next year. Or maybe I am just having a shitty day and need to call them when I have more time and I'm not hangry. In any case, what is most important is giving yourself the time and space to recenter yourself and your values, needs, and wants. Don't do something simply because you have always done it. That doesn't work anymore. Remember, all bets are off. Guard your calendar like you guard your home. No one gets in unless they are invited, take off their shoes, and are an enjoyable guest.

Every friendship is different. There is no one-size-fits-all model, no automatic path to long-term success. Not even in a book. In this super-connected world, everyone has their own expanding dartboard of circles, and therefore is experiencing a range of pressures and expectations to keep those dynamics intact in their own way. I have good friends that I used to see in person a few times a year, but as our families grew, our careers changed, people moved, the circus hit, and the world got wilder, we see each other only once a year. I had to get comfortable with that cadence and internalize a new truth that *physical time spent together was not a reflection of the strength of our bond* (just like I had to accept that making my calendar full didn't mean I was necessarily getting anything out of my social life). This required communication. I had to get comfortable asking friends, *Does this cadence work for us? Is it okay? Should our annual meetups be over the course of a weekend so we get really deep time together? Or should we prioritize the friendship in our calendars so we can see each other more often?* Friendships grow and change. They call on us to grow and change with them.

Or not. There are some friendships that you shouldn't feel pressured to continue, or salvage. I am all too familiar with this struggle. Before the circus, I "broke up" with an old friend—let's call him

Fred—whom I had fallen in love with when I was twenty-three. Unfortunately, that love was unrequited. We became "friends" after a very short-lived stab at dating, and we remained so for almost twenty years. I settled for friendship because I still wanted him in my life. But every time I saw him or hung out with him, I was annoyed. I was upset. I was uncomfortable. Because I had loved him once (and for many years continued to), I excused his inability to have a truly meaningful conversation with me. At some point, I realized that keeping him in my life, always seeing him when I was in town, always going out of my way to make plans for dinner and drinks, was keeping alive and well the core truth of our relationship: he had rejected me.

I could have taken the advice of other friends, even from a trusted counselor, who suggested that I just back away, stop calling, and retreat from our social interactions (also known as ghosting). But something in me told me that I had to end the friendship. I had to unsubscribe, for good. So, I took him to dinner, explained how I had been feeling for nearly twenty years, and told him that we could no longer be friends. It was one of the hardest conversations I have ever had in my life (and I have had a *lot* of hard conversations), but ultimately, it was like a spell had been broken. Suddenly, I was aware that for years I had believed—at times consciously, at times subconsciously—that being friends with people who rejected me romantically meant that *I was strong and could weather the pain of love.* That is some martyr bullshit. It wasn't strength. It was masochism. And it sucked. I stayed loyal to that belief for decades before I realized that my entire social life was full of men who had rejected me romantically. Good humans. Some great men. But not good friends, for me. Once I started to unsubscribe, I knew I had to unsubscribe from *all* of those friendships in one form or another. Keeping these "friendships" (subscriptions that were keeping me and us on autopilot) was truly standing in my way of finding real love in my life. And it was only when I then subscribed to the belief that *I only keep in my life people who respect, appreciate, and accept me for all I can offer* that my love life changed. And it changed instantly. And in a massive way. This was my experience. It may not be yours. I share it in case it resonates.

Work Team(s)

Next on the board, we have work. This is more of a sneak preview, rather than a full exploration, since work as a larger subject will come up in a later chapter. I wish I could just limit these circles to who comes and goes within our personal lives, but let's be honest: our work lives and our home lives are now forever intertwined, and it would be dishonest to ignore an entire group of people who are a consistent presence in your day-to-day. (Slack, in some ways, has become the "family" group text of the modern work-place.) This ring can be small or large, depending on where you work and how you make money. It also can depend on how your work is structured. In the physical world, we are usually divided into teams, departments, cohorts, or the like—you may be part of a larger corporation, but the people you consider to be within your work circle are the people and teams with whom you more commonly interact. Or you might work for a smaller company, where you engage with higher levels of management. Or you might just work for yourself. You might work a number of jobs and therefore have a number of smaller circle rings within this layer of your dartboard.

In any case, "work teams" are the people to whom you are subscribed via the same underlying policies, practices, and digital and physical systems of some sort of organization (e.g., the company org chart, payroll, the HR intranet, etc.), as well as its mission, vision, and values: spoken or unspoken. To start, think about who within those spaces *could* be pared down. Unlike the other circles, this will be a delicate dance between preserving your sanity and preserving your employment. If you choose to disengage more seriously, that should be your choice, not mine. For now, consider how you might be able to put up a boundary between certain people or attitudes within your work space, or how you can draw a firmer line between your work life and your nonwork life. If you can't or don't want to cut ties, use digital and physical tools, like autoreply, proactive communication, or the Busy function on Slack. Go to your calendar and see what could be removed workwise, whether it's that monthly happy hour or that check-in lunch with a former client that is scheduled out of pure habit. Once you do, you'll come to realize a hard but liberating truth: you are not obligated to do anything at work except what you have committed to do for your immediate boss. Stay tuned.

Now that you've moved through your large and medium circles, you have arrived at the inner sanctum. *Small circles* are ones that are meant—traditionally—to last a lifetime. (Or, if it's a roommate, at least the length of your lease, which can also feel like a lifetime.) These circles include anywhere from one to ten other people, generally, and are built around a sort of inverse equation: the smaller the circle, the more powerful the subscription. We call our role in these circles "partner," "husband or wife," or "mother," etc. They can be heart-wrenching to unsubscribe from, or even renegotiate, so tread lightly and do so with great kindness, communication, and consideration. The reality is that there are bonds within your small circle that you cannot remove, but we can minimize their negative impact, if there is one.

Immediate Family

The first in the sequence of narrowing circles is your immediate family, those who are closest to you either emotionally or in proximity. For some, it includes only you and your partner. (For others, it includes children, live-in parents, relatives, or in-laws.) This might be everyone who lives under your roof at home or for whom you are directly responsible.

Unsubscribing from this level of relationship can be difficult, and doing so is tied, in many ways, to having some degree of privilege—it assumes you have another place to go, a means to support yourself, and options about how to proceed once those bonds have been altered. But the first step, like it has been for all the others, is to simply take a break. No big decisions need to be made yet. If you can, try to remove yourself from the physical space for a time—any period of time. Or, if that's not feasible, remove yourself from the day-to-day habits and rhythms that run your household and your collective life. Get off autopilot. Is it making clear that one night a week is yours and yours alone? Is it picking up the phone to call parents or siblings only when you're in a good mood, and not just to vent? Is it allowing your partner to do the thing they love (but you hate) alone, so that you're not driving one another crazy? Is it having a conversation about what the expectations will be for aging parents, for what happens if there is an emergency and someone needs to come live in the house?

If removing yourself is an impossibility, or could cause harm or negligence to others, then be the source for broader change. Lead the group in unsubscribing *as an immediate family.* Focus on the *we.* Together, review your group purchases, take stock of commitments that drive you out of the home constantly, commit to phone-free zones or tech-free times. If you're not the kind of family that breaks bread every night around the table together, put a weekly family dinner on the books. If you are the family that eats nightly, try one night a week off. The point is: break up your habits so you can re-evaluate whether they are on autopilot, and whether you want them that way. *Why* do you do what you do as a group? Is it out of joy or obligation? Is it out of tradition or present-tense bonding? Not only will this help you; it will help them. Maybe it will empower them, even, to initiate the same process in their own lives and help them grow. Sometimes they just need permission to speak up about what they want and need.

Romantic Partner(s)

As mentioned previously, your romantic or domestic partner is a member of your immediate family circle, part of the clock that keeps your day-to-day life ticking. But they also occupy their own space—the next smallest circle on the board. You mean something to others as a unit, but you also mean something to each other as individuals, and it's important to keep that distinction in mind. The experience of clearing out the other noise in your life from the Big Forces and these larger circles can be valuable for many reasons, but perhaps the most valuable is the opportunity to see how the lives closest to you are being potentially obstructed by that noise. As we clear away that noise, we can get a better sense of how important certain relationships are and what state they're in—especially this one.

If the relationship is working well, my only recommendation is to ask for support as you go through this process. Explain what you are doing and why you are doing it, ask them to give you the time and space to lower the volume and reassess. Maybe even ask them to join you in unsubscribing from the relentlessness of modern life. That will likely mean changes—some major, some minor—to how you relate to the world around you. It may change what your home looks like, where you live, how you spend your time together, even how you communicate with one another throughout the day. Take your relationship off autopilot by committing to spending time together that is not brokered by any third party, especially a corporate one. Take the commercials out, the phones, the texting, the robots. Take this opportunity to discuss how you relate to click-up economics, individually and as a couple—where you put your eyeballs, clicks, dollars, time—and whether your habits and subscriptions are fortifying your relationship or distracting from it. Reconnect to what made you click Agree to this very meaningful subscription in the first place.

If, on the other hand, your relationship is *not working* the way you want it to, it may be the right time to think deeply about whether to resubscribe. (Wow, that sounds clinical and cold—I don't mean it to be—but sometimes we have to look at these things that way, in order to see them clearly.) Ask the hard questions. How has your relationship been faring? Have there been changes in your relationship, or have you changed? As you look ahead to what is next, do you want to keep going? Think about each stage in the relationship, and how each set of subscription criteria has applied: (a) How, when, and why did you sign on? (b) How do you feel about the ways that you renew the relationship, together and individually? What is on autopilot? Does the autopilot help or hurt? (c) What are the terms you seem to have agreed to, with or without your awareness and consent? Can the relationship be made better or more joyful if terms are renegotiated?

Tough stuff. I've been there. Only you have the answer, but know this: you are not alone in searching for it. Millions of us have either been in (or know stories of) couples who decided to part ways because the stresses of these years have illuminated truths or needs that had never come to the surface. There has been tectonic change beneath our feet. We are no longer living in Normal Times. It is impossible not to be affected by the world around us. Nor by the circus itself. For some of us, we were heartened by what we saw, what we learned about, and what we experienced with our partners. Others were confronted with clear confirmation that it is time to unsubscribe, either temporarily or for good. That may not be a "bad" thing for our culture. It all depends on what you think of divorce. Is it a horrible, drama-filled admission that you have failed, or is it a reorganization of your most intimate relationship based on changing needs and joys? However you think of it, you have some underlying subscription—an idea, notion, or belief—about it. Best to look at that first. (We're about to talk about underlying subscriptions in chapter 12.)

Whether your most intimate relationship is working well or not, creating the time and space to go through this process will be rewarding in the end. It may not be comfortable—at all—but it will be rewarding.

You

The center of the dartboard is, of course, you. And the you that is there is the you that is shaped by the pressures of the rings surrounding you. At this stage (in this chapter and in this larger process), you are aware of who fills these rings, how they impact you, and how they might be reshaped. There is a lot at stake here: if everything is well distributed, with healthy boundaries and empowering subscriptions, your circles stay intact and offer joy and satisfaction; but if one ring starts to take up more space or exert more energy than another, the whole thing warps. What matters most now is keeping everything (everyone) in balance.

It's time to feel some of this in your hand. Take a piece of paper and write down the names of thirty people in your life. (Or one hundred or ten—whatever works.) Don't bother with online platforms.

Don't run to Facebook and LinkedIn and such. Just sit alone and simply jot down names. Next, identify which circle each of these people is in. Are they a friend? A community member of some kind? An acquaintance in the Supercommunity? What role do they play in your life and what role do you play in their life? What role do you *want* them to play in your life and what role do you want to play in theirs? Be honest, radically honest. This is private. You can tear up, shred, or burn this paper when we're done.

Now sit with the list and simply observe how you feel when you see certain names. What images come to mind? Are you tense or calm? Do you immediately recall a fond memory, or do you know, deep in your gut, that you only maintain this relationship out of habit? Circle the names of the people who light you up, the ones that you look forward to seeing, the ones who empower you to be your best, the ones you connect with—or *can* connect with—deeply. Put a dot next to the ones that you are unsure of, the ones that are neutral. (That dot represents a pin. They're in the parking lot.) And put a small *X* next to the ones who make you feel less than whole, taken for granted, upset, or annoyed. Think about how much time you spend with each of these people. Do you actively seek out the ones you circled? Do you maximize your time with them? Do you spend too much time with the others? Why? What is it that keeps you in an automated state, constantly going back to those who annoy or take you for granted?

Think about what it would mean for your life if you could "rack focus." Racking focus is a filmmaker term that describes changing focus from the background to the foreground (and vice versa). When I did this exercise, I realized immediately that there were all these *amazing people* in my life that I kept in the background, on whom I did not focus. Why? Habit. The infinite loop. I was spending all my time focused on those who were in the foreground, many of whom had either put themselves there or had been *placed* there by automated social platforms. I decided to rack focus and shift my attention to those I had neglected (and with whom I truly enjoyed spending time). It has wildly changed my social life. I have reconnected with some of my best friends in the world, many of whom simply drifted to the background.

This is a simple "people audit." I know it seems very clinical, but modernity requires these kinds of strategies. Funny enough, we think nothing of the fact that Facebook has ads between our friend posts, but an exercise like *this* seems so impersonal. That is how much the practices of the Big Forces have twisted our senses. A people audit can help you get clear about who you want in your life. It is, after all, a choice. And you can choose to put people in and you can choose to take people out. How? We may need some new language to help.

Nine
How to Talk About It All

As the famous saying goes, "The pen is mightier than the sword." In the battle for our behavior, words are most powerful. I often find that when I want to change my behavior, I have to change my language. (I was also an English major in college, and I geek out on new words.) I have come to realize that language can really shape our reality. If we are always "struggling" and life is always "impossible," it will continue to present as such. But if we are always "ready for a challenge," we begin to relish the problem-solving that comes along with seemingly impossible situations we find ourselves in. Our outlook and our language come from the very same brain. They are completely connected, and they can influence each other.

Language is also how a society inculcates its beliefs. The sheer magnitude of the Big Forces has warped our beliefs because the Big Forces are the ones doing most of the talking in our society right now. Since language created this system, new language is required to change it, resist it, confront it, interrogate it.

Language is also a little club. When you spend your life crossing into different communities, you become a bit of a social anthropologist noticing differences in language and social custom. When I first got to college, I realized that wealthy people spoke differently than the working class. And as I began to explore career paths, I saw how, in some ways, a big part of any graduate training is learning to "talk the talk." The lawyers learn one language. The engineers learn another. The doctors another. All require highly specific language to solve highly specific problems.

At this point, we all understand the language of click-up economics. We get the visual and clickable grammar of it all. The Big Forces have trained us. We know how to manage our marketing preferences and accept or block certain cookies from websites, and we are increasingly aware of the games marketers play to get us to stay tethered. More or less, we know how to detach ourselves from the *surface subscriptions* and the bullshit they bring into our lives. We find the Unsubscribe button or the Cancel button—wherever they may be hidden—and we click. And when we are asked why we are unsubscribing, the language is provided to us: *I get too many emails, the emails are not relevant to me, I never signed up for this list,* etc. While the process is draped in sappy language like "Oh, so sad that you're leaving! We'll miss you! It's so hard to say good-bye (to your money)" to trigger our emotions, there is not much actual regret.

But with people—people we know and love, humans who deserve kindness—we are often far less equipped. We often can't find the words. We don't know how to explain it, especially in a situation like this, where parting is more for our own holistic benefit rather than because of a clear wrongdoing on their part. We don't want a confrontation. We avoid. We dodge. We ghost. It can be agonizing, especially when there sometimes is simply not a right or easy way to do it. No other cohort of humans—ever—has had to manage this many relationships at once.

Sometimes, you just need a few words to get you started.

Here is some sample language that I have found to be effective when having these types of uncomfortable conversations. Amend to your liking. You can use these in an email or a text, but if the person is a genuinely good egg, challenge yourself to say these in person, face to face, heart to heart. It is very difficult to show emotion or communicate compassion with digital tools. Emojis just do not cut it. Let's all stop pretending that they do. You'll save yourself the dreadful waiting for a response, and you'll train yourself in one of the most important tools for a life well led: how to have hard conversations. Hard conversations are hard because we fear change. We know that if we communicate authentically, we will pop out of the infinite loop. And that can be scary. It's well worth it so that our relationships sit on a bed of honesty and authenticity. The truth is that none of us has the patience left for the bullshit. It's exhausting. Our happiness is at stake. So, it's time to get comfortable with getting uncomfortable. We'll go circle by circle.

The Supercommunity

When you need space
Use these to put a people subscription in the parking lot so you can reevaluate. This can be a preemptive message to the masses, either in a post or through an email, or a blanket response to those trying to get in touch.

- "Hey, all! I am taking a digital detox. I hope life is good on your end. I'll be back online after the holidays."

- "Information overload. (Love you all, but) I have to take a step back."

- "Hope everyone's doing well. I'll be offline for a bit."

- "What's up, all? It's time for me to unsubscribe. Here's my email. Let's stay in touch that way."

- "I just read this (amazing) book about unsubscribing. I'm going to take a beat."

When it is time to end it

Use these to unsubscribe for good.

- "This group has been really helpful to me. I hope I have been the same. Thank you. It's time for me to take myself out of it. I send my best."

- "The terms of membership here just don't work for me anymore. Be well, all."

- "I've decided to not move forward. I'm oversubscribed all around."

- "Gotta take myself out of this group. Life just morphed. I have to morph with it."

- "It's time for me to unsubscribe. (Sending love.)"

Best to avoid

These kinds of messages breed our illness. They infect large circles with toxicity. You may want to say these things, but chances are the world is a better place if you don't.

- "This group is a bunch of assholes. I'm out."

- "Not interested in more of this crap. Bye."

- "You guys are part of the never-ending bullshit."

- "I don't want to be part of this insanity anymore."

- "Count me out, bitches!"

Community Institutions, Associations, and Organizations, Extended Family, Work

When you need space

- "I only schedule Zooms two days a week now. I'm limiting my digital time. Can we do Thursday instead?"

- "Please count me out for now. Talk soon."

- "I have to bow out and restore so I can live to fight another day."

- "How can we streamline this so I can give you as much of me as I can afford to (or as my schedule allows)?"

- "We have to put some boundaries in place here."

- "This schedule doesn't leave much room for family time. We can commit to the kids being there once a week. More than that gets tough for us."

When it is time to end it

- "I did some deep thinking, and I have to end my membership. I'm oversubscribed all around."

- "This hurts, but I have to step away (for good)."

- "I am really grateful we got to work together or spend so much time together. My life just looks different now."

- "We've decided not to participate. The schedule doesn't give us enough family time."

- "This has been weighing on me. But I know it's not personal. I just have to make some changes."

Best to avoid

These kinds of messages double down on your weakness. You are not weak.

- "I can't continue. I don't have it in me."

- "I have nothing left to give here."

- "Are you guys kidding me? You push and you push and you push. When is enough enough for you?"

- "I don't have the bandwidth for you."

- "My plate is too full. I can't handle it."

Friends

When you need space

- "We're not making plans until next month. Can I get back to you?"

- "Dinner every Sunday is tough for me to commit to. I'm finding that as I get older, I need more downtime before I start my week."

- "(I think) I want our friendship to look a little different than it used to."

- "I have to step back. It's not forever. I just want to give some thought to how we go forward. We both deserve that."

- "I want to say yes but I have to say no. I'm running on empty right now. I want to recharge."

When it's time to end it

- "I will always have great affection for you (or love you). We don't work the same way anymore."

- "I just don't accept the terms you need for this to work."

- "I really don't have any ill will. Our lives just look different now."

- "This feels terrible, but I have to walk away (or set this down or leave this be)."

- "I think the answer is we have to let it go."

- "I never imagined you wouldn't be in my life, but I have to mourn this and accept it."

Best to avoid

- "I never really liked you anyway."

- "You are an awful person."

- "I've been faking it this whole time."

- "Please unsubscribe, thanks!"

Immediate Family, Romantic Partner

When you need space

- "For the summer, 6:00 p.m. to 7:00 p.m. in our house is Unsubscribe hour."
- "The family room is now a tech-free zone."
- "I'm not sure where we go from here. I want time to think about it."
- "I want you to fuck off right now. Love you. But please . . ." (if being that frank is how you operate together).
- "I want to find a day a week that we can each take to ourselves."
- "I've decided to step back for a bit."
- "I don't get to be who I want to be when we are together. That has got to change."

When it's time to end it

- "This simply doesn't work."
- "We, together, are not a functioning team. Do I love you? Yes. Did I want this to work? Always. Will it work in the future? Not for me."
- "The core truth of our relationship is that _____. That doesn't work for me."
- "This is painful, but I will not accept this idea that love is suffering or that staying in an unhealthy relationship forever is brave or some sign of strength. I won't teach our kids that."
- "I have taken every step I know how to take. They keep leading to the same place."

Best to avoid

- "You screwed this up. I didn't!"
- "I want out. I never loved you."

- "I'm moving out, and there is nothing you can do."

- "You are the devil incarnate."

- "I thought you would change."

That was a lot. If you need to sit with these for a bit, go for it. I'll still be here. But if you're ready to continue, let's still take a moment and think about what that felt like, what impact those scripts had. If you had some unexpected (good or bad) reactions, reflect on why. Write your thoughts down. Or maybe just go for a walk and think. Processing is part of the unsubscription process.

Great. Now, if you're ready, we'll keep going.

Sometimes, as we all know and have experienced, it's not about the words. It is instead how we deliver them that communicates healthy boundaries or compassion, empathy, and love. Important, too, is what we do next. We said what we said. Now what? Do we back it up with equally kind gestures? Or do we undercut our message with counterproductive behaviors? An awareness of *why* we are behaving the way we are is key. Are our behaviors based on present-tense beliefs about the world? Or are they based on old and tired conceptions of what certain relationships are supposed to look like, sound like, and feel like?

Before we go one step deeper and look at the *underlying subscriptions*—ideas, notions, and beliefs—that often put our behaviors on autopilot, I promised to discuss work. What you have done so far has, for the most part, been about you as an individual. In your personal space, you are in charge. But in an office or workspace, sometimes our agency is limited, and things are less on our terms. For many, work is a world unto itself, where power dynamics, money, and group hierarchies can be completely different. Let's see how we can navigate it through the lens of unsubscription.

Ten
Ugh. Work.

I have given work its own real estate here because it comes with a unique set of parameters and problems. We spend one-third of our lives at work, and the United States is considered by many to be the most overworked developed nation in the world. In many ways, work is the ultimate subscription.

Think about it: we sign up, we agree, we log in, we show up; then we renew over and over again on a "recurring basis," day by day, year by year, paycheck by paycheck, mind-numbing Zoom by painful Zoom. Along the way we accept (and accept and accept) the terms and conditions of the job, whether they change or stay the same—what the work is, what services or labor we provide, how and how much we will be compensated, etc.—all in exchange for a salary (material benefits) and the feeling that we are stable, secure, and productive. (If we are lucky, those terms and conditions might be laid out in an actual contract that we get, in theory, to negotiate, but many of us never get that clarity.)

Like shopping online or constantly scrolling social media, our reward isn't just tangible, it's emotional. At work, we get to experience validation, praise, pride, triumph, confidence-building, and teamwork, and overcome fear, anxiety, insecurity, and disgust. We find ourselves within a community and contribute to its mission and growth. We get to be leaders and followers, hunters and gatherers, farmers and farmhands. Some of us even get to be kings and queens, lording over our peers from our perch in the C suite.

Even with these benefits, though, working in a capitalist economy is tough. Unsubscribing from a job means forgoing a salary, and that means potentially wreaking financial havoc on our checkbook, our future, and the lives and futures of those who are dependent on us. (In case you need the reminder, the world is expensive. I paid $41 for a salad the other day. WTF.) Havoc also means, for many of us (80 percent of the population), losing medical insurance. And unlike in other countries, health care is not a protected right in the United States. Those of us who grew up in working-class and middle-class homes know this conversation well:

YOUNG PERSON: "I got a job! It's what I love to do. And it's kinda well paid."

OUR PARENTS: "Um, are they giving you benefits? Medical? Dental? Vision?"

In most European countries, a universal health care system provides at the very least a widely accessible public option. It varies, of course, country by country, but workers—from mine laborers to retail managers to consulting executives—have the freedom to unsubscribe from a job without fear of racking up a $200,000 hospital bill. That's not to say that all our American leaders are blind to this particular challenge. During the 2020 presidential election, future vice president Kamala Harris proposed separating health care from employment, a move that would have allowed hundreds of millions of us to make choices about where we work without deep fear of what might happen if we fell and broke our hip, but the proposal was lost in the media swirl of a loud and messy election season.

Work is also a challenging subscription to grapple with because it is universally mismanaged. While some of us may have varying degrees of trouble with brands, banks, schools, tech, friends, family, partners, or politics, most everyday Americans, whether they work in entertainment or in Silicon Valley, as a teacher, firefighter, or Walmart cashier, will likely tell you that the way we work in this country is broken. Pre-2020, too many people worked too many hours and commuted too far, all for way too little compensation. The ability to put work on our phone or laptop turned 9-to-5s into 8-to-7s or 6-to-10s—and that was just our day job. If we needed more money, the side hustle emerged as a standard rite of passage (TikTok calls it "the 5-9 before the 9-5"). People stopped taking lunch breaks, opting instead for a "sad desk salad." Or if you worked for a startup, the company just encouraged you to be in the office for all three meals by providing them, as well as other life "needs" like a gym, game room, and dry-cleaning service. All in the building. Think about it: Google has *campuses* in California and New York. People literally do not have to leave to perform the basic functions of their personal lives. The result: a dystopia where CEOs make 320 times the average worker, an exhausted workforce is cool and comfortable but abused, unprotected, and scared shitless to take a day off or even step away from their phones to address vital health care needs or to cast a vote, and workers all along the socioeconomic spectrum—from Twitter to Visa to Whole Foods—just hate what they do all day.

During the circus, we were given, for the first time, an opportunity to stop. Friday, March 13, 2020—the day after New York City declared that offices and businesses were closed—might have been the only time in corporate history that workers (except for essential workers, of course, and we are eternally grateful to them) were told to work from their own spaces or take the day off entirely. And, it turns out, we liked it. We discovered that, actually, we like being "on the go" less. We may not have enjoyed being trapped at home with some of our family members, but we liked a life that was less hectic. It showed us that we could achieve the basic functions and goals of our work on our terms, without the added noise of office gossip, overpriced sandwiches, money spent on constant travel and business casual attire, or meetings about meetings about meetings.

Suddenly, work became something very *different*. For so many of us, it became an element of our lives, a very *important* element, but not necessarily the core piece of the much larger puzzle. It was a walk down the stairs and into the den or dining room or small corner we were able to carve out among the kids' toys in the basement. We turned the laptop on and started our day—no train, no "express" bus, no carpool lane, no subway. (For many, no pants.) We were no longer trapped in a cubicle or tied to a desk. We could take a five-minute walk to get or make ourselves a coffee. We could have lunch with our families and use the time we would have spent crammed onto a commuter train. Some of us came to realize that, actually, this job that was keeping us in a city or state we didn't like—or that forced us to work under conditions that no longer served us—did not *have* to be the answer.

Jobs that had been overlooked or taken entirely for granted at best (and exploited at worst)—poll workers, delivery workers, sanitation workers, teachers, nurses, doctors, lab techs, public health officials were suddenly being celebrated as the unsung heroes of our age, applauded every night at 7:00 p.m. on the dot by entire cities—and their work seemed so much more critical than our own. We gained a perspective about what was important, what was controllable, what was human.

And then the circus kept going. And going. And the new utopia started to show cracks, because we were still working within the old system. It was clear that everyone was accessible at home, with nothing else to do, so emails and pings and meeting requests came through at any hour of the day. Office phone lines were abandoned and business moved to your personal cell phone, spreading your number to far too many you would prefer did not have it. Women, in record numbers, were forced to leave their careers to supervise the sudden at-home education of their children or help to care for aging or ill family members, the most susceptible to the initial outbreaks of COVID-19. The economy tanked. People were laid off and companies consolidated, leaving employees to manage double or triple the workload with no pay raise.

And when the world opened back up, we were expected to all just go back like nothing had happened. Business as usual. Sorry, *what*?

Knowing this now, having seen it play out, what does *it look like* to unsubscribe in the workplace? We have talent. You have talent. I have talent. We have skills, aptitudes, ways to solve problems and contribute. Many of us are just employing those in ways that boost productivity, wealth, and power for others, but not joy, wealth, or power for ourselves.

It is time that we unsubscribe from jobs and careers that keep us unhappy, abuse our talents and hard work, or rob us of the freedom to design our calendar—and our lives—to best suit us. It is time we unsubscribe from the tyranny of asshole bosses. And it is time that we stop giving our superpowers to companies that do not align with our values. We are all too comfortable with—fully subscribed to— the idea that *it's just a job*. Well, it is not. It is where we spend thirty to eighty hours a week, where our lives are led, where we fit into the machine of click-up economics. It is where we learn behaviors and adopt attitudes that carry over into our personal lives. Let me say that again: *it is where we learn behaviors and adopt attitudes that carry over into our personal lives.*

So, for a moment, picture unsubscribing not as quitting, as telling your boss to shove it, and simply not doing your work. Think of it instead as unsubscribing to your current relationship with the work that you do in order to evolve and improve it. (Though, of course, if you really feel you need to quit and have the means to, knock yourself out.) Take the power back. You are not an employee of their company. You are an employee of your own. You are selling their company your talents today. And maybe not tomorrow.

In our day-to-day work life, we inherit three major subscriptions from the companies we work with or for (big, small, corporate, or independent): their *mission*, *vision*, and *values*. These are part of a company's DNA, and writers like me are paid a lot of money to get them on paper.

For those less familiar, let me explain what they are and why they are so important.

A company's *mission* is generally defined as the reason it exists in the world. It is customer-focused. It defines what the company provides (products and/or services) and to whom it provides them. It states the company's goal. It often starts with an infinitive verb. For example, Tesla's mission is *to accelerate the world's transition to sustainable energy.* Patagonia's is *to build the best product, cause no unnecessary harm, use business to inspire and implement solutions to the environmental crisis.* Coca-Cola seeks *to refresh the world and make a difference.* Slack wants *to make work life simpler, more pleasant and more productive.* Now, you and I know that some of these are authentic, and some are complete bullshit (the ones that are complete bullshit are, to no surprise, the ones that are most responsible for flooding our modern world with even more bullshit).

A company's *vision* is basically who they want to be when they grow up, where they see themselves in five and ten years, what their long-term vision for the business is, and what they intend their impact on the world will be. For the Alzheimer's Association this means *a world without Alzheimer's Disease.* For Disney, it's *to be one of the world's leading producers and providers of entertainment and information.* Southwest Airlines: *to be the world's most loved, most efficient, and most profitable airline.* (Ha! Um, Southwest, how about just getting us all where we were supposed to be for Christmas? Baby steps.)

Lastly, a company's *values* are the ground rules set for behavior as individuals within the company and as a collective. Kellogg's demands *integrity, accountability, passion, humility, simplicity, results.* Salesforce wants to see *trust, customer success, innovation, and equality.* Google, appropriately, wants more: it has a list of ten value statements.

These statements are important. Consultants put companies through the often super-annoying paces of crafting them because, like a constitution, they give a group of people a starting point from which to invest in the company, and the company a starting point to develop policies, guidelines, and practices that keep the engines going. Whether they are honored or not as business picks up, either way, our hard work amplifies these three statements in society at large. Our talents grow their businesses. Our power creates more power *for them.* Make no mistake: where we work matters. And we have more agency than we think. Because we can also determine our own mission, vision, and values.

Paper time. Sit down with a piece of paper, and a pen or pencil, and think about what your mission, vision, and values statements would be if you, yourself, were a company. Don't stress. Just write whatever comes to mind. Let whatever wants to float to the surface go there. This, too, can be revealing: what you've written down might be something like, *to make a positive difference in the lives of schoolchildren* or *to make the world a more beautiful place* or *to help people find their dream home.* If this isn't what you already do, maybe it's what you should be doing. If it's what you are doing, maybe there's more that can be done. (A quick aside: A lot of modern pop self-help tells us that what we see as our mission should also be our "purpose." I disagree. Our work mission is our work mission, and that is valid in and of itself. It does not have anything to do with our purpose or value as a human. No one is put on this earth to sell condos. They may get a lot of joy from that work mission. They should. Rock on. But it's not their *purpose.* We are all here to love. And to be part of each other's story. More on that later.)

Next, tackle your vision. Where do you want to be in five years, ten, twenty? Your vision might be *to make a lot of money* or *to be the number one salesman in the territory* or *to become the best camp leader in the country*. Next, your values. How will you behave to bring that vision to life? What will you honor in yourself and in your circles? Your values might be *empathy, teamwork, fair pay, gender equity, responsibility to the very planet we all live on and that we're hoping to give to our kids*.

Once you have these in place, and you have really considered them deeply, see if they match up with those of your employer. In fact, take a minute now and search around your employer's website or your employee handbook to see what their mission, vision, and values are. Do you feel those values really have been represented, that that mission has been a guiding force in your experience working there? If you're looking for jobs, do the same. Turn on your bullshit meter. Ask around. Are these big words real? Do they influence the running of the business, or are they just part of the never-ending bullshit? It is fully fair game to leave a job because the day-to-day experience of working there conflicts with the mission, vision, and values they purport to honor.

Notice where the differences are and think about how willing you are to manage that delta. Trust your gut. Trust that you can see things now for what they really are. And that is a truth that companies will try to suppress: Workers see the bullshit. And they are tired of it. We understand that our values are not being lived out by the companies we turn our time and power over to. We watch as they exploit us, our colleagues, each other, and our peers. Perhaps there was a time in America when a less media-savvy public could be manipulated easily into believing the spin. Not now. We have seen behind the curtain. We cannot unsee. It's not an almighty wizard. It's a person at a desk, with the same human frustration we have. And likely the same dreams and desires: to lead a happy, satisfying life.

Each of us has a role to play in whatever job we do, and we must do it well and deliver, as it were. Yes, that is part of the agreement we make with our employers. No one is refuting that. That is a *given*. But we must also place our own individual, professional mission, vision, and values up alongside and within the context of our larger organizations. We must stand firm and put up both *digital* and *physical* boundaries in order to honor them—and to protect ourselves, our families, and our physical and mental health. That requires renegotiation of some of the terms and conditions of our work subscription, and a reclaiming of our personal power. When we finally experience our personal power at work, the work changes all around.

Fresh with personal power, you have the chance to amalgamate that power with your colleagues. For those who may not know the full scope of labor history: Unions are a major reason that workers flourished in the twentieth century. They were a primary means of merging individual personal power into collective power, and of renegotiating (literally) the subscriptions that control our behavior at work. In the latter part of the twentieth century, the Big Forces found this kind of collective bargaining to be, well, inconvenient, and so they banded with the government to "break" unions in any way that they could. I know this, because it affected me directly. Instead of raising taxes on the wealthy—or exploring any number of options to avoid this fate—the budget of New York City is typically balanced on the backs of workers. As a kid, I spent days making posters for my father's bus-driver union. One of my first memories is of using a huge black marker to write the word STRIKE on poster board.

Unions represent everyone and anyone who is not the owner(s) of the company. Anyone who files a W-2 at tax time. The average person. In other words, *the majority*. Click-up economics has been ferociously successful because unions have been suppressed. They were suppressed consistently over the latter part of the twentieth century. Countless dollars and meetings and backdoor handshakes have been directed to keeping the conversation about them out of the workplace. Once the word is whispered—"union"—corporations start to lose control.

Let's look at the case of the formation of a union at the *New Yorker*, one of the nation's most successful magazines. Overwhelmed by the relentlessness of their work and underwhelmed by their pay, a group of staff members across departments—editorial, copy editing, design, art, and others—created a union to fight for a fair contract. After banding together, organizing support, and raising their voices, they were able to negotiate a contract with Condé Nast—one of the oldest companies in the nation—that allows for salary minimums, defined working hours, and specific regulations for disciplining and firing workers.

This is unsubscribing in action. Instead of quitting en masse, which might have made a statement in the moment but ultimately would have amounted to, at most, an annoyance for the hiring managers (after all, companies like this argue that the prestige of the institution will always have people in the wings waiting for a job), the union members rewrote the subscriptions (the actual contracts) that underlie how the corporation functions. They didn't quit. They didn't burn their lives down. They changed their employer's behavior by changing their own. They didn't accept what was *realistic*. They changed their reality by pushing into the *unrealistic*.

What happened at the *New Yorker* got even more intense at HarperCollins when that publishing company's union went out on strike in late 2022. It's been happening all over the country. Nurses are striking. Teachers. Rail workers. Baristas. Hollywood writers (in what basically amounted to the first major strike against AI). Yes, it's encouraging to see that Americans are no longer willing to put up with the utter bullshit, but bear this in mind: we have a long way to go to get back to a fairer balance of power between corporations and their employees. Union membership peaked in the US in 1954, when nearly 35 percent of Americans were represented by a union.

In 1979, 21 million people were union members. Now? Just over 11 percent of Americans belong to a labor union.

Short of a union that can literally rewrite the subscriptions that keep a corporation running, what does unsubscribing within our work space (and workforce) look like for the rest of us?

When we speak up at work, when we find a voice that is respectful but clear, we can effect change. But that requires us to confront, wrestle with, make peace with, and then maybe unsubscribe at an even deeper level from our entrenched ideas, notions, and beliefs about work.

Let's take a closer look. The first, most common refrain: *I need this job*. When you believe you need a job—or a client or a project—that your career will fall apart without it, that your kids will starve if you leave, you are operating from fear and turning over your power. (You are not wrong that it will impact your life, but that impact sits on a spectrum, and we tend to focus on the most extreme potential outcome.) Employers know this, which is why they let you keep a picture of your kids on your desk: that way, you're constantly reminded of their theoretical hunger. It's why they (reluctantly) give you a vacation: to remind you that you need something to pay for it.

Consider instead subscribing to the belief that *I could walk out of here tomorrow and it would be okay*. What does your day-to-day behavior look like if you subscribe to *that* notion? How do you carry yourself and interact with your boss and team? What do client calls sound like if you take the "I need" out? How long a lunch do you take? Do you actually *take* a lunch? How long of a vacation do you take? How often do you go to the dentist? I am not advocating for you to not give a fuck. (Sarah Knight does that brilliantly. See her book.) I am challenging you to look at every minute of your behavior throughout the workday and ask this question: *What idea, notion, or belief is controlling how I behave?* Am I being controlled by my fear of being unemployed or by my love of this job? If you are not motivated by your love of the work, it is time to make a change—a big one.

For some of us that is a risky and privileged idea. I understand. For some, especially those who work in institutions that rely on strict process and protocol, like hospitals, or those who are brand new to the workforce, or those who work minimum-wage jobs that keep their kids fed, it can be dangerous or threatening to think or act outside the norm or to challenge entrenched power. If this is the case, it's important to seek out those who have more power than you do.

Let's say you're a nurse, and you worked nonstop during the circus. Now, work has calmed a bit, but the hospital simply didn't learn the lessons from the crisis. It's the same old thing. You're overworked. You're underpaid. You can't even control your own schedule. Where can you find support outside of the hospital? Are there nursing associations, groups, or organizations that you can turn to even just to *vent*? Do they provide a space for you to learn new tactics that might shift the power dynamic at work? You are not the first nurse, and I am not the first writer who has wanted to fucking scream. (Go scream. Then come back.)

What is critical about finding support outside your usual circles is that any organization—even those that are casual—has a mix of power. Someone is a leader. And you can learn and grow from them. You may not shift the power dynamic at work overnight, but exposing yourself to people who are powerful themselves teaches us how to access the power inside of us. You'll notice a few traits that stand out: powerful people are calm not dramatic; they choose their words carefully and after thoughtful consideration; they strategize and take one step at a time. These are important lessons.

Next: *I am successful and hardworking only if I am constantly busy.* Like Ben Franklin said, "Motion does not equal action." In this future—the one you and I are living in post-circus—we must learn to move less. These times call on us to find greater value in being still. We must admit that constant motion—to endless meetings, constant events, even serving on countless committees—lets us avoid some of the painful truths of our lives, and we must learn to be still and face those truths.

The answer, I have learned the hard way, is never *there*. It is often *here*. The circus showed us we have a *here* to attend to that has been neglected. At least mine was. And often that *here* is somewhere at home with the people we love. How many meetings do you attend that you don't contribute to, but feel you just need to be seen at? How many lunches do you go to that you hate, just so you can hand over a corporate card at the end of it or be seen leaving while everyone else is stuck at their desk? How many hours are you spending, unable to clock overtime, just to make sure your boss sees that you sent an email after they went home? Stop. Go home. Water *that* garden. This one has been sufficiently watered today.

For me, unsubscribing in this realm has been a major challenge but has brought relief and much calm and focus back. Much of my work as a filmmaker is about being connected, being seen, and being seen as connected. So much image-making. Too much image-making. In entertainment, the relationships and calendar you maintain, even your casual weekend social media pics, speak volumes about how in-demand you are as an artist and as a person. I reached a breaking point. Enough. It's taken a lot to disentangle myself from these behaviors and from the internalized thoughts that beget them—they are the product of an immigrant upbringing, a competitive educational environment, and a business where the personal and professional are essentially one. In order to confront my anxieties, I had to name them, which meant writing them down. When I did, I saw ten major underlying subscriptions—ideas, notions, and beliefs—that I had to unsubscribe from in order to redefine and renew my work life. Here they are. Perhaps some of these will resonate with you.

1. *Success in my field requires me to physically be in [insert city here]. A lot.*

2. *I have to maintain every business contact I have or I am irrelevant.*
3. *If I don't make millions—billions—I am a failure.*
4. *If I close my company, everyone will think I am uncommitted and unreliable.*
5. *Busy equals productive. Productive equals successful. Successful equals happy.*
6. *Work is a measure of my value as a person. I have no worth without it.*
7. *I can't be without a job for a month. It is not financially possible.*
8. *My work determines my place in the social and class hierarchy.*
9. *A pandemic is not reason enough to make any major changes.*
10. *My work is my life. I take great pride in it.*

The list, honestly, could go well beyond ten. But I'll spare you. What's most important to note is that looking at a list like this can be really daunting. When it reflects your life back to you, ouch, it can hurt. To be totally open here, when I first wrote these down, I was depressed. Wow, I have taken on a lot and somehow made it all *part of me.* I didn't think I really thought like this. But I did. I looked at these thoughts, suddenly out of my head and on paper, and I realized that I had signed up for all these subscriptions. These are emotional contracts between me and me (some are even spoken or unspoken between me and many of my circles). Whether I clicked Agree or not, I had consumed these beliefs and lived them out year after year after year. I watched other people live them out, and I mirrored their behaviors. I heard them spoken by colleagues, and I parroted them. I saw the damage some of them had done to people around me, but I thought I could rise above it. The hard pill to swallow is this: we are all connected. You cannot escape consuming these ideas and taking them on as your own until you unsubscribe from all the bullshit that keeps these ideas alive and well in your brain and heart.

Eleven

How to Unsubscribe from Work or at Work

Now that we've clarified what unsubscribing in a work context means, it's time to do it. Where to start?

The same place we do in our personal lives: on the surface, with all the pinging and ringing. There is no reason that our laptops, our desks, and our offices—be they in the dining room or in a skyscraper—need to look and sound like Grand Central at rush hour. It is neither necessary nor cool to always be connected. Those days are over. Unless someone's life is on the line, that phone call does not need to be returned in the next twelve seconds. That text message is not a reason to stop everything you are doing.

We do not need more ways to access each other. Instead, we need strong boundaries in place to structure that access. Your cell phone is the perfect example. It is not a work device (*especially* if your job is not paying for it). Treating it as such is why we work so much: our entire office is in our pocket, and everyone knows it. Enough. Communicate with management and company policymakers about texting, email, and group work policies, about what expectations are before 9:00 a.m. and after 6:00 p.m. and on weekends, holidays, and vacations, and how together we can all put in place limits and healthy guardrails. If you feel more comfortable having backup, go to your employee handbook and see if there are policies that you can cite and explain that they are not being followed. If there is no official policy in place, raise your voice and tell management you want one.

How? Make it a graceful approach. Kindly request a meeting with your work management to discuss communications expectations. For some of us, this will be excruciatingly uncomfortable. The power structures inherent in office life—especially between newer team members and leadership, or between working generations—make this seem like a total impossibility. But this is a lesson in personal power. It's also a good moment to learn how to manage up. Completely politely, ask your immediate manager (or boss or supervisor or owner—whomever you report to), "How do you like to communicate? What's the best way for me to communicate with you?" That will open up the conversation. Then, make it an ongoing priority. Check in from time to time. When you are comfortable, tell your immediate manager that you are "doing my best to limit the noise that constant email creates so I can be more productive. How can we institute or create a communications policy?"

If that is laugh-out-loud funny to you because it sounds like total bullshit, here is some alternate phrasing. "Damn, the email in this place is killing me. Isn't it killing you? Any advice?" See below for variations on the theme.

If you *are* management, it would serve you and your office well to be the one who starts that conversation. It would be my guess that the people under you on the ladder are exhausted by how accessible they have been made to be and feel in the modern workplace—and they are not saying so. They understand you're dealing with new ways of working (remote, from home, hybrid, etc.), but group-text services could be making it all worse, not better, if there isn't clear direction from you about how to use these tools to make the business work well while respecting their boundaries.

While we're at it, it is time to unsubscribe from meetings that accomplish nothing, from committees that do not align with our personal values, and from extracurricular work activities that are *designed* to make us work more. These types of changes may be daunting, but they call on us to be leaders. Most of the time, you'll realize that you aren't alone in your thinking.

Me, a leader? Yes. You. Leaders do three things when they want to effect change: (1) they ask their colleagues in similar positions at different places of work how it's done in their world, (2) they think through whom will be affected by that change and how they can minimize any negative effects, and (3) they explore new language and approaches to ensure that when they do raise their voice, it is clear, calm, respectful, and effective. For example: the Monday check-in that was instituted three years ago but now everyone talks about hating and not getting anything out of. If you're in a position to do so, take stock of who seems inconvenienced by it, gauge whether your suggestion would be favorable to the majority, and think about a tactic to achieve your ultimate goal. Maybe kindly and privately propose to those in power changing the *cadence* of the meeting. Maybe it becomes a biweekly event, and then if things don't improve, a monthly thing. Or that an agenda be circulated beforehand, and if no one has anything to address, the meeting doesn't happen at all. I'll bet you'll see smiles of relief and gratitude on the faces of most people in that meeting.

Cadence is an important consideration for all of our life commitments. How often are we doing, meeting, attending, driving, participating, paying? In a post-circus world, *slowing life down*, taking it off and out of the infinite loop, may mean that what is annual becomes biannual, what is monthly becomes quarterly, what is weekly becomes monthly, what is daily becomes weekly. For millions of us, work is relentless because the very cadence of the American economy is based on quarterly goals, reports, and accounting. It is stunning just how much is affected when the Big Forces set their quarterly goals. The whole society must move at that pace. Perhaps in this new future we are building together, there are business leaders who are brave enough to change that. Why divide the year into fourths? Why not thirds? Halves? Doing it all the way it has always been done will give us the same madness it has always given us.

Back to the office. I'm not suggesting you stage a hostile take-over. Workplace politics are very real, and the last thing I want is for you to put yourself into a precarious spot. But know your role within the group (and your power) and use it appropriately. If you struggle with how to effect change or don't feel that you can be the person to initiate it, you can still follow those three leadership steps, just in different ways: First, have a phone call or drink with a few friends from different industries and see how they are handling your particular problem or how they've seen their colleagues handle it. Then, find an ally at work who feels similarly and talk through what the change might *look* like, what underlying policies or protocols at work would need to change, and who would be most affected by that change. Then, use some of the language at the end of this chapter to craft a kind and reasonable approach to management.

Managers respond well to proposals, not complaints, to solutions, not more problems. No one wants to hear it. Frame your change as a proposal, one that you have considered, researched, and thought carefully about, one that you are asking they consider implementing. Also, think about how it could benefit them—or if they are your immediate supervisor and you report to them, how the change could benefit your workflow, which would in turn benefit them. Within traditional work structures, power is apportioned very intentionally. You must meet leaders at their level (empowered) by being a leader (empowered). Being cranky and whiny about how much email you have and how overworked you are (disempowered) triggers all sorts of emotions in people. You might remind them of their mother or father, or their spouse, or an awful roommate they once had. Don't give anyone reason for an easy *no*.

• • •

With that, we'll move from our surface subscriptions at work to our people subscriptions at work. Yes, I hear you. *I can't just unsubscribe from coworkers. I work with these people every day!* I know you do. But it is time for a conversation with either them or with your manager to restructure what is expected of the working relationship, how communication flows, and what your collaboration should look like for you to be happy. Power dynamics are real and strong. You may not be able to disentangle yourself completely from managers or office mates, but it is possible to reduce interactions with those who are not critical to your workflow—colleagues who spend their days complaining, gossiping, and generally poisoning the well, or who demand responses or work product on a certain schedule when *they* are the ones who didn't plan well; clients who require that you have lunch in *their* part of town only; bosses who hold their power over you—socially, sexually, financially. It's time to unsubscribe from working relationships that bear no fruit professionally, and even higher bosses who demand undying loyalty from us in the name of year-end profits for ventures in which we have no other financial stake than our salary. We have discovered that it is just not worth it.

Does that mean you can't be ambitious? Absolutely not. But do it on your own terms. Find ways to reduce the bullshit.

Perhaps the most effective and meaningful way to do this is to unsubscribe from the idea that *our work team is our family.* This is a very strange, completely inappropriate practice that only came into our professional consciousness over the last twenty or thirty years. Families (are meant to) provide unconditional love, pick us up when we have fallen for the nineteenth time, and provide the necessities of life. Work circumstances are different, but they are *close enough* that employers use the similarity to exploit workers—both unconsciously and consciously—employing the same emotional tactics that some families use to keep your behavior on autopilot. Yup, I'm talking about the twin devils: guilt and shame.

Click-up economics—with its Steve Jobs casual look and its artisan coffee and its open-plan offices—has completely mutated the role our colleagues play in our lives. When the physical space we worked in was different, when what we wore to work was more formal, and when we worked at human speed, boundaries were clearer. We had offices. With doors. We didn't have tricked-out common spaces or high-end kitchens or even employee benefits designed to keep us there longer. We clocked in, and we clocked out. No scooters. No pinball machines.

Now, we stay past seven if the office is comfortable, even fun. *Hey, we can expense a cab home.* We will get in early if breakfast is served on-site. We will feel more connected and committed to a company mission if it feels like everyone is working from sunrise to sundown to achieve a common goal, and the company furthers that connection into the familial by adopting family behavioral patterns: team dinners, coworker nicknames, birthday emails, baby showers.

I'm not trying to be ridiculous. There is nothing wrong with enjoying the company of your colleagues. But there is a fine line. When that line is blurry, problems arise. A blurry line makes us much more susceptible to all the emotional manipulation that we were (or are) used to in our family units, because we're playing out those dynamics within our work life. Guilt, as much as we hate to admit it, works on us—*Don't you feel bad leaving early?* So does shame—*You have to come for drinks! Don't abandon your work wife!* We put up with passive-aggressive behavior, microaggressions, and sometimes even a small level of emotional manipulation—*You should send in that testimonial about your colleague for their promotion, otherwise no one will do it for you when you're up for one*—so as not to rock the boat. Some put up with way more. Our colleagues may be incredible people. They may be or become friends inside and outside the office. But we work with them. We work for them. They work for us. These are not family dynamics. They are work relationships. The two are different.

Building boundaries, big and small, between yourself and other people is key. The word *boundary* sounds scary. But think of it as a fence, not a wall. That fence has a gate, and you choose who can come through. Just know up front that everyone will test your new boundaries. Humans love to test boundaries. They love to see what they can get away with. They love to push and poke and see how far they can go. They don't do it to be assholes. They do it because they are human beings. *What are you doing after work? Any weekend plans? Want to grab dinner and talk through that proposal? When did you lose your virginity?* I mean, talk about blurry lines.

Putting limits in place will be revealing, but other people's *reactions to those limits* will be even more so, and that is what you should really pay attention to. Do people seem to respect whatever changes you're clearly trying to make? Is it impacting your role on the team, the conversations you are privy to, the access you have? If so, that says more about them than it says about you—and in some cases, just knowing that is enough to release you from the guilt of doing it in the first place. In others, it might be another piece of evidence that perhaps this isn't the right place for you.

I have been a freelancer for decades. But I started my career in a corporate office tower in Midtown Manhattan, in the Time & Life Building. Even though I truly loved the job and came to love some of my colleagues as friends, I knew I wanted to be an independent creative artist. I couldn't do it in those halls, no matter how homey and hallowed they were.

Despite what my résumé and education might lead you to believe, working independently has not come without great financial strife. There is a heavy price to pay for working outside the norm. It has come with worries and anxieties about health insurance and cash flow and credit scores and all sorts of utter madness. At some point in my twenties, though, I understood that if I was ever going to be able to write for an audience larger than me and my mother, I was going to have to step away from the corporate model. It was my decision, and I rode the rocky waves (very rocky waves) that resulted up and down as I forged a career and strengthened the muscles required to make my work profitable enough to earn a living.

Along the way, I learned about contracts firsthand. At first, I fell on my face. Flat on my face. Being a people pleaser and an entrepreneur can be an unproductive mix. But over the years, I learned how to write work agreements (subscriptions) that spell out the specific terms and conditions of a gig (a "project engagement"). I never have unlimited power to dictate those terms and conditions. I still need to negotiate within reason, but I have way more power in the very process that ultimately determines my calendar and the flow of my life.

If you want to be happy with your work, in both the short and the long term, you have to understand that: (a) you get to choose your work, whether or not it feels that way and whether or not there is incredible pressure from family, society, your children, any of your social circles, or your credit-card debt and student loans; (b) you have the option to not renew (people change jobs every single day); and (c) the terms and conditions need to suit you, align with your values, and engender your joy, not crush the fuck out of it; if they do not suit you, propose changing them to whomever it is who holds the power to negotiate with you.

Before we move on, let's organize and categorize the people in your work life. What's the purpose? To see these work circles as living, breathing units that require us each day to subscribe, subscribe,

subscribe, and to engage actively and intentionally. Again, this process is not meant to rob you of joy in your work. In fact, it's exactly the opposite. I want to guide you through cleaning it all up so you can see it clearly and, no matter what you decide, truly experience joy at work. When you create the time and space to unsubscribe, whether that's a week off, a sabbatical, a job move, a garden leave, or just a weekend or day off spent taking a deep breath, here are some key questions to ask yourself as you move through each ring of your work dartboard.

Your Industry

- What are the values that the industry embraces? Does my company align? Does my team align? Does my boss align? Do I even align? What "seat on the bus" do I have to sit in to bring my work experience more in line with my values? Should I change my role in this organization or perhaps work in a different *part* of this business?

- Am I finding or taking opportunities to lead in the industry? How can I step up and lead in ways that empower myself and others? How can I make the industry reflect more of my own personal values?

- How are we as an industry fueling and automating the ills of click-up economics? How can we automate society's wellness instead?

- What actual written or spoken agreements, contracts (subscriptions) do we have in place that dictate our work? Do those need to be updated to reflect and respect where the world is after the circus? (As we'll look at later in this book, what are the inequities and abuses built into these agreements and contracts, and how do we challenge and rewrite them?)

- How do I feel working in this industry and fueling its power in our society?

Your Company

- Are my expectations set "correctly" with respect to my future at this company? Are there paths forward to grow, or am I deluding myself here?

- Who is the leadership, and what kind of human beings are they? Do I want my talents making them more powerful in the world?

- What are this company's mission, vision, and values? Are each of those reflected in my day-to-day experience, or are they bullshit? How can I work inside this company to effect more authenticity and transparency?

- Whom is the company in bed with, subscribed to, or contracted with, and what is our relationship with these partners amplifying in our society? Am I on board with this? Where is that all written down or where and when is it spoken?

- How does it feel to work here every day? Am I satisfied by that feeling, or does it leave me severely wanting?

- What do I get from this relationship financially (in both the short term and the long term), professionally, socially, and emotionally?

Your Clients

- How much of my mind space am I willing to turn over to their needs and concerns? Is my relationship with them healthy and productive?

- Are the terms of our relationship clear? Are they written down and properly structured? Are they being honored? Do they need to be renegotiated? How willing am I to walk away if they are not being honored?

- What needs to change about our digital communication habits so I feel in control of my work, my calendar, and my mental and physical health?

- Am I behaving—speaking, writing, responding, reacting—in a way that respects my own time and boundaries? Or am I letting people walk all over me because I am walking all over me, too?
- Do I need or want this many clients? Do I need or want more? Fewer? Who is dictating and making that decision, and how can I be more responsible for who I have to work with or for?
- Am I valuing my time and talents? If I charge more, can I have fewer clients?

Your Team

- Why do I continue to participate in the work of this team? What is my real "why"?
- Do they treat me like a friend or like family? Or is it clear that we are work colleagues? Are the lines blurry? If they are, how can I create boundaries and clarity while still enjoying our time together? In what ways does my behavior reinforce this?
- What needs to change so I can be happier in this position? What agreements—spoken or unspoken, written or unwritten—need to be renegotiated so that the terms of this role work for me?
- What needs to change about our digital communication practices to turn the volume down day to day and make this a calmer environment—one in which I can focus, concentrate, and be productive?
- How much of the rhythm of my work schedule is dictated by that of the team? How can I change that? Also, why on earth do we need so many meetings? What are we getting from that habit and how do we change it? How can we be productive as a team without constantly wasting time? On the flip side, what do we need to be in the same room together to accomplish?

Your Boss

- Why do I continue to work for or with this person every day? What is my real "why"? Start here: Do I like this person or enjoy working with them? How much does that matter to me or doesn't it?

- Are the terms of my job clear? Are they written down? Have we actually discussed what they expect me to do in order to earn my salary? Or am I flying blind here?

- Am I an easy person to manage or am I the nightmare? (Don't gloss over it. Look inside. For me, I know that I am a total nightmare if I haven't eaten or slept well. I am a hangry monster. Know thyself.)

- Do I behave in response to their behavior (good or bad), or am I proactively creating the behavioral habits that govern our relationship?

- How do I interact with them? What am I expecting emotionally to get from our exchanges?

- Why do I feel I need or want to get that from my boss? How does needing or wanting to get that affect my life and my emotional life outside the workplace?

Once you have considered these questions, it's time to think about next steps. What changes do I want to make? Which relationships need to shift? What terms of my subscription with a particular person or group do I want to renegotiate? Do I just set a rule for myself, or do I have to have a conversation? This can look, as we've said, like a few things. It could mean quitting. It could mean looking at opportunities in a different department or part of the company you're already at. It could mean not volunteering for the committee that plans your holiday party, or attending that meeting that says, in writing, that attendance is optional. It could mean just taking your hard-earned paid vacation days and *using* them.

In my case, I stopped having lunch with colleagues. Do I have to eat? Sure. But can I take an hour or two out of the middle of my day to do so? No. The work I do requires momentum and uninterrupted hours at my laptop. I get lost in the beauty of a story or in the rhythm of a paragraph. Books don't write themselves. Nor do screenplays. So, whenever I get an invite to lunch, I respond politely with this: "I would love to, but lunches are out for me. Can we do a drink at six p.m. instead?" There is no reason to be an asshole. But there is a real reason to structure your day in a way that works best for you.

If restructuring a relationship requires a conversation, here is some sample language to consider. You can use one of these sentences, or two, or many. Mix and match. Choose your own adventure. Hard talks are not easy.

If you can make these conversations open, ongoing, and regular, then there won't be so much pressure on you when you really feel you must set a boundary or unsubscribe. If you are a leader or manager, intentionally bringing this language into the office culture is a gift to your team. It lets them know that you are thinking about their welfare, their mental health, their balance. The world has changed. We are not going back to the way it was before. So, find ways to be generative about making the office a better place. If you don't—and you squeeze your team into the old ways—don't be shocked by a negative response. The circus was a reckoning. People want to talk about new schedules or frameworks, fair and dignified pay, equity, and boundaries.

When You Need Space from Certain People or Groups

- "Let's pick one day a week to have lunch. I want to use the other days to [exercise outside]." Choose your healthy solo activity.
- "I'm not making plans outside of work for a bit. Can I get back to you?"
- "Deep work time! I'm going to close my door for a little while."

- "I promised myself no alcohol till Christmas. I'll skip drinks, but let's have coffee Friday, me and you."
- "I want to step off that committee. I don't have anything to contribute."
- "I would just love a phone call. Call me. I am reserving video just for clients."
- "I need space right now. Respect and admire you. But please . . ."

When You Want to Streamline or Set a Boundary

- "I really want to say yes, but until I finish my deadline, I can't focus on that well."
- "Can we round up and establish a new way to communicate as a group?"
- "I think our office needs to look a little different from how it used to."
- "Our schedule isn't leaving me much room for family time. How can we make some changes?"
- "I want to have a standing day each week [or hour(s) each day] to just focus on my inbox."
- "For the summer, let's set a dedicated lunch hour so we're all on the same page. How does everyone feel about that?"
- "I think it's time for us to renegotiate the terms of our work relationship."
- "I feel like this is not working. How do you feel? What can we change here to make this work?"
- "I think we all need to unsubscribe from this idea that . . ."

When It Is Time to End It

- "I will always have great respect for you. I just don't want to work for you."
- "We have had a great working relationship, but it's time for me to start a new chapter of my work life."

- "I just can't (don't) accept the terms you need for this to work. No hard feelings."
- "I assumed a lot. I invented a lot in my head about what working here would be. That is on me. The reality of this job doesn't work for me."
- "It is time for me to unsubscribe. I can't support who our company is in the world right now."
- "Do you really believe we are living our values as a company? I don't buy it. I have to walk away."
- "I've decided to resign my position at the end of the summer."
- "I'm not sure where I go from here. I think the answer is I have to step down."
- "I wish you and the team only success. My needs and wants are just different now."
- "I have family commitments, and I'm seeing them in a totally new light these days."
- "I just read this (amazing) book about unsubscribing. I think it's time to unsubscribe from this job."
- "We have to put some structure in place here."
- "Boundaries, please."
- "I had this idea I would be here forever. I have got to unsubscribe from that. It'll be healthier for me."

Twelve
Our Sticky Stories

As our conversation about work revealed, our day-to-day behaviors are very often rooted in powerful *underlying subscriptions*. To create real change in our lives, we have to unsubscribe from these, too. Welcome to the next phase of the Great Unsubscribe.

Our underlying subscriptions are ideas, beliefs, and notions we each have about who we are, how the world works, and what our place and role is within it. They are the subscriptions at the very core of each of us. These are the deeply held beliefs exploited by advertising and the messaging of the Big Forces. (See figure 10.) These narratives, in the marketing and brand world, are called *sticky stories*, and business teams *live* for them—so much so that they pay writers and consultants good money to teach them how to put them together. (I know because I used to be one of them.)

Storytelling is a powerful art, but for a story to make an impact, it's got to be memorable. We know that from movies, heartfelt celebrity interviews, and expensive Super Bowl commercials—but we also see it in our own lives. Every thought we think about ourselves, every behavior we know we should probably change, every fear or dream or goal we have stems from a memory or moment or school lesson we experienced that clawed itself into our brain and won't let go.

The reason it won't let go is that it has become an "automatic thought." The concept of underlying subscriptions comes from the world of cognitive behavioral therapy (CBT), which was popularized by Dr. Aaron Beck in the 1960s. (Psychoanalysts have been

FIGURE 10
Core
Underlying Subscriptions

making similar arguments for the last century.) In 1979, Dr. Beck outlined three "interrelated levels of cognition": core beliefs, dysfunctional assumptions, and negative automatic thoughts. Not only is CBT the basis of much modern talk therapy, but its insights have also been used—and abused—to exploit consumers. Basically, the Big Forces use our "negative automatic thoughts" to sell us shit we don't need.

While I have personally found CBT a useful tool over the years, its power crystalized for me during the circus. The greatest lesson I took from my unsubscription is that even my beliefs about myself and the world around me are *temporary* (*impermanent*, as my Buddhist friends would say). Perhaps like you, I had never quite understood that before. I thought that once you start believing something, it is forever. I thought that once you take on a quality or a behavior, it *merges with you* and becomes part of your identity. Nothing could be less true. Click-up economics may be well served by that misconception about human psychology. The Big Forces want their storytelling to stick forever. Organized religion wants the same and may be equally well served. So is racism. So is nationalism. So is fascism. But a healthy society is not. Our souls are not. People grow. We change. We shed old behaviors so we can embrace new ways of being that fully honor our humanity.

According to CBT, it is our *interpretation* of the situations of our lives that influences us emotionally, behaviorally, physiologically, more so than the actual situation. What does that mean? Something happens, and our brain makes us a good story about it. The reason that story sticks is that it gets trapped in an infinite loop. Not only is that loop reinforced by more experiences that seem to prove the belief, but we form friendships, develop relationships, and join groups that support these beliefs, or at least that never challenge them. Same with our jobs: they reflect these beliefs. When we look at our lives as a whole, what we do, think, and say are often based on these beliefs. That's why I have organized this process in the way that I have: to help us all unsubscribe layer by layer so that we can really get to the core of who we "are" or who we believe ourselves to be. From *that place*, and that place only, can we truly and authentically renew our lives.

So, how do we unsubscribe from the sticky stories? Well, first, "Stop believing everything you think." If there are five words in this book I really wish I had written, those would be them. Alas, I did not. I first heard them in the Broadway musical *Some Like It Hot*, written by Matthew López and Amber Ruffin—insightful words of caution from one character to another to be mindful that not everything that swirls around in our heads is worthy of the emotional investment of our *belief*. Brilliant. It is our choice to believe the messages we get. In other words, it is our choice to make up an *empowering* story about the message or a *disempowering* one.

How do you do that? First, be mindful of that choice. Start to pay attention to all the messages that come at you in any given day and to the sticky stories you make up based on them—about yourself, about the world, about work, about family, about money, about love. Notice if you actively process those messages and consciously craft your stories or if they just sort of seep into your brain. Do you hold each of these messages up to the light as they come in to examine them? Or are you unaware that they're taking up real estate in your mind? I have news for you: the Big Forces understand your mind's storytelling power, and they are hoping you make up disempowering stories so their products and services can be your emotional salve. Stop believing everything you think.

Another effective way to unsubscribe from sticky stories is to first examine where they come from in your personal history. For me, they tend to fall into five buckets of beliefs: inherited beliefs, experiential beliefs, educated beliefs, cultural beliefs, and narrated beliefs. Are there some crossovers here? Yes, of course. I'm going to use this chapter to lay those out, so you can start to understand and trace how your own stories have been shaped. As I go source by source, start to notice all the underlying subscriptions that come to mind. Write them down on a piece of paper. They are the contracts, commitments, promises you have made to yourself about how the world works, and how and where you fit into it. The truth behind the curtain: stories stick more in *moments of high emotion* or when they come from *people for whom we have great emotion*. Here we go.

As an Individual

Inherited beliefs

These beliefs come from our families, our parents—basically, our smallest circles—which makes them most foundational and potent. Most of us won't even remember when we "signed up" for these, when we allowed them to become part of who we are and how we behave. They were modeled for us by people we love, people from whom we wanted respect, admiration, and validation. And milk. They were passed down, carried on from one generation to the next. These can be empowering or disempowering, seemingly incidental or formative.

In my own life, I inherited the belief that *if I am gay, I am a bad person*. No one directly told me that nor asked me to subscribe to it. I never clicked a button that noted my agreement or approval. But the people I love had inherited that story generation after generation, and so they passed it on to me. They did not do this with malice. In many ways, they did it out of love—to protect me from a cruel world.

But my subscription to that belief was renewed over and over in larger circles through constant reinforcement of that same message in casual chats, bad jokes, judgmental glares at gay people in the street, in discussions at community gatherings or church, or in movies or television. A message I subscribed to at home was validated and strengthened circle by circle.

When I finally did come out, it was liberating, but only surface-deep, as I would come to learn. I had fully expected that just saying *the thing* would be the end of it, but it turns out that it was just the beginning. Through my twenties and thirties, I battled deep depression and unrelenting guilt about the decision I had made to live my life on my own terms. I had unsubscribed from all the surface subscriptions that I associated with being a straight man: straight porn, intense weightlifting (that one would return because much of gay male culture is equally focused on hypermasculine bodies, a direct response to the devastation of the 1980s), talking about girls, season tickets to the Mets. Looking back, I did a lot of that unsubscribing pretty inelegantly. I would disappear whenever my straight friends threw a gathering that I just felt was too intense for me. I avoided group dinners, even phone calls. I didn't show up for bachelor parties. I didn't even respond. I took refuge in living a "gay life" in Southern California. I had changed my circle of friends and no longer engaged with relationships that only seemed to add to my guilt and shame.

But I was still unhappy. I was in great pain. I was bitter and angry that my straight counterparts had "an easier life." I smiled through it, refusing to share with anyone just how unhappy I was. My "velvet rage," a term coined by Dr. Alan Downs, was affecting my behavior, my social relationships, my love life, and my career. It all looked good. I made sure of that. But it was a perfectly crafted image, one that the rise of social media helped me curate. As I worked with a number of professionals—therapists, coaches, workshops—the takeaway was always the same: I hadn't yet done the deep work of addressing just how angry I was. I still had a voice in the back of my head telling me that being gay was wrong, that I was a bad person. I couldn't do much about what I had inherited, but I could do something about how I had internalized it, the story I told myself about it all. To fully unsubscribe from that belief, I came to understand that I had to rewrite it.

Experiential beliefs

Experiential beliefs come from—you guessed it—our actual life experiences. We create our sticky stories based on specific "good" or "bad" moments we've participated in, witnessed, or been directly involved with. An example: When you're a kid, you watch a random man on the street steal your mother's purse. You tell yourself (or maybe your mother tells you, too) that *strangers are bad*, or that *people you do not know are dangerous*. Or you're in middle school and you tell a secret to a friend. You think that it's a safe one to tell, but the next day you arrive at school and other students are staring at you. That "friend" told them your secret. You tell yourself that *you must be careful about being vulnerable. People don't care about you the way you might care about them.* The more intense an experience is, or the more frequently we experience it, the stronger our subscription to that belief becomes. Because we build evidence. We look for proof. Constantly. That "evidence" powers the loop. *See! You must be careful about being vulnerable.*

How much of our behavior as adults is run by the belief that *you can't trust people*? Seemingly innocent moments—big or small, internal or external, true or interpreted—can impact us for years and influence our larger behaviors, thought patterns, interactions, and self-identification.

Learned beliefs

These are beliefs we subscribe to because we are taught they are *correct*. This group can include a wide range of beliefs—educational, moral, religious/spiritual, cultural. They can be informational (*Columbus discovered America*) or behavioral (*getting an A on a test will get you positive attention and praise from your parents and community*). In either scenario, we are presented a clear case of right and wrong, a clear set of stakes and outcomes. When we're young, these beliefs are reinforced and celebrated with validation and reward. As individuals, we carry these beliefs in our brains and in our bodies.

We can also learn them collectively. The way our school system functions is an interesting case study in learned belief. As a society, we are subscribed to certain beliefs about education that are reflected in how we structure that school system. Standardized tests and streamlined roads to college and careers dismiss alternative ways of learning or applying information, while at the same time overemphasizing the importance of taking the same path as everyone else. All of which leads to millions of highly educated twenty-two-year-olds seeking well-worn paths directly into the same dozen or so white-collar professions, all convinced that *school is preparation for a high-paying job. There is no way I can possibly be happy unless I make $400,000 a year and live in the heart of a major city.*

Likewise, paying our teachers poorly and crowding our kids into packed classrooms demonstrate physically and psychologically our collective beliefs that *education is a mass event, not a personal journey*, and *jobs that bring personal joy and that are "good for society" should absorb a trade-off: a shitty salary*. These beliefs ultimately inform and direct our budgeting and policymaking. Active-shooter drills and armed guards outside classroom doors—as well as inaction in protective legislation—underscore the belief for both children and adults that *the world is not safe*, and that *you are only worthy of safety if you live in a well-funded district*.

When I was growing up, the local high school was a jail. Literally, the building was designed and constructed to be a prison before the City of New York decided it should be a high school. Can we really say with certainty that its students did not walk away from that experience subscribed to the belief that *life is a prison*?

Is it any wonder children go from school and into the rest of life subscribed to disempowering beliefs about community, the state, and the nation? I know I am being extreme, but our subscriptions are powerful forces, and if we want to effect change, we have to get real about what we are teaching our kids about the world. And if we are truly going to meet the moment as we undergo this transformation into a future of mass labor automation, it is high time we start examining these underlying subscriptions—and rewriting them.

As a Group

This brings us to *collective beliefs*. Collective beliefs are ones we subscribe to as a group, as opposed to the ones we subscribe to as individuals.

Narrated beliefs

These are beliefs that we subscribe to collectively because we are told (or sold) a story or narrative. A classic: *America is exceptional*. Collectively, 335 plus million of us claim to believe this. We never signed a piece of paper that said "Check this box if you believe America is exceptional," but we collectively subscribe to this belief—and renew it—through national practices that remind us of it and reinforce it: speeches, songs, the way we teach our history, holidays, ceremonies, and civic rituals. Like inherited beliefs, we keep these underlying subscriptions strong through repeated and intensive exposure. But unlike inherited beliefs, these get "adopted" en masse, which makes them more powerful.

We also learn these beliefs from media, specifically from (a) news media, and (b) our primary national storytelling apparatus: Hollywood. In the twentieth century, cowboy movies narrated our collective experience of "settling" the West. As a nation, we watched and we subscribed to the belief that *bringing law and order to the savage West is right and just* and *white men bring enlightenment to the rest of the beasts of the world.* What enormous bullshit. We watch love stories on television and collectively subscribe to the belief that *love is a man and a woman who hardly know each other, but because they both moved back to the same small town from the big city they should hook up and have babies.* Ah, Lifetime.

Today, America and all Western societies are now seeing what happens when you put very powerful storytelling tools into the hands of malicious actors. It certainly isn't the first time. We saw it throughout the early twentieth century, when fascists used propaganda (and bold graphic design) to mask heinous and unspeakable crimes and to stir up nationalist fervor in their constituents. Now, we're no longer dealing with flags, newspapers, and radio. We have highly sophisticated media that reach millions and billions. And technology that makes deceit nearly undetectable. Ever use a photo filter? Or heard of a supercut? A deep fake? The Alex Jones InfoWars podcast? If each of us can now "remove unwanted objects" from our photos with a "fun" tool on the latest smartphones, how much more (large-scale) media is being manipulated so it's clean, camera-ready, digestible—or so that it supports the extreme beliefs of the media maker? (Worse, imagine if the "media maker" isn't even human.)

A battle to control the collective narrative(s) is raging in our society. "We live in a world," Jonah Sachs wrote in *Winning the Story*

Wars, "that has lost its connection to its traditional myths, and we are now trying to find new ones—we're people, and that's what people without myths do. These myths will shape our future, how we live, what we do, and what we buy. They will touch all of us. But not all of us get to write them. Those who do have tremendous power."

Without guardrails in place (regulations, public policies, etc.) to ensure that very powerful psychological and storytelling tools are used for the greater good, these bad actors, who well know the robust might of tech-fueled storytelling, are wielding it to secure mass subscription to very dangerous collective beliefs. We have seen it on our own televisions: the narrator himself, perhaps at a rally, gets you worked up emotionally so that you are primed for mass subscription to very extreme ideas. Click-up economics has not only altered how we tell stories. It has altered what it is that we believe.

Cultural beliefs

Very often, cultural beliefs are group responses to specific ceremonies, rituals, and collective practices that are meant to create an explicit, externalized standard of behavior. (Sometimes, these beliefs appear, quite literally, as taglines, slogans, or on banners or printed communications materials at these ceremonies, rituals, or collective practices.) We often say we collectively "adopt" them. They are the collective beliefs we are raised around, even if we don't necessarily individually subscribe to each nuance of them or internalize them as reflections of our own worth.

For example, Roman Catholics believe that *God is a three-part being*. Every week (or holiday) at church, we gather to repeat this belief, talk about it, sing about it, and give our little collection envelopes to support it.

Italian Americans—a community made up largely of Roman Catholics—believe that *Sunday is family day*, born out of the tradition of rest and attending Mass on the holiest of days. Many of us who are first- and second-generation Americans can tell endless stories about the moments when "family day" conflicted with the American notion of "Sunday Funday," and how negotiating that difference created conflict. In my own life, the two have always been at odds. So, I renegotiated the terms of this subscription with my family. We have family day every three weeks. My fiancé and I spend Sunday with friends every three weeks. And on those third Sundays, we rest. Yes, we go through seasons when that is more formalized than in others, but that's generally how it lays out now. Initially, this took some getting used to, but it took the pressure off everyone, including my mother, who is used to cooking every Sunday for the full clan. Adjusting the cadence proved a useful way to honor traditions old and new.

Mass experiential beliefs

Just like individual experiential beliefs, collective mass experiential beliefs are the ones we subscribe to as a group when we have intense collective experiences, good or bad—and they can be used to fuel narrated or cultural beliefs at large. For example, the night that Barack Obama was elected president, many of the 69 million people who voted for him burst into tears. Across the country, we had a collective emotional experience. For those of us on the left, it was one of the most exciting days in our civic lives. We had worked incredibly hard to get the nation to unsubscribe from a very strong collective belief that *American presidents are only white*. Together, we rewrote that sticky story, and the emotional experience allowed many of us to collectively subscribe to the belief that *you can create change in the political system*.

The other side of that coin is collective trauma. As I detailed in part one, 9/11 was a collective traumatic event that led to a burst of patriotism and service. That burst was then manipulated by our own government to mass subscribe us—via policy (an actual written subscription)—to the belief that *with patriotism comes a decline in personal freedom* (the Patriot Act), that *the world is made up of us and them*, and *the only reasonable response to violence is more violence* (the Iraq War). Politicians know that moments of collective trauma present opportunities to rewrite policy, because emotions are high.

This is why politicians (and preachers) tell stories: to evoke emotion, so that they can get a group of people to collectively subscribe to the beliefs that they hold, in the hopes that being aligned with those beliefs will drive them to the polls to vote.

You can see the power of collective beliefs. These subscriptions act as code in the larger machine. If we are collectively subscribed to sticky stories that pit us against one another, that feed our selfishness and our nastiness, that rob us of our equity, our freedom, and our dignity, we will continue to see great conflict around us. Automating this—which is what the Big Forces have thus far done—is making it all worse. It is giving us more and more of the same. It is scaling up our illness. It is magnifying the worst of us. If we do not correct course, what is to come will be far worse. If, on the other hand, we can collectively unsubscribe from these sticky stories, challenge them, reevaluate them, and clean house, we stand a chance to rediscover ourselves, our collective power, and our collective wellness. We can create change. We can transform.

This is a chance to think about our collective sticky stories and about your own. What are your underlying subscriptions? What ideas, beliefs, and notions have you subscribed to about yourself that may not actually be true but are controlling your behavior? Write down what comes to mind for each kind of belief. Were they the beliefs you expected to emerge, or did some come out of the woodwork? Do other things suddenly start to line up and make sense? How have these different beliefs shaped your worldview, past and present? How have they affected your behavior? How have they helped you, but how have they kept you subscribed to problematic systems, thoughts, or relationships in the infinite loop? How easy do you think it would be to shift them in a new direction?

Most directly related to the rest of this book, consider this: How have they influenced your subscription to certain people, groups, and even the products and services of the Big Forces? Let's look at how *underlying subscriptions, people subscriptions, and surface subscriptions* all fit together. If I have an *underlying subscription* to the idea that, say, *strangers are dangerous*, then I am likely to only bond and form relationships (*people subscriptions*) with people and groups who look, talk, and think like I do. *That which is strange or unlike me is threatening.* I look for evidence of this belief everywhere I go, consciously and unconsciously. This belief affects my friendships, my schooling, my romantic partnerships, and on and on. And I am primed to feel that threat day to day, making me more and more susceptible to messaging from the Big Forces about everything from expensive alarm systems (that can "protect" and "secure" the ones I love) to indestructible tank-like SUVs to cable news that reminds me daily that "foreigners are taking all the jobs" (all surface subscriptions). My life becomes a big proof that *strangers are dangerous*.

Now that we have located and identified our own individual sticky stories, as well as the collective ones we have all been subscribed to, the next step is to use language to interrogate them. Call them out. Make vocal your desire to *unsubscribe* from them. Here is some sample language you may find helpful, and you can use it with yourself or with others. I have included a mix of "woo-woo" and "straight talk." California and New York. Beer and wine. Choose your adventure.

As individuals

- "I realize I have been operating under the idea that every email needs to be responded to immediately. That's not healthy for me. I have to unsubscribe from that idea."
- "I can't keep subscribing to this notion that my self-worth depends on your approval. Turns out, it doesn't."
- "I just kept telling myself this fucked-up story that success is for other people, not me. Complete bullshit."
- "Sorry, I just no longer believe that I am my work. My last day will be October 1."
- "You know, much of my life I have believed that men only want sex. That has kept me from allowing myself to get close to men. I no longer subscribe to that belief."
- "I learned a lot these last few years. This just doesn't work for me anymore. It's total bullshit."
- "As a couple, we have to stop thinking of ourselves as just roommates in this apartment. I want us to make changes to not only our schedule but also to how we think about who we are to each other."
- "Wow, that's a good story. But it was just a story. I no longer believe I am unlovable if I am overweight. I am going to rock the fuck out of this bathing suit. Sorry if you think only the razor-thin can sport a two-piece."
- "Our family no longer subscribes to the idea that our car represents our value. We'll drive a less expensive car, and we'll still be happy and amazing."
- "We moved. We unsubscribed from the old-school idea that a bigger house is a better one. We love living in a condo and having more disposable income."

If those seem way too wordy for you, here are a few new phrases to experiment with when other members of your circles vocalize a deeply rooted belief about you, your circle, or that which is is disempowering:

- "Sorry, no, I don't buy that anymore."
- "Nope! Not taking that bait again."
- "Uh, no. I cannot keep supporting that idea."
- "That is bullshit. I don't believe that anymore."
- "Please unsubscribe, thanks!"

(Yes, I use the word *bullshit* a lot. It's because most of the bullshit that floods our modern lives is—intentionally or not—exploiting our negative underlying beliefs about ourselves. It doesn't uplift us. It doesn't empower us. It finds our weaknesses and tramples on them. Your life, my life, our happiness is too important not to call it what it is.)

As a group

- "We have all been operating under the idea that every email needs to be responded to immediately. That's not healthy for us."
- "We cannot keep subscribing to this notion that people over forty are old. It's a joke."
- "We just kept telling ourselves this story that the American way is the best way. Other societies have had much longer to figure these things out."
- "You know, we all seem to believe that working till midnight makes us a dedicated team. How about we actually rest and enjoy our families after six o'clock so we can come back to work tomorrow ready to do our jobs well?"
- "Haven't we all learned a lot these last few years? Can we please unsubscribe from the belief that universal health care is a bad idea?"

- "It is time for us to reevaluate our company communications policy. We can't subscribe to the idea that what worked in 2019 is going to work now."
- "Wow, that is a powerful story. But it is just a story. I don't actually believe that immigrants are bad for the economy. I don't think we should keep reenforcing that."
- "Let's unsubscribe from the idea that renting means you're less successful. The whole world has changed. I don't buy that anymore, and we shouldn't as a group."
- "Yes, that worked in 1982. Not now. It is time to unsubscribe from the idea that greed is good. Also, let's unsubscribe from 'it will trickle down to you.' It didn't."

That is *how* we unsubscribe. We first cut the cord and disconnect ourselves from the tethers of the surface bullshit. Then we take a step back from the people and circles that are standing in the way of our greatest joy. Then we identify and call out the underlying ideas, beliefs, and notions—the sticky stories—that are powerfully calling the shots deep in our brains and hearts. Keep that list of sticky stories. We're going to use it as we sit in the dark well.

PART THREE

The Dark Well

Mourning and Morning

FIGURE 11

You in the Dark Well

Unsubscribing brings greater challenges step by step, harder conversations, and trickier interpersonal and personal dilemmas for us to sort through and sort out. And, when it's all said and done, we land in one very tough spot. I call it *the dark well*. Welcome.

I have given the dark well its very own real estate in this book because it is that important of a moment, a stage, a place—when you have muted the very noise around you and inside you that keeps you going, going, going. I have no interest in contributing to that noise, so this chapter sits alone here, a space for you to return to should you want, without the noise of what has come before and what will come after.

The dark well is as dark as a cave and as vacant as a church parking lot on Monday morning. It is as hollow as a vase and as barren as a desert. It is tall and short. It is new and old. In it, you are starving and sated. Lost and found. It is a strange space. Like, *really strange*. It will feel like you are living someone else's life. It will feel like you are without aim or goal or purpose or motive. It will feel like you are going through withdrawal. (Yes, the addiction metaphor is apt.) It will be lonely. Your inbox will feel bare, your phone will be quiet, your mailbox will be empty, and the group at your dinner table may be smaller. It will create moments of panic, of fear. You may not know what to do every morning the moment you wake up. You may feel isolated or out of touch with the world you once took an active role in. Life may actually feel empty, because it kind of will be (unless, of course, you have kids or other people in your home). The closest thing that you might be able to relate it to are the opening weeks of the circus. Yes, it all comes back to that.

It might feel great at first. Freeing. Full of possibility. Joyful.

Then it may just feel like shit.

Once the reality of unsubscription hits, a rush of emotions will likely follow. We may feel a rush of regret for doing it all at once. We might feel selfish. We might feel foolish. We may feel ashamed that we let ourselves get to this point in the first place. We may feel like we have failed, like we are not *good* at friendship, relationships, or parenting. We may feel like we are not successful or ever likely to succeed now that we have taken a step to separate ourselves from all these Big Forces, people, situations, and beliefs that keep us in our own personal infinite loops.

We may feel like we have not lived into the promises of our youth, like we have let ourselves down or let down people who have supported us, or who are genuinely proud of how hard we work and how successful we are, or who truly value what we do for a living. We will feel vulnerable. We will feel *bad*. We won't feel like a participant anymore. We will no longer be on autopilot, so we'll feel almost like an exposed nerve, overwhelmed by even the simplest decision we'll have to make, because it was once taken care of for us. We'll want to rush right back to all our old habits. (I have news for you: we developed those habits to avoid feeling exactly how we will feel in the dark well—empty, lonely, disconnected.) We will feel like an outsider, a feeling that we avoid like the plague in our day-to-day behavior, because, at a primal level, not being part of the group makes us feel unprotected, more likely to be singled out by a flying beast or run down and gobbled up by a speedy predator. It feels, in a word, unsafe.

At least, this is how I felt.

But we must move through it if we want to win the battle for our behavior, if we are ever to change the trajectory of our lives and that of our nation. So, there is great value in going through this stage with as much reflection and grace as you can muster. But it is not easy.

The dark well is a scary moment because it is then that you realize that you are no longer getting from the world what you feel you need or want from it. You are not validating other people's bullshit, and they are not validating yours. You are back in the slow morass of human time. People, quite simply, may not get it or understand why you're doing it. There will likely be resistance from partners, children, neighbors, and friends. You will have to dig deep and pull daily from whatever reserves of love and patience you have inside you. Trust me, those reserves are much deeper than you think. When you unsubscribe, you are stating publicly that the status quo just doesn't work for you. You are saying that you want something better, something that makes your life more satisfying, meaningful, joyful—and that will scare the shit out of people, because it will immediately trigger them to wonder if they, too, should be doing the kind of questioning that you are. Many people will perceive you as a threat to their own infinite loops. They will hear judgment when there is none. They will feel rejection when there is none.

In short, they will make it about them. And that's not because they are terrible people. We are all humans, and we need each other—but that need, in extremes, is precisely how we shame one another into social conformity. It will take strength to resist this. That strength is in you. It is your personal power. It is a muscle—the very muscle that click-up economics has atrophied in all of us—and the more you use it, the stronger it gets. As subscribers, consumer power does not work within a system of highly consolidated Big Brands. Independent and critical thinking does not mesh with Big Media. Divergence, discovery, and present-tense living do not work with the behavioral automation Big Tech perpetuates. Conscious spending, robust personal savings, and slow banking do not serve the interests of the Big Banks. As voters, power of the people does not align with the Big Parties who are more loyal to lobbyists, corporate interests, and the very highest strata of our society.

As the saying goes, "Life is a series of doors opening and closing. But it's hell in the hallways." The dark well may be the longest and emptiest hallway of your life. But in it, there is simply more time and space. There is more time and space for you. There is more time and space for your partner and your kids, if you have children. There is more time and space to engage in activities that humans have practiced for thousands of years, and you will quickly realize how much of your day is spent engaging in activities that humans have practiced only since the year 2000. The dark well is a sacred time for you to discover or rediscover what life is like without the constant pinging and ringing, the exhausting running and going, and the endless need to be better, bigger, stronger, faster, richer.

Here is what the dark well is *not*: it is not a windowless room with no contact with the outside world. You can, um, do things (more on that later). Make this stage of life as comfortable as possible. Be kind to yourself. Resist the instinct to go out and buy new clothes, new furniture, new lotions, new *stuff* to comfort you in the dark well. You're not here to perform change or dress it up in new athleisure wear. You're here to feel what it feels like to take away the noise.

You also get to determine how long you are in it. Is it a week, a month, a season? Is it a summer, a year, or just the length of your work vacation? Growth and change and progress and reflection are not linear, and they certainly do not conform to modern automated time. I know this is hard to hear, but there is no right answer. In some ways, it takes as long as it takes. But best to at least put a limit on it, at least for the first go-around. The dark well can become self-indulgent. You can spend too much time in it. You can wallow in it. You can get so used to it that you forget to get on with life.

• • •

Now, *practically speaking*, life changes when you unsubscribe. When I unsubscribed from the surface subscriptions, my life got quieter. But that quiet did not always feel good. At first, the idea (and later reality) of a life without Big Tech was unpleasant. It called for a total overhaul of my relationship to information and how I accessed it. Life without Big Media was so much calmer, but it did feel unexciting. I felt uninformed and, uh, out of the loop. I felt disappointment when I couldn't keep up with the cultural conversation and even disapproval when those I used to seek validation from figured out that I hadn't watched every movie nominated for an Oscar for Best Sound Mixing. I started to be able to separate *life* from *drama* (heightened life) once again, and I learned to sit in and fully embrace the "unexciting."

Big Brands were another tough one to let go of. The way that tech makes us feel smart, or media makes us feel connected, brands make us feel special. They are a curation tool, a pathway to a certain image or idea of what life *should* look like. And without those daily reminders—the newsletters, the email blasts, the sales announcements—I felt like a part of my identity had gone missing. (Sigmund Freud called this the "ego ideal.") Life without the Big Banks, on the other hand, was glorious. No overdraft fees, no clunky websites, no dodgy charges. I pulled all my money out of Wells Fargo and put it in a local nonprofit credit union. I spent much of my time in the dark well redefining my relationship with money, auditing all my finances, really being honest with myself about how I spend and how many dollars I just give away freely. And once I turned off the television, and unsubscribed from messages from the Big Parties, the daily street fight vanished.

Life without my people subscriptions was tough. I picked a small circle of people, maybe three or four, to be in touch with over the phone. They kept me sane. They kept me from wilting. They kept me engaged with the world.

It finally got quiet, and that quiet offered me the chance to listen to the thoughts that I had spent decades ignoring, brushing aside, and shutting down. I had ignored them before because the clanging of a life full of commitments and people and travel and go, go, go seemed more urgent, because I was fully subscribed to the idea that *other people know more than I do about how to live*, and because I knew somewhere in myself that if I ever really listened to it, I would have to change so many things about my life that it seemed overwhelming, daunting, terrifying.

But as I sat in the dark well longer and longer, and it got quieter and quieter, the voice got louder. And I finally listened and heard what that little guy was saying. Funny, surprising thoughts popped up, like *I like calligraphy. Sushi never makes me full. I love bourbon.* He also said some more important things: *I'm not actually enjoying all the random hookups I am having. I am spending too much time on this fucking app. I hate cooking. Some of my friends bore me. I miss talking to my cousins. I want to be a father. I want to love someone again. I have everything I need in this world.*

Those are some of the discoveries the dark well gave me. Now it's time to figure out what it can give *you*. To do that, we need to figure out how you'll spend this sacred time. Here are a few suggestions. You can use them as inspiration or use each as an exercise to fill a day until more personalized things come to mind. At first, doing any of these will feel super uncomfortable. You will have to immediately confront your fears, conscience, imagination, and all the voices in your head that tell you that you are being weird, self-indulgent, and all the other bullshit that swirls around in there. I encourage you to keep going, to push through. There's a wonderful world on the other side.

Experience minimalism

Minimalism is the logical response to a culture of maximal consumption. The minimalism movement is gaining ground in our popular culture, a complement to slow food, for example, and all things *slow*. For me, the first act of living in a new way was to clean out my apartment. (Thanks, Marie Kondo and the Minimalists.) Creating a clean, well-ordered space for myself to be in the dark well helped immensely. And my sock drawer never looked better. What minimalism gives us is less: less to manage, less to process and worry about, less to clean, less to give a single fuck about. (Thanks, Sarah Knight.) In many ways, unsubscription is a call for minimalism, too. Just get rid of all the crap that gets in the way of living a satisfying and meaningful life. Being oversubscribed is what gives us too much to manage, process, worry about, clean, and care about. Hopefully, what you take away from this book is that minimalism on your screen, in your inbox, in your social circles, and in your brain and heart are a pathway to a more satisfying and meaningful life.

Read a printed newspaper

I know what you're thinking: *You just told me to unsubscribe from Big Media.* And therein lies my point. Big Media is not journalism. Twitter is not the newspaper. A newspaper, in its purest form, is curated, edited information, and at this rate, the purest form of newspaper you'll get is your local one. Read it. Reading occupies both of your hands, so you can do nothing else but focus. It reminds us of the power of editorial—someone chose this story because it is important. And it even reconnects us to paper, which came from a tree. (You may call that crunchy bullshit, but if we are going to solve our climate crisis, it might be helpful for all of us to value trees again. Newspapers are not causing climate change.) Reading also consolidates "the news" in one time and space. It doesn't update every millisecond. It slows the pace of your consumption and allows you the time to digest before the next issue hits your doorstep in the morning. Read it, get up to date, then get on with life.

Run and walk

I continue to be astounded by the benefits of walking. It is a practice I started in my dark well and then carried through into my life after. Walking without electronics—nothing in your ear, nothing in your hand, nothing pinging and ringing—is an opportunity to think about the questions that arise in life when you unsubscribe. Or you can do a walking meditation. You may start to notice things you haven't before: the person singing an aria out their window (is that Brian Stokes Mitchell?) or the new display in the window of the store down the street. A simple walk (or a run, if you're feeling ambitious) reconnects you to your local world, to the people who inhabit it, and it reminds you that a healthy life should only move at the very pace your legs can take it. You don't need a gym membership; you just need yourself.

Care for everything in your home

What I found most remarkable when I cleaned out my apartment was that having access to the objects (and clothes, appliances, papers, etc.) that I loved—sitting with them, looking at them, actually using them—made me want to clean them, polish them up, fix them, and bring some of them back to life. The act of caring for your belongings can be revolutionary in a world that tells you to throw them out and buy something new the moment something goes wrong. It also gives you a place to direct your energy and love while you're unsubscribed. If you are a gardener, you know the great value of growing food, plants, and caring for living things. We can garden everything, living or not.

Work with a therapist or coach

Despite having come from a family and culture that believes therapy is for crazy people, I have worked with both therapists and life coaches for over twenty years, and I firmly believe I am a better and healthier person for it. Our mental health is as important as our physical health, especially in this modern world. Working with trained professionals can help you navigate the dark well, well . . . well. They provide accountability and feedback as you ask and answer some of the questions that present themselves when you unsubscribe. And they can help you contextualize the emotions that arise. If a therapist is not immediately available or is an impossibility, start to do the work you can where you are: document your thoughts, journal your feelings, the goings-on in your life. Read books about behavior and psychology. Look at your own patterns. Do a people audit. Think about what you would want to focus on, were you to seek guidance from a professional.

Resensitize yourself to money

Just as slow banking can wake us back up to how we spend our money, where it goes, and just how fast it flies out of our checking account in a digital economy, touching cash can be a profound reminder of the value of money. You'll think I'm nuts, but in the dark well, I ironed my cash. At first, admittedly, I did it because I thought it would kill any coronavirus on the bills. (And also because I am a compulsive ironer.) But then, I kept doing it for a few weeks after, because I enjoyed having crisp dollars in my wallet. It made me pay attention. It made me less likely to spend it on something frivolous. And it made me much more aware of what I could and could not buy with a crisp, green Andrew Jackson. (I also spent one evening reading about Andrew Jackson, because I figured if I was carrying him around all day, I should at least understand what he'd done to get himself a spot on our currency. That conversation is for another day.)

Talk to strangers

You need not actually spend this period alone. The only people you need to hold off on communicating with are the people in your parking lot or those to whom you don't have an immediate obligation. Everyone else is fair—and encouraged—game. Take the opportunity to talk to the people you may not normally exchange more than a greeting with—the grocery checkout guy, the woman at the bank, the dry cleaner, the person who sells you your newspaper, your coffee, or shines the shoes you just found when you cleaned out the closet. Click-up economics keeps us talking to, interacting with, and engaging with people we already know, our face glued to our phone, and our ears plugged with headphones. Most of the algorithms that run our lives now are not designed to foster empathy, and it's hard to cultivate that (or belonging) when we only ever talk to people with whom we have the most in common. Pluralist societies—those in which multiple groups coexist—require an ability to see the world through someone else's eyes. Without divergent experiences that shift us out of our bubbles, nothing changes. And you won't get a sense of the pure possibility of those divergent experiences unless you expose yourself to newness whenever you can.

Cook your food

Despite my Italian heritage, I hate cooking. That's what the little voice in me said when I finally listened and admitted it, and so I tried my best to honor that truth. I don't like spending time putting recipes together and bending over a hot stove, but I do see the value in going to the grocery store, sourcing your daily bread and juice, and preparing a meal for yourself or your family. If you're like, hey, *I cook every night for my kids*, then switch it up in the dark well. Go out, order in, and give yourself time out of the kitchen. (Or, if the kids are old enough, have them help.)

• • •

The most important work you can do in the dark well is to *rewrite your sticky stories.* Remember that list you made as you were locating and identifying your underlying subscriptions? Revisit it. Sit with it. Think about how these beliefs have affected your life, for better or for worse. Are they affecting your health? Your love life? Your finances? Your career? Are they limiting you? Do they have you convinced of "truths" about yourself that you know, in your heart of hearts, are simply untrue and counter to your very nature?

Look closely at the ones that are most obviously disempowering you: For example, *life is a prison. I am trapped in that prison.* Now, take the disempowering belief and flip it, reverse it, rewrite it in an empowering way. How do you know the difference? Empowering ideas give you power instead of taking it away. They inspire you. They light you up. They get you out of bed. They give you energy. They give you peace. They calm you. They are based on the core truth of who you are as a loving, honest, joyful human. They also give and extend that power, peace, light, and energy to people around you. *Life is not a prison. I am not trapped in that prison.* Or even better: *Life is a playground. I am free to explore that playground.*

Consider doing this in thirteen areas:

Health	Romance
Finances	Family
Intellectual	Extended Family
Spiritual	Friends
Play	Community
Career	Supercommunity
Space	

This list is synthesized from a few sources. It comes from a life-coaching "life wheel" used by any number of coaches, gurus, and personal success cheerleaders. It comes from the eight different kinds of love that the ancient Greeks taught. And it comes from the very social circles that I outlined earlier. (See the Resources section at the back of this book for more information, if you'd like to download a worksheet to help.)

As you rewrite your beliefs in each, pay attention to your tendency to limit yourself. We all do it. Resist. There is no right answer. This is not an assignment. No one is grading you, and no one else ever needs to see it. Make these right for you. Make sure they represent your inner truth, your inner voice, your authentic self (all the buzzwords). Your limits keep you in your comfort zone. To help, I offer you examples from my own life, one from each area (in no particular order).

Health

I am human with a finite life span. I have to be good to my body if I want it to last. This replaced my old notion that *I am young, healthy, and invincible. Other people get sick, not me.*

Finances

I am worth more than any amount of money can ever reflect. I am worthy of love and all good things in my life because I am a good man. This replaced my old notion that *my only worth is financial. If I don't make millions and billions of dollars, my life is not worth anything.*

Intellectual

Learning continues well after our formal education. It is a lifelong pursuit that expands the mind and keeps us sharp. This replaced my old notion that *whatever I got from my schooling is what I get to build a life on. My degree is everything. I have to use it. Taking a class as an adult means you are unclear about your career path.*

Spiritual

God is everywhere and in everything. God is loving and good and wants the best for me. This replaced my old notion that *God is this angry man in Heaven who watches me constantly so he can punish me if I step out of line.*

Play

Play is for everyone. It's a necessary part of restoring our energy, creativity, and love. This replaced my old notion that *play is for kids. Work is for adults.*

Career

I can work in multiple creative forms and arenas. They feed each other. The only limits that exist are in my head. This replaced my old notion that *professional success only comes if you prove you can do what everybody else does.*

Space

I have all I need. I don't need anything more than this apartment. And a fucking dishwasher. (I'm still working on this one.)

Romance

I am worthy of love and ready to love in a healthy partnership. The right partner adds to my joy and success. This replaced my old notion that *I am not worthy of love until every part of my life and body is perfect. Partners get in the way of success. They drag you down. It is one or the other. Marriage is a toxic battleground that will wound you forever.*

Family

Family is a source of endless joy. I want one. These replaced my old notions that *family is a source of stress and anxiety. I'm fine single.*

Extended family

Family provides boundless love. I can totally be myself when I am with my family. Also, I am strong enough to maintain healthy boundaries with my family. It means we are modeling healthy behaviors to each other. These replaced my old notions that *family provides conditional love. I have to follow the rules to be loved. Boundaries are not for family; they are for outsiders. Boundaries mean I don't love my family.*

Friends

Friendship supports, uplifts, and challenges me. It extends my joy. My real friends love me just the way I am. They require no performance. This replaced my old notion that *people only like me because I am funny, entertaining, and please them. Friendships are a proving ground for how special I am. Friendship is a quest for validation and approval from the whole world.*

Community

The world is full of good people. Time in the local community around me is important and can be exciting. This replaced my old notion that *online communities are the only, real, and right way to work with people for a better world. This is the future!*

Supercommunity

The world is full of good people. I can connect with them in specific and structured ways to improve our collective conditions and improve the world. This replaced my old notion that *the world is a mess, filled with complete assholes. The point of having access to all of them is to scream at them.*

Even now, I am exhausted reading the old ideas, beliefs, and notions that ran my life and controlled my behavior. And now that I have some distance, it's much clearer how they came to be. (I could probably write a book about each one of those and when and how I subscribed to them.)

Everything Everywhere All at Once is an incredible 2022 film, nominated for eleven Oscars, winner of seven. Directed by Daniel Kwan and Daniel Scheinert, starring Michelle Yeoh, Stephanie Hsu, and Jamie Lee Curtis, the movie centers on Joy Wang, the owner of a laundromat, who channels her newfound supernatural powers as she travels the multiverse of her life. (The theory of the multiverse, for those who may not know, is that outside of our observable existence, there are many, many more. Think: alternate universe or parallel lives.) Along the way, she rediscovers her relationships to her daughter, her husband, and herself. Story aside, the movie is powerful because it literally uses (and creates) chaos on screen as a visual metaphor for the chaos the protagonist feels inside her heart and brain. For an audience in a movie theater, it is almost dizzying. But when it stops, when the chaos of the action ceases, Joy (that's her name on purpose, I imagine) is resensitized to the beauty of her life, understanding the beauty in a life of "laundry and taxes." In turn, the film itself resensitizes the audience to human emotion.

That is what all this is for. No matter how many lists you make, how many recipes you cook or books you read or days you spend walking outside in the beautiful light of day, the very best way to spend your time in the dark well is simply to resensitize yourself to your own life. Our lives have been swept up in a digital tornado for the last two decades. It is constant chaos. It is relentless. It is loud and needy. It is poking and prodding. It is invasive and intrusive and unapologetic. It is designed that way so that, no, you never get a break. You must take that break. Unsubscribe. Breathe. Resensitize yourself to your living space, your body, your money, your loved ones. And give deep thought to what it is that you truly believe.

Why should you do any of this? Because we need you. We need your talents, your brain, your heart, your love. We need your collaboration and ideas and partnership. And if you and I never shake hands, there are people around you who need you: your partner, lover, wife, whatever you call your significant one (or ones), your kids, your family, your neighbors, your friends, your town. Sure, if what you came to in the dark well is that you would rather tell us all to go fuck off, well, that is your call. But I don't believe that any of us is wired for solitude, even the introverts among us. We are all on this train together. No one is meant to live outside the tribe, even if the modern world has made that a very viable and seamless option. We are wired for cooperation. We are wired to share our best. And those around you need the very best of you.

How do I know the dark well so well? Well, I had some practice earlier in my life. The dark well is not a new place, created by a post-circus world. It's where you end up whenever you make the choice to unsubscribe. As I mentioned in our chapter about sticky stories, I went through a period in my life that required major unsubscribing, when I was nineteen years old and decided to come out of the closet.

I do realize that, at this point in the world and in media, and in this very book, a coming-out story does not break much ground. But I want to tell you about it, because it might demonstrate that sometimes you don't need an earth-shattering, generation-defining, worldwide circus to make you realize that things need to change. Sometimes, it's just you.

First thing you have to know: I was a really gay teen (I have the pictures to prove it), and the last person to realize it. Not only did I perm my hair at twelve so that I could look like Kirk Cameron from *Growing Pains*, but I was also madly in love with both a boy at school and the sixth-grade substitute teacher who was teaching us pre-algebra. Middle school and high school were a constant emotional struggle as I pretended to be even remotely interested in *Playboy*, forced myself to learn how to spit (a strange 1990s affectation that signaled to everyone around you that you were "macho," like the WWF star Randy "Macho Man" Savage), and awkwardly added the word *man* to every sentence out of my mouth—*Man, I hate school. Man, I need to get a job. Man, I am such a man*—just to really hammer it home.

Six years later, a male college classmate kissed me, angels sang, and the world was never the same. As I came out, I had to wrestle with very intimate and deep-seated ideas, beliefs, and notions about identity, sexuality, love, attraction, desire, and God—*Gay people are weird. Gay people are sick. There is something wrong with gay people*— and push through anxieties like *My friends won't want to hang out with me. I will never have friends. I will never get married. I won't ever have children.* Even worse, *I am not worthy of love. I don't deserve a relationship. Gay people can't have healthy relationships. I am going to die of AIDS.* Yes, this is what the '80s did to all of us.

Without doing it consciously—or writing a book about it—I had to unsubscribe from all of it. *Hustler* and *Penthouse*, magazines with big-busted centerfolds (I just did not understand everyone's obsession with Cindy Crawford) and outings with the guys to the women's college to pick up girls? No more. Friendships with colleagues who thought I should be quiet about my sexuality? No more. All of the rituals, customs, and traditions that nineteen-year-olds engage in constantly to impress girls and court wives and sex partners—not to mention old-school Catholic, Italian, and Italian American ideas, beliefs, and notions that you are going to hell if you lay with another man? Good-bye. Pretending that I gave a single fuck about the World Series? Absolutely never again.

Once I came out to my family, I lived in the dark well for months. It was painful. I lost friends. I lost the support of some family members. I was lonely and scared. But I had to sit in that dark well until I could find new and empowering sources of love, validation, and friendship, and until I could explore enough to subscribe to new ideas, notions, and beliefs about who I was in the world. Because I had declared my being queer publicly, I had burned the boats. There was no going back. (This is why I will forever advocate that, yes, as long as we live in a society that praises conformity and strict gender roles, there is a reason to publicly "come out." To say that you are different and that you unsubscribe from a whole set of beliefs and practices is powerful.)

While there was joy in my liberation, it was the most frightening experience of my life. It would be years before I would feel safe again, but when I did, it was a whole new life. I went from living a life that was inauthentic and on autopilot to one that is genuine and conscious and alive. That shift could not have occurred in earnest without a void—a sacred space—in between *who I was* and *who I am.*

It also required deep mourning. You cannot renew your life until you properly mourn that which is forever gone or that which will now never be. I had to mourn the pristine image I had of what my life was going to be like as a happily married man with a wife and kids. And my parents and sisters had to mourn the same. (Yes, I can have children if I want to, but in the late '90s that was not something one might imagine.)

(Before it even enters anyone's mind or blog review: no, I am not suggesting that you and every other reader "go gay," as my dad would say. I am suggesting that transformation—real transformation—is only possible when we peel back the layers of our life and dig deeper than the relentless modern world allows us to dig, and when we challenge the underlying subscriptions that make up our identity, as individuals and as a people. If we want to change "the system" or "dismantle" it, we would be well served to dismantle, reevaluate, and rebuild the architecture of our own lives first, so that our calls for change in the greater society come from a place of experience and of wellness. We cannot effect systemic change, at any level, until we effect it around ourselves, in our own personal systems. Only then can we endeavor to extend that change circle by circle.)

During the circus, trapped at home alone, I realized that I hadn't done the mourning. Quite literally. Since I stepped on the treadmill of "go to Hollywood and become a rich and famous director," I hadn't stopped to mourn each of my three grandparents who had died along the way. I hadn't stopped to mourn my first boyfriend, whose kiss had freed me and forever changed my life; he died at thirty-nine. I hadn't stopped to mourn my professional mentor, who became a "mom" of sorts to me as I entered the professional world, and whose guidance and love restored my confidence after I came out; she died at fifty-six. I hadn't stopped to mourn my first boss in Los Angeles, who taught me about growth and patience and friendship and transformation; he died at forty-four. Nor had I stopped to mourn a very special old boyfriend, truly the kindest man I had met in my life thus far; he died at thirty-six.

As New York City was losing a thousand people a day, it was impossible not to recognize the mourning I hadn't done before COVID hit. It is no cosmic mistake that a year into the crisis, I had the chance to be with my last remaining grandmother on her death-bed. I took it. As painful as it was to be in that room, I sat vigil with my family as Grandma Margie died at home, at ninety-six. I held her hand as she took her last breath. And I said good-bye not only to her but also to an entire chapter of life.

The dark well will include mourning of some sort. It may not be the mourning of actual people. It is more likely that what you will lay to rest is who you used to be and what you used to believe about yourself and about the world. Breaking out of the infinite loop—in the world, in our circles, and in ourselves—requires a breaking. In that breaking, promises might shatter. Our own personal systems might fail. And our sticky stories might die. And that's okay. Sometimes the only way to truly live is to let go of the story of your life. Or the stories that make up your perspective on your life.

The dark well is also likely to include opportunities for forgiveness. It offered me that, and I hope that it can do the same for you. Doing some of this "work" prior to the circus, I had learned to forgive my father for much of the chaos of our childhood. Truly forgive. Because of that, I had convinced myself that I fully understood forgiveness, as a concept and as an act of love. And then I met a woman named Sarah Montana. Sarah is a writer here in New York. Both her mother and her brother were murdered—yes, *murdered*—by a neighbor, when Sarah was twenty-two. She gave a talk in 2019 in which she shared this with the world. ("They" refers to the three main characters in the story of what happened: her mother, her brother, and the neighbor.)

> They were characters, just offstage, waiting in the wings, the rest of us on stage, talking about them. But my story was about the three of them, always. To get free, I had to get clear on exactly what contract I was shredding. Once I did that, I found myself alone, center stage, in the spotlight, with endless possibilities. Real forgiveness has to let go of all expectations. You can't expect a certain outcome. You can't expect them to reply. You can't even expect to know who you're going to be on the other side of it. Forgiveness is really tricky. It's one of those tools that is only properly wielded when we have healed just enough that we have nothing left to lose.

Not only did her talk make a puddle of me (holy shit), but I continue to see in her talk confirmation of the importance of shredding the contracts we have written in our brains and in our hearts. Very often, you cannot get to forgiveness until you have unsubscribed from the nasty stories that keep you trapped emotionally. Forgiveness quiets the torture of the soul.

That's a lot. Truly. When you feel ready, when you have done your mourning and your thinking and your feeling, get up, get moving, and get out. I know I had to, at some point. In my experience, you will know when is enough and when it is time to remount the horse of it all. It might be scary, to reemerge into a world where you won't control the conditions, where you may be tempted to go back on autopilot and submit to the Big Forces, but just take a deep breath. You have the tools, the patience, and the grit to move into this next phase.

It is time for renewal. The sun is shining. It is time to shake off the slumber and wake up. Good morning.

PART FOUR

Renewal

What Is and Is Not on the Other Side

Thirteen

You and I

Adele said it best, "Hello from the other side." Renewal, like unsubscribing, is an active process. It begins when you emerge from the dark well, armed with a new perspective on how you'd like your life to look, feel, and *be*, and the tools to maintain that new existence. And it continues through the rest of our lives. This renewal is a renewal of life and living. As individuals and as a society, we are always starving for something better. If we have any hope or expectation that we can create it together, we must first create it for ourselves—every one of us. Like with everything else so far, you are in the driver's seat.

To be clear: when I say "renewal," I do not mean "starting a cycle over." In our society, the word *renew* has come to mean just that: *sign up again*. Its etymology reveals a subtlety well worth pointing out. The word's original meaning was closer to "bring newness again." To what is barren, bring fullness. To what is dry, bring water. To what is dead, bring life. Funny enough, the icons we use in our society for renewal (see figure 12) only reinforce that blurriness. Renewal is not simply starting a cycle over, as these icons would have us believe. Instead, I propose we use a different icon to mean renewal (see figure 13). Yep, these all look like flowers. That's not a coincidence.

There are two types of renewal that are worth considering and engaging with in practice: *individual* and *collective*. Let's first look at individual renewal—how you and I use what we have learned from unsubscribing and from our experience of the dark well to transform

FIGURE 12
Renewal Icons

FIGURE 13
Better Renewal Symbols

our lives. Then, in chapter 16, we'll look at how we can apply the same process to effect a collective renewal—a renewal of our collective beliefs and behaviors.

At the personal level, renewal is a new state of being in which, quite simply, you love your life. You are happy, instead of feeling that you have to constantly pursue happiness in the relentless noise of the Big Forces. The best way to kick it off, I've found, is reversing the process that got us into this conversation in the first place: start inside at the core and move outward, adding back ring after ring intentionally and with great care in order to create real balance (see figure 14).

We start with new core ideas, notions, and beliefs—new *underlying subscriptions*—and we communicate them, privately and publicly, to the circles that matter most to us, and/or to the circles that subscribed us to an old version of these ideas in the first place. That is *key*: communication. We have to break the contract and resubscribe to a new one or revise the terms of the emotional contract that is dictating our behaviors. Then, we go out and *live* these new underlying subscriptions

FIGURE 14

Renewal. Layer it back with intention and great care.

New *Underlying
Subscriptions*

Revived and New
People Subscriptions

Purposeful and Valuable
Surface Subscriptions

New Balance

by making them the cornerstone of our new life, choosing new activities and goals, and choosing to spend our time, attention, energy, and focus on people and circles who can support them (i.e., making new or reviving our *people subscriptions*). Later, if we want, we can resubscribe to some of the *surface subscriptions*, if and only if we truly feel there are tech, brands, banks, media, and parties that align and can support our renewal (see chapter 14). In effect, we build a new life—inside-out—that supports, celebrates, and makes manifest our wellness.

Or, if you really like concrete steps:

Steps for Renewal

1. Question your *underlying subscriptions,* your ideas, beliefs, and notions.
2. Rewrite them so you have new empowering ideas, beliefs, and notions.
3. Communicate these privately and publicly to related people and circles.
4. Make them the cornerstone for a new life. Fill that new life with revived and new *people subscriptions* that support and align with these new ideas, beliefs, and notions.
5. Consider resubscribing to some valuable *surface subscriptions*, in limited and structured ways, if and only if they align with your renewal.

Most pop psychology can help us understand and do number 1. Maybe it can get us to number 2. But that's where it all tends to stop (posting "I'm a good human being" on a yellow Post-it note on my bathroom mirror and reading it every morning is probably not going to change my life). I hope this process of unsubscription and renewal takes you and us further. This is values-based living.

Intention-forward living. Living inside-out. Living consciously. Call it whatever you want or don't want, but don't miss the point. You are a critical component, because you have to define your values according to what matters to *you*, and then *you* have to commit to them and live them in *your* life.

Let's go step by step.

In the dark well, we wrote our new set of ideas, notions, and beliefs. Now it's time to communicate them and have some hard conversations. Why are they hard? Because we have spent our lives in infinite loops that revolve around and reinforce our old beliefs about ourselves. When you sit people down and tell them otherwise, it can be very unsettling.

The hard conversations are your chance to communicate your new stories to your smallest circles. Why is this helpful? Because you do not exist in a vacuum. The very act of living—and living well— will always include at least one other person, if not tens or hundreds. We cannot experience deep personal change without renegotiating and communicating with others, especially those who matter most to us or with whom we made the original emotional contract. Subscriptions, after all, require two entities to make an agreement, even if that agreement is about *who you are*.

For me, renewal began like this: during my time in the dark well, I had rewritten several old beliefs about how I measured my own value. The new ones: *I am worth more than any amount of money can ever reflect. I am worthy of love and all good things in my life because I am a good man.* I chose to subscribe to this new story and was doing well with it on my own. But to "manifest" it in my life (to make it real), I had to physically say it to the people I loved and then to the rest of the world. I had to go out and *live that subscription.*

What did that look like? I sat my immediate family down (my

father, mother, and two sisters—the original clan before our parents' divorce) and said these words: "My whole adult life I have believed that my only worth is financial, that if I don't make millions of dollars, my life is not worth anything. I can't live like that. I no longer believe that. I am worth more than any amount of money can ever reflect. I am worthy of love and all good things in my life because I am a good man."

You said that? Yes. And let me tell you: it was not easy. In fact, it was a nearly impossible conversation. My body fought me. My lips could barely get the words out. (Working-class kids do not go to Harvard then say shit like this. Or so I used to think.) Hard conversations take physical energy because they actually *require* it; they call on our bodies to make new shapes and use new muscles. Being vulnerable like this triggered all sorts of deep feelings in everyone at the table about salaries, money, business, risk, credit scores, the purpose of education, wealth and class, why I even went to private school, college, and graduate school. I had taken a core value that was buried deep in me, put it out on the table, and burned it in front of those who matter most to me.

And then, something really incredible happened. The conversation, the response, turned into something loving. One sister teared up as I did. The other grabbed me in a full embrace. As did my parents. My family could hardly believe that I had been carrying that sticky story around for so long. We talked. And talked. And together, they helped calm me. This is the beginning of renewal. Is it messy? Sometimes. Is it sappy? Sometimes. Is it life-changing? All the time. (Of course, they had one last question: "Is this what your book is about?" Um, yep. It, like, *is* the book.)

Once that conversation was over, I had it again, this time with my fiancé. (Yes, he is in a smaller circle than my family. Why didn't I choose to start with him? He's only been in my life for a couple of years. This shit was *decades* old. I had to clear it out first with the people who had been there all along my journey. Then, I could discuss it with him.) That discussion was a supreme nonevent. One of the reasons I proposed marriage to this man is that he sees my worth. And I see his. No bullshit necessary.

Once I did that, I then moved wider—circle by circle—to further communicate this and some of my other new beliefs to the people who mattered the most in my life—sometimes formally, sometimes casually. I chose to physically speak with the smallest circles. For the larger ones, I simply started living differently. And writing publicly about these ideas. And speaking publicly about them. There are no hard-and-fast rules here. You do you. I recommend the hard conversations. They can forever renew you. In those, your goal should only ever be this: just get the words out. Do it with love, yes—don't be an asshole (the world has enough of them)—but just get the words out. Don't worry about what you look like, sound like, how you're sitting, or what the response will be. (In the end, as much as you might hate to admit it, you cannot control the response.)

One practical matter. *What if the person who most reinforced one of my underlying subscriptions is no longer with us? What if I made a promise to them about who I am, but now they are long gone?* Write them a note. Say what you have to say. And put that note in the back of this book on your bookshelf. Or create some other meaningful ritual for yourself that will help you move forward.

With the hard conversations out of the way, we now can double down and make our new *underlying subscriptions* the cornerstone for our new life. What does that mean? *Do I have to move? Do I change my name? Do I shave my head?* No, no, and please don't. Simply fill your life with people and groups (and places and activities) that support and align with these new promises that you have made to yourself. Take advantage of a clear calendar and an empty inbox (I know that's still a pipe dream for a lot of us, but stay with me), and use that space to fill your life with a job, a romantic partner(s), friends, family, books, dinner dates, anything else that reflects this new value system you have created.

You can jump in or go slow, but stay present enough to keep asking yourself this test question: *Does what I am doing right now (or what I have on the calendar tomorrow) support, strengthen, deepen, and amplify what I identified in the dark well as my true values, my ideas, beliefs, and notions about myself and about the world around me?* If the answer is yes, keep going. Think about Nietzsche again. Is this something I would choose over and over again?

If the answer is no, stop right now. Identify where you can do even more unsubscribing.

In my own life, for example, I am now committed to the belief that *gay people are incredible. Gay people are healthy. There is something special about gay people.* I had to unsubscribe from a lot of bullshit to get to this place, and what I have been left with, through that space and additional growth, is the notion that *I will have children when and if I want them. It is okay to have new friendships that reflect where I am now in my life.* Even further, *I am worthy of love.* To get there, I had to commit to relationships with people who believed those things, too, and whose values aligned with mine. I had to take myself out of environments that were disempowering and dispiriting—including, for me, some larger Hollywood circles that endlessly reinforced the idea that *your worth as an artist is measured by the size of your house, what car you drive, or how many people follow you on Instagram.* And I had to stop dating people who would not let me love them. The people in my life now help me to reinforce the empowering beliefs I now have about myself, allow me the time and space to prove them out, and support me in creating a life that is rooted in these beliefs. That effort was not easy or frictionless. It has been long (because I resisted for *so long*) and lonely (because the dark well sucks) and uncomfortable (because it exposed every wound that

I had carried for the last forty years). It was full of discomfort, displeasure, disappointment, disapproval, and disgust. I had to ask to see the manager. The manager was me.

The truth is that if you set out to build a new life, designed around these beliefs, you won't have the space for the bullshit that you used to put up with. There just isn't room for it. You'll also fine-tune your bullshit meter—that little voice in your head that says, *Hello, this is not working for us. No more of this crap, this humbug, this malarkey, this balderdash, claptrap, hokum, drivel, buncombe, imposture, and quackery.*

Here are some important reminders as you engage in renewal.

Make It Really Actionable

One helpful practice I have employed is printing a set of "Ground Rules" or "House Rules." I post them in my kitchen. And I update them every few months or so. For example, *Go for a walk, even a short one, every day.* That is an actionable behavior that supports my new belief that *I am human. I have to be good to my body if I want it to last.* As it turns out, it also winds up supporting other beliefs: *Time spent with others locally is important and exciting. God is everywhere and in everything. Learning does not stop after our formal education.* No, I do not walk around Manhattan telling local merchants, "Time with you is important and exciting." But I have found great joy in new behaviors that support my actual values, instead of, say, walking on a treadmill at Equinox and feeling bad for an hour that I don't have a six-pack. This is living from your personal foundation up, rooted and solid, instead of swimming in the surface bullshit and never going deep.

You Don't Need to Perform Change

Renewal is not about proving to the world that you are changing. It's not a new haircut or new clothes or a new car (if you've made it this far in the book, I hope you now realize who and what wants you to think that it is). You may choose those things into your life as you become aware of new needs, wants, and joys. But change doesn't need to be performed. It needs to be communicated. Those are different. You will feel the change. And so will those around you. Choose hard conversations and moments of vulnerability over moments of performance. And don't buy more shit to show the world that you have changed. That is literally the opposite of what I am advocating. As a wise and pretty popular man once said, "You will know a tree by its fruit."

Renewal Requires Action with Others

You are not an island. You are not a self-help sticky note. You can never make change with a mantra or a hashtag alone. You exist in a society. This is why you are the center of a larger dartboard. This is why behavioral therapists recommend replacement behaviors to take the place of old habits, and why addiction specialists recommend you socialize with other people who want to end their addictive behavior. You must make commitments that empower you and reconnect you to circles that don't just accept your wellness but *magnify* it. Can you do that over the Internet? Sure, if it helps to kick-start or support you. But in the end, nothing is more powerful than taking action in the society immediately around you—in your closest circles—physically.

Make Short-Term Commitments

As you renew, make short-term commitments and block out time for reflection. Take it slow. Set benchmarks and check yourself. Resist annual and lifelong contracts for a while. Do nothing for more than three months, then breathe and recommit forward for another three months. (Or whatever period you deem helpful to you.) Check in with yourself from time to time. See if those new commitments are serving you or not and adjust accordingly. Nothing is permanent. These "rules" are yours to craft.

Be Patient

Remember, new ideas, notions, and beliefs take time to reinforce, to manifest, and to make an impact on our behavior. They are up against twenty, thirty, forty, fifty years of habit, after all, not to mention two hundred, three hundred, four hundred years of collective patterns. As much as the circus showed us how fast change *can* happen, it truly was a unique moment. And as much as I have presented unsubscribing and renewal as a process, it is more accurately and importantly a practice. Keep repeating. Keep discussing, questioning, challenging. Keep exploring. Keep discovering. Keep calling out your renewal publicly. Watch your words; they matter. Be kind. The world needs kindness right now. Not Care Bears kindness, actual real fucking kindness. I see you and honor you, and you see me and honor me, because we are both human beings living on this planet together and we have to make this work.

Before we move forward, I want to address people and circles specifically. Over the course of my renewal, I struggled a lot with how to choose who got to come back into my life. In the end, the question to ask is this one: *Who supports my joy?* In my darkest moments over the last few years, I worked with a brilliant therapist who very astutely said these four words: *Run to the love.*

Because my life before forty had taken me to so many different (and intimidating) environments and communities around the country, I had developed a habit of seeking out those who questioned my presence in those environments and spending endless energy proving to them that I belonged. I didn't do it consciously.

I was on autopilot. The people around me were always a mix of two groups: those I genuinely wanted to spend time with and those whose presence helped me support that very disempowering notion. *Run to the love* helped me shift the focus of my energy by challenging me to focus actively on the former group: the people I loved (no strings) and who loved me. No endless quest to prove my worth.

This, of course, crystalized in the dark well. I knew I had incredible people in my life. They had just been lost in the crowd. I couldn't see them or hear them in the overwhelming noise of my life. I totally lost the thread. I also discovered, quite painfully, that the noise was covering up what was missing most: a partner and a family of my own. Look, some people are fully fulfilled single. I am just not one of them. After ten years of being single, I had perfected the relentlessness to avoid what it really felt like to be alone. The dark well forced me to confront it. I realized that I wanted to run to the love.

Look back at that list of people that you circled in chapter 8. These are the people to bring back. For me, I started with the people who delighted me, who I could not *wait* to see. I wanted to spend time—actual human time, not text time, screen time, Zoom time, or even phone time—with them. I called them on the phone. I set a date. I recommitted to quality interactions.

Billy Baker, an author and writer for the *Boston Globe*, wrote about another way to do this. In his book *We Need to Hang Out: A Memoir of Making Friends*, Baker explains that after quitting social media, maintaining relationships with his male friends meant finding ways to spend time with them doing what he called "stupid" stuff: treasure hunts and high-school-style Skip Days, even a '90s cruise. I don't know Billy, but I love his version of running to the love. He chose to make *play* an integral part of the process as he actively brought people back into his life. He had to get off autopilot, disrupt his day-to-day routines, and make a point to spend time with the people he really enjoyed. And he decided to do it in *fun* ways that fostered childlike joy and reminded him why these had been his friends in the first place.

I think we all came to some version of that realization during the circus: Oh shit, *these* are the people who matter. These are the people I have been missing because I am so busy. These are the people I need and *want* in my life.

My brother-in-law had a very similar experience—one that I would wager to say reflects a lot of people's life-changing epiphanies. Phil is a forty-two-year-old software salesman. He was the first in his family, like I was, to get a college education and cross over from the back-breaking labor of the working trades to the skyscraping buildings of New York City office life. Phil likes his work. And he loves his family. But like millions of others in the tri-state area, a hellish commute was keeping him from truly enjoying both. Phil has three boys. As his family grew, a four-bedroom house with a yard was no longer affordable in any area with a reasonable commute to Midtown Manhattan. So, for the last fifteen years, Phil has commuted one hour and forty-five minutes, each way, via "express bus." (Trust me, I've done it, there is nothing express about it.) If you do the math, which I always like to do, that's 910 hours a year on a bus. Thirty-seven days. More than a month spent, every year, commuting. As my nephews got older, Phil was not only missing dinner but also soccer games, football games, parent-teacher conferences. Then the circus hit.

Luckily, Phil was able to keep his job and work from his basement office. These years have given him a new perspective. His time at home—reconnecting with my sister and his boys, coaching their teams, volunteering for the boys' lacrosse association, eating family meals together, having the energy left at the end of the day to watch a movie with his wife—made one thing very clear: he would not go back to his old life. A five-day commute was costing too much. He was able to unsubscribe from the belief that *time away from the people who matter most is worth it if the money I make supports them.* Now, with the experience of these last years, he subscribes to a new belief, one he is very vocal about: *Being there for my family comes first. Period.*

Phil is fortunate that technology affords him the chance to still do his job without the horrendous bus commute. That may change. But if and when it does, he knows he will have to give great consideration to going back to the way things were. He understands the trade-offs now, deep in his bones. No matter the circle, whether it is your family, your neighborhood, or your friends from college, what is important is that the people around you (and on your screen) are a reflection of your wellness. Run to that love. Prioritize that love. Add to and be part of that love. It may not always be easy. It may not come without many moles popping up that you'll want and need to whack. But your happiness is at stake. For real.

Lastly, it is important to clarify one very critical element of this conversation. The effort to bring our world in alignment with our values is not meant for us to ever socialize or interact only with people who *agree with us*. Their beliefs need not mirror ours, but they also need not constantly nor violently counter them. There is a significant distinction to be drawn between agreement and alignment—a nuance click-up economics has steamrolled over. Alignment is a state of peaceful coexistence. It is the best we can do as a society of very emotional, messy humans. It allows us to have plenty of relationships with those who look at the world very differently. Turns out, when we are empowered and stand confidently in our beliefs, others become way less of a threat to our peace and calm. We don't have to agree with everyone, but we can endeavor to align. That alignment must be the basis of our collective renewal. Without it, we're fucked.

Fourteen

To Resubscribe or Not to Resubscribe

The process of individual renewal will inevitably lead you back to the outermost ring, to the surface bullshit you read this whole book to escape in the first place. What commitments do you want to make in your life—either physically or digitally—that support the beliefs and values you have reconnected to or discovered? If this next phase of life is meant to be a true renewal and is meant to demonstrate those values, how do you *design* your day-to-day? You are the architect. How do you earn a living? How do you get the news? What do you eat? Where do you shop? Which subscriptions are going to keep the bullshit at bay and let you just *be* happy? And which lead you right back to where we started? The relentlessness is never that far away. And there are plenty of people and forces more than happy for you to get right back into the infinite loop.

For me, I challenged myself to root any new subscriptions directly in the new ideas and beliefs that I had spent so much time reconstructing, to ensure they aligned from the start. Here's what it all looks like now. I offer it in case it is helpful.

Health
I am human. I have to be good to my body if I want it to last. I walk in the park in the mornings and resubscribed to a very basic (local, inexpensive) gym for the fall and winter—one that offers month-to-month commitments. Then, I unsubscribe for the spring and

summer and go back to running outside. I want a healthy body, so I eat only foods my great-grandmother would recognize as actual food—a suggestion I took from author Michael Pollan. I drink socially. I eat cake. I love bread. And I don't spend a single second counting calories or feeling bad. We go the grocery store almost daily. We buy fresh food. We cook it. (Well, my fiancé cooks it. I hate cooking. I clean the dishes.) If we order something, we call it in and go pick it up. I see the doctor three times a year. I wear a mask just on the subway (ugh, so many people, so many germs). I have prioritized my health now that I am in my midforties. This body can all go one way or the other in the next ten years.

Finances

I am worth more than any amount of money can ever reflect. I am worthy of love and all good things in my life because I am a good man. I walk to my new bank every Friday morning and take out $200 in cash so I have some pocket money. I pay my bills once a month online; no autopays. If I can't afford to do something or go somewhere, I say no. If I can, I go and do. We have made this an ongoing conversation in our home. *Is this in the budget this month or not? Yes? Great. No? Okay, I'll cancel.* I do my best to minimize the drama. If I can't afford something right now, it is what it is. It is not *I am an unsuccessful and terrible person who will never get what I want out of this life!* I have learned to breathe and take it all down a notch.

Intellectual

Learning continues well after our formal education. It is a lifelong pursuit that expands the brain and keeps us sharp. I go to the bookstore once a week and buy a new book. I read it. I could go the library, but I like keeping books in my home. We pick one TV series at a time.

We turn the TV on only to watch that series. I only maintain my digital subscription to that network. (Right now, we're on season 2 of *The Americans*. I had never seen it. Great show.) I chose three magazines I love. They come in the mail. I take them on the subway. I read the *Times* every Sunday.

Spiritual
God is everywhere and in everything. God is loving and good and wants the best for me. I joined a local Episcopal church. I go once a month. Weekly doesn't work for me. It's too much. God and I are good once a month. Every night after dinner, I look at my fiancé and I say, "Hey, thanks for cooking for our family." That's God to me. I also dance when I can. Nothing is more spiritual to me than dance.

Play
Play is for everyone. It's a necessary part of restoring our energy, creativity, and love. My fiancé and I are learning how to play tennis. New York City has free courts. We bought inexpensive rackets. We fumble our way through it, but it's fun. Right now we're good enough to play one another but not yet good enough to play anybody else. We get to be competitive and playful with one another. We also try to spend as much time as we can with my niece and nephews. Kids know how to play.

Career
I can work in multiple creative forms and arenas. They feed each other. The only limits that exist are in my head. I take projects as they come. I put my full heart into each. If I am mistreated, I walk away. I don't plan in quarterly goals anymore. I plan "what's next" from a bucket list of dream projects. I put the kibosh on everything else. I don't work weekends. I stop at 6:00 p.m. Does that always work? Nope. But I do

it most days. I take off for doctor appointments, holidays, important family moments. I read the major trade magazines for my industries online once a week. I have dreams and ambitions, but they no longer consume me. I took the *need* out and made my goals *wants* instead. If I die having achieved my goals, I'll be thrilled. If I die having not, I'll be dead. It won't matter anyway. I refuse to constantly prove my value. I am valuable because I am alive. And I get up every day ready to contribute.

Space

I have all I need. I don't need anything more than this apartment. We recently resubscribed to our lease. We still don't have a dishwasher. We'll buy when we're ready. I threw out everything that I didn't love owning. I didn't hire the cleaning woman back weekly. She comes once a month now. I clean weekly otherwise. And do the laundry. And the fucking dishes.

Romance

I am worthy of love and ready to love in a healthy human partnership. The right partner adds to my joy and success. My fiancé and I live together. We support one another. We put up with zero bullshit from one another. We're honest and loving. We're not sure marriage is supposed to be much more than that.

Family

Family is a source of endless joy. I want one. My fiancé and I call each other *family.* And we have started the process to have a child. As a gay couple, it is not as easy as, well . . . it's not as easy. Let's leave it there.

Immediate and Extended Family

Family provides boundless love. I can totally be myself when I am with my family. Also, I am strong enough to maintain healthy boundaries with my family. It means we are modeling healthy behaviors to each other. We take the train to New Jersey every two to three weeks to see my family. We unsubscribed from "every Sunday is family day" and resubscribed to a more sustainable cadence of visits. I call my mother, father, and sisters often. I couldn't be with or hug them during the circus, so I'm not missing out on loving them as much as I can in this life.

Friends

My real friends love me just the way I am. They require no performance. Friendships are an opportunity for shared joy. I see my dearest friends as often as I can now. Or I call on the phone. Or I email to set a time to do a video call if they live far away. I highly limit my texting. I don't message unless I am late to meet someone. My fiancé and I host a game night once every few weeks. I send birthday cards again. I don't go to parties, events, or dinners with people I don't enjoy spending time with or who require anything more of me than *me.* I picked the people I truly missed in my life and put them back in. And when I put them in my calendar, I put the commitment in for four to five hours, not forty-five minutes (so I can run somewhere else).

Community

Time spent with others locally is important and exciting. I spent last summer here in New York exploring the city. No travel, no planes, no chaos. I challenge myself to remember the names of the dry cleaner (Masood), the pizza guy (Joe), the laundry man (Jin), the gym guy (Philip), and the coffee lady (Judy). It's very Mr. Rogers, but these are the people in my neighborhood. I support their businesses. I say "Good morning." They say it back. If I need a tape measure or an extra egg, I knock on my neighbor's door. Jennie is happy to help.

Supercommunity

The world is full of good people. I can connect with them in specific and structured ways to improve our collective conditions and improve the world. I have "social media" scheduled into my calendar, twice a week. That's my limit. I use social media to connect with larger circles, not my closest ones. Those closest circles have been the focus of my personal renewal. They come first.

Sometimes, things don't fall directly into these buckets that I've created; sometimes they fall back into the categories of the Big Forces, because the world is largely (for now) still run by them. Here are some examples of how I've reconciled my renewal with structures that are still somewhat out of my control:

Tech

I now subscribe to the notion that *technology serves specific goals in specific moments for specific tasks.* Some digital wellness experts will ask, *How can we use tech to empower us, teach us, connect us?* That's a fair but flawed question, for all the reasons I have argued in this book. I don't want it to do anything for me. I want less of it. Yes, I have a website and limited social media. I dedicate those two blocks per week to using all of it. I don't use any messaging across the platforms. I check email each morning, and I often set an autoreply on my personal email that tells people they are welcome to call me on my phone if it's urgent. I do my best not to be obnoxious about all this, but it does require a lot of explaining. It's worth it, though. I get to choose my behavior day to day. I get to touch paper and pens and notebooks again. I get to print and frame photos. I get to talk instead of type. (Who knew the future would include *this much typing?*) My renewal has made my life more tactile, more interesting, and more joyful.

In the end, a low-tech life may be impractical for you. It is my hope, though, that at the very least you can gain ample time and space to consider its place in your life. Tech is not "the future." It is part of the future. The rest of the future? We get to create that. We get to determine together what role tech plays. Let's give tech a supporting role. The lead is far too important a part.

Brands

Personally, I have had a lot of fun with this one. I now subscribe to the notion that *well-chosen items that will last a long time are worth the money.* Most of my shopping is clothing, so I unsubscribed from J. Crew and found a new retailer—a small men's shop here in Manhattan. I only shop in person. The clothes are a little more expensive, but the shop guarantees them for life. I have gotten to know the manager of the store personally. (And because I have been walking each morning like grandpa at the mall, I am maintaining my weight, which reduces the amount of clothing in varying sizes I accumulate.) I no longer have an Amazon account. I'm happy to be *that guy.* In our house, now we ask, "Do we have one already?" If not, "Can we make one or borrow one?" If not, "Is there a local shop that sells it?"

Banks

I now subscribe to the notion that *money is a means to an end, not the end itself.* Like everything else, you can make the choices that are best for you and that honor and support your beliefs about money. Full disclosure: you may never completely figure this one out. There's a lot of baggage that will come with it. I continue to fight. But I am fighting now with much more focus, with much less noise, and with much more information. There is more control, more intention, more maintenance. However you choose to engage with your new commitments to banks and financial institutions, remember these important questions: *Did they support me when I was down during the circus? Will they support me and my financial needs should another crisis of epic proportion fall upon my desk? Who is making money in this relationship? Is it me or them?*

Media

As you renew, it is important to wade back slowly; digital media is a tidal wave that will take you right back under. How loud do you want it all to be? How much do you want to interact with it? What is news to you? Why do you give your attention? It is time for all of us to stop giving it so very liberally. I now subscribe to the notion that *my heart and brain only deserve significant, important, and meaningful information and stories.* This has changed the flow of my day, what my apartment sounds like, what my ringtone sounds like, how much time I spend on social media, and how much news I consume. It's over. I don't want—nor do I need—Facebook, Instagram, Twitter, TikTok, LinkedIn, CNN, MSNBC, CBS, a digital copy of every magazine and newspaper, Netflix, Hulu, Disney+, Discovery+, Apple Music, Pandora, Spotify, and every other subscription service available. Time to make choices. Time to limit the madness.

For those of us who work in entertainment, the pressure is real (and constant) to have read, seen, and listened to everything. We put each other through these culture tests, cool tests, with-it tests to make sure the people we are working with are as cultured, cool, and with-it as we are. It is *exhausting.* And annoying. Even for us, we can be engaged and informed citizens and storytellers without surrendering a limitless amount of our time, clicks, attention, and dollars—on autopilot—daily. I have gotten highly comfortable saying, "No, I didn't read that. Tell me about it," "No, I didn't see that. What's it about?," "No, I didn't listen to that one podcast episode. You know there are 500,000 podcasts on Apple, right?"

Parties

This one was fairly simple. I have unsubscribed from the major political parties. That doesn't mean I don't vote for their candidates or that I do not educate myself about policy and government. I watch debates between candidates. I do my reading. I research them. I write about society online. (I try to do this thoughtfully, in the spirit of collective renewal, not in the spirit of "Fuck you, you're wrong.") I have taken all the time I used to spend consuming politics and put it into civic work. I write. I speak. I serve on the board of select community institutions that I love. I'm not interested in a text message "from Jill Biden" asking me for $2. *Please unsubscribe, thanks!* It is critical for each of us to understand that politics and government are different, and for each of us to find a healthy role in this democracy. Let's choose government. Let's walk away from politics.

As I write all this, I realize how little of life now requires the products and services of click-up economics. Unsubscribing has kicked the Big Forces out of my life. I tap into them when I need them. I tap out when I don't. No infinite loops.

It is time to play "hard to get" with brands, business, tech, media, government, and the banks. Make them work for your money, your click, your attention. Make them spell out what actual value they are bringing to your life and how exactly being in bed with them supports what you really believe about the world and about yourself. Demand transparency and accountability and actual customer service. Demand equity. Demand a space for your personal power to exist. Or walk away.

This has been a long process, and it is my greatest hope that my work on these pages has been meaningful for you. Welcome to life outside the infinite loop.

Fifteen

The Elephant

We're not done yet. There is still a very large elephant in the room, and the elephant is this: if you and I engage in the process of unsubscribing, does the world just magically transform? No. Sadly, it doesn't work this way. A happier and healthier you and a happier and healthier me do not a happier and healthier world instantly make. Can we each affect the people and the society around us? Yes. Absolutely. But we cannot rely on social wellness to go viral. The systems in place are simply not designed for that, and whatever good does go viral is bound to be dwarfed by the illness these systems are automating.

So, I propose we do two things after we effect our own individual renewal. First, we engage in civic renewal projects in our circles. Next, we demand of our representatives that those who hold the reins of power in this society stand up to the Big Forces and act for the common good. We already have a collective mechanism to create large-scale social wellness. It's called democracy.

Oh, shit, here comes We horse! Remember him? We horse is back in the game! It is only through active citizenship that we can reclaim this democracy and, in the process, effect a genuine collective renewal for our country.

In a powerful report for the *Guardian*, George Monbiot, columnist and author of *Out of the Wreckage: A New Politics for an Age of Crisis*, details how corporate marketing has reframed many of the issues of our day to make us believe we are solving problems with individual solutions instead of collectively challenging the major structural beliefs underneath. For example, fabric bags may or may not be better than plastic ones. The answer is to buy less, period. And change our laws and business-incentive structures so that we consume less. Electric cars may or may not be better than gas ones. The answer is to drive less, period. And change our laws and business-incentive structures so that we use fewer fossil fuels.

Monbiot admits, "I'm not saying the small things don't matter. I'm saying they should not matter to the exclusion of things that matter *more*. Every little bit counts. But not for very much." Monbiot goes on to explain that "the great political transition of the past fifty years, driven by corporate marketing, has been a shift from addressing our problems collectively to addressing them individually. In other words, it has turned us from citizens into consumers. It's not hard to see why we have been herded down this path. As citizens, joining together to demand political change, we are powerful. As consumers, we are almost powerless."

I would add only this: as automated subscribers, we are even more powerless.

This is why paper straws and culture wars over gas stoves and soda calorie counts—whatever the collective rage is about tomorrow morning—it's all *surface bullshit*. Does debating these things feel good? Yes. Do policy changes move the needle somewhat in specific communities and in specific ways? Yes. Are these changes "bad" things? Certainly not. But it is not tectonic transformation. To get back to our primary role as citizens, we must unsubscribe from our automated role as subscribers, and that calls on us—as I hope this book illustrates—to dig deeper.

And while I agree with many of Monbiot's points, small personal behavioral changes very often illuminate the underlying beliefs that control us. They are often our first awareness that these sticky stories even exist. Yes, in order for individuals to collectively demand change at a policy level, we must confront our collective underlying beliefs. But before we can do that as a group, we first have to see *our own* and get used to locating them and pointing them out. Once we have begun to engage in individual renewal, we make collective renewal possible.

Big elephant. Important elephant.

Sixteen
Collective Renewal

The world needs you. On this side of the dark well, you have a new perspective to share with the circles you belong to—from the smallest ones to the largest. You may have decided you have *zero interest* in playing a part in some of your previous circles (screw it, stay unsubscribed), or you may have discovered that some of your previous circles mean so much more to you now. Chances are that, like I did, you have discovered that less is more and that deeper is better, that there is great value in getting rid of the extra fat and focusing on the circles that actually make your heart beat and bring you joy and satisfaction. You can help those circles do their own deep work. You can help them renew.

If you do that and I do that, the collective renewal ahead is not some infinite loop of chaos and bullshit. Instead, it is circle after circle of belonging, shared purpose, and mutual respect. As we proceed, we have to be open to the idea that *it will all look very different than what we are used to*. There is risk involved, but a common goal: that we all rise. We have only ever known imbalance, inequality, and endless drive for growth, on a ruthless quarter-by-quarter basis. We have only ever known the fight for a seat at the table. We have only ever known the relentlessness of our day-to-day. What does sustainability and shared success look like? The truth is that we don't know. We haven't built it yet.

We do know, though, what we *want*. In the grand scheme, we want America to live up to its promises of equality and freedom. We want the country to expand its resources and gifts to as many of our fellow Americans as possible—without invalidating our own success or taking away the great pride we feel in how far we *have* come as a society or as individuals. We want to be proud of our country and how it functions here at home and in the world. And, at every level, we want more power in the whole system. We want to share in the success of the nation. If we are integrally part of creating it—which we are, every day—then we want to benefit from it. No more performative rage, selective accountability, or moving the goalposts to screw millions out of sharing in that success.

As consumers, we want to be heard. We want respect for our time. We want food and water that is healthy (wild idea), customer support that is effective, and services that truly deliver. Sure, we want to be stylish, hip, modern—all that means is that we want to be seen. We want to be visible. We want to know we mean something to the world, that we're not just a demographic, a number, an anonymous follower. We want businesses and brands to see our humanity and live into the promises that they make us. We want to know that our money, our email—and our lives—didn't just go into some black hole. We don't want to be automated, mindless subscribers. We want to be fully fledged and active participants.

In our communities, we want to be—and be surrounded by—happier people, healthier people, people who are free from unnecessary suffering, hunger, physical and economic pain, violence, and crime, or who are prepared to respond appropriately to what is unavoidable about the human condition. We want to give a shit about each other again. In our families, we want connection and joy. We want to know each other, appreciate each other, and feel like we are raising kids in our own image, not anyone else's. We want products and services that help us achieve the goal of a richer life, not one that is busier, bereft of nourishment or quality time with our loved ones, but one full of happiness, meaning, and satisfaction.

In our hearts, we want lives that "work." We want to matter. We want, when we leave this earth, for someone else to know that we were here. We want to know that our hard work paid off, too. We want to know that the sacrifices we make every day for our families are worth it. We are good people and *a* good people. We deserve that. It is all a tall order, yes, but none of it is too much to ask.

How do we get what we want? To truly experience a collective renewal, we must face this truth: we cannot get there through automation. The only way to do this is through citizenship.

I know that when the word *citizenship* appears, most people back off. We hear flags and passports. Immigration and border walls. Volunteering in a soup kitchen. We have flashbacks, perhaps unpleasant ones, to fifth-grade social studies. (We all do.) That's not what I'm talking about here. I simply mean this: people. A return to each other.

If consumerism centers on products, citizenship centers on people. The process I have detailed in this book is my call for us to cut our ties with rampant consumerism and reengage with one another, in the flesh, so we can express what is most human about us and get our experiences of positive emotions from one another, instead of from the products of click-up economics and its algorithmic middlemen. A renewal of our role as citizens—a return to each other—offers us an untapped well of pride, satisfaction, respect, hope, power, contentment, creativity, joy, belonging, and love. Yes, love.

Our desire for love is an essential human need. In fact, the Greeks, the very founders of democracy, practiced, taught, and built social and community bonds based on eight types of love. Our modern project is to disentangle our system, rugged individualistic American capitalism, from how it has been practiced thus far—including how it is executed and warped with digital tools—and rewrite its rules so that we can practice it in a more loving way. Please don't cringe at

Please Unsubscribe, Thanks!

this earnest appeal. I know I lay it on thick sometimes, but do you prefer a world full of hate or a world full of love? I simply mean that our transactions in a renewed economy, and the subscriptions that govern them, must be rooted in mutual respect and shared success among all of our circles, so that when these subscriptions are automated—by high-powered systems that scale up instantly and massively—we can truly magnify societal wellness.

The people furthest on the left claim that this is an impossibility, that capitalism itself is irreparably flawed, that the inequities between capital and labor can never produce widespread justice or happiness. On the other hand, the people furthest on the right claim that anything that resembles a rule infringes on their freedoms and on the free market. Many have abused and contorted the basic principles of capitalism to excuse injustices, overlook massive imbalances, and justify the hoarding of resources, capital, and material success. We must remember, though, that even the formalizers of capitalism conceded that abuse of customers (and labor) was bound to occur, but that it is the responsibility of the government to stop such abuses. Adam Smith made that very concession: the government has a responsibility to protect its citizens from abuse by the market.

The American government has not fully owned that responsibility, and it must. It has never even been fully *funded* in order to own that responsibility, and it must be. Some of the clowns in Congress don't even understand that this *is* their responsibility. Fighting on Twitter is not. *This is*. Before we throw out the baby with the bathwater, this moment in the world demands of us that we fix our system, not replace it.

Operating from extreme and limiting underlying beliefs about success, wealth, class, and legacy—beliefs that have been passed down by generations and reinforced in social and business circles from New England to New Mexico, from Washington to Washington—we have gutted, defunded, and expunged many of the agencies and institutions that carried the real weight of that responsibility to protect. Those very institutions and agencies have historically maintained our guardrails, our collective limits.

It is our responsibility to turn to one another and protect one another. We can demand that protection from our government, *and* we can help our circles effect their own renewal using the principles of subscription and unsubscription.

This is the civics work at hand. It will call on us to be leaders when we haven't been, vocal when we have been quiet, involved when we'd rather just go home and watch cable news all night. Modern citizenship is not about undying loyalty to partisan media. It's not even about phone banking or mass texting or social media organizing. That is the fallacy of the digital era: that every problem can be solved immediately with a post, a video, or a snarky comment. This only *adds* to the bullshit.

That type of change-making—one that employs digital media on a mass scale—is powerful and effective in specific ways and for specific purposes. For example, the Parkland High School students (now alumni) who, brokenhearted, organized the global March for Our Lives, have leveraged technology brilliantly. They broke through the noise so they could be heard. And they helped put pressure on Congress to pass the Bipartisan Safer Communities Act, the first major gun reform legislation in decades. The hard truth is that their success is an anomaly, and their actions and strategies are not a one-size-fits-all solution for all of us to create tectonic transformation.

So, how do we, ourselves, fix the system and effect this collective renewal? How can we redesign it all to foster mutual respect and shared success? My proposal is to look at our shared subscriptions. Let's use our talents and relationships to help our existing circles locate them, reconsider them, break them, rewrite them, and then redesign their models and forms to honor a renewed vision for a more equitable world. It is time to join your local social club. It is time to join your condo board. It is time to join that church group. Pick something, anything that commits you to working with other people to effect positive change. It is time to return to each other and renew the circles, institutions, and organizations that make up our society.

Challenging collective subscriptions could even be a conversation you have with your friends over a beer. *Where do we all get this idea from that college friends are only supposed to see one another at reunions?* You could even just start with your family. *Where is it written that we can't have dinner together every night? Where is it written that we have to? Maybe we should write it down and actually commit to it?* Writing a family constitution can be an incredibly rewarding experience. (See Resources at the end of this book for more information.)

In all our circles, large and small, here is what that process looks like:

Steps for Collective Renewal

1. Identify the surface bullshit the circle is putting out into the world. Most of it comes from the *surface subscriptions* the circle requires and takes the form of social media posts, logos, advertisements, and marketing communications of all kinds. Depending on the circle, its size, and its resources, these may be homemade and local, or mass-produced and overly polished. Either way, it will serve us well to ask these questions: *How is this circle contributing to the noise of modern life? How is it engaging with or fueling click-up economics? How is the communication between the circle and the outside world extending our collective wellness or illness? What is on autopilot? How do we take it off?* Put a pin in these questions for now. First, just locate the bullshit. Name it. List it. Point at it.

2. Locate the *people subscriptions* that govern behavior in this circle. These will ultimately control how people treat each other within the circle and how the circle (as a whole) treats the people it engages with. These look like group rules, policies, protocols, agreements, contracts, handbooks, guidelines, ground rules, customs, traditions, and codes and blueprints of all kinds. Some are written. Some are only spoken. The real work is locating them. Figuring out where and what they are. Then discussing them. Calling them out, putting them up for debate, and collectively unsubscribing from them or not. For now, put a pin in these, too.

3. Go deeper—to the same place that we went in our individual unsubscribing and renewal: consider the *underlying subscriptions* that control behavior. These are truly governing the circle. Locate the cultural, narrated, and experiential beliefs that keep the circle on autopilot. This is where the hard conversations are bound to be had. *Where are these written? How and when are they spoken? What is being communicated to the circle—overtly or not—that causes people in this circle to behave the way that they do? How are the incentives aligned or misaligned in the very design of the circle that produce these results? How do these notions stack up with mutual respect and shared wellness? Are they extending love and well-being into society or are they extending illness?* The best work we can do as citizens, the greatest service we can offer each other, is to help our circles identify these, debate these, reevaluate these, rewrite these. And then redesign how our circle functions.

Systems do not simply develop. They are designed. At some point in the creation of the circle, someone made a problematic choice that locked the system in an infinite loop. The effort to challenge systems is to call those architects to account. They may be long dead. But we have a responsibility to fix their mistakes. Not to bitch and moan about their mistakes. But to fix them. Collective renewal happens when we then reverse from number 3 to number 2 to number 1. We help write the circle's new ideas, beliefs, and notions (number 3). Then we execute these within the circle, in the form of new organizational and business models, and systems, policies, regulations, rules, traditions—whatever is appropriate for the circle (number 2). Then, and only then, can we consider and rewrite the surface communications (the surface bullshit, number 1) that the digital world is so very obsessed with.

Writing new ideas, beliefs, and notions can take time. But the process can create tectonic change. I know this well. Over the last twenty years, I have watched my family renew itself. After the drama and chaos of my parents' divorce in the late '90s, each of us was broken in two. No one escaped unscathed. It would take many years, seemingly countless moments of vulnerability, to unearth our buried sticky stories about who did what and who hurt whom. After the day my father left our home, the five of us would never be alone together in a room ever again. We would welcome husbands and wives and grandkids. And they would bring new life and energy to our family. As each entered and they learned the full story of our family, each of us was forced to name heroes and villains, to explain *why* we did what we did when we did it.

The process revealed that even among the five of us, the "story" of what happened was really a combination of narratives we had told each other about my parents' marriage, and of hundreds more we had told ourselves over forty years—and for forty years before that in each of my parents' childhood homes—about what marriage, divorce, loyalty, betrayal, and healing mean. No, I never sat them all down and talked to them about "collective renewal," but as my niece and nephews were born, their births begged us to synthesize all these stories and rewrite our collective definition of family: *family is love*. And as long as there was love between us all, there was family.

The wild part of it all is that now, twenty-five years after the divorce, my parents have become friends. With the love and support of each of their new spouses, they both join for holidays. They both join for special moments. Last fall, they shared a table at a local fall fair to each sell their retirement crafts. Mom sells homemade Christmas goods that she makes in her garage. Dad sells homemade American flags that he woodworks in his garage. (You cannot make this shit up.) Take it from me and my sisters, renewal is possible. If our nightmares can come true, so ought our dreams. Polyurethaned flea market flags and personalized Santa stockings were not the dreams of our youth. But a lasting peace between our parents was. We are living in our collective dream now because we refused to give up. We never stopped wrestling with our definition of family. Even as its form changed.

We cannot give up on our fellow Americans either. And so we cannot let the Big Forces off the hook. Their transformation can be built on the same principles, even if it looks different. It all starts with an open interrogation of the underlying ideas, beliefs, and notions that define them. An example: In the summer of 2019, as part of a corporate governance project with Business Roundtable, a Washington-DC-based nonprofit association of CEOs, 181 executives from America's leading corporations, including Citigroup, Apple, PepsiCo, and Walmart, issued a "Statement on the Purpose of a Corporation" (known as "the purpose"). Moving away from the commonly held belief that *making money for shareholders is the primary purpose of the corporation*, the statement centered on five major commitments: "delivering value to our customers, investing in our employees, dealing fairly and ethically with our suppliers, supporting the communities in which we work, and generating long-term value for shareholders." Together, they recognized that their (often outsized) role in American life constituted a responsibility to our society.

This was an attempt to rewrite their collective subscriptions (the contracts and promises that govern their businesses). The statement the group released was a clear departure from more than fifty years of "profit is king" thinking, orthodoxy ingrained in business circles, based on the work of economists like Milton Friedman, of the University of Chicago. But it was a half measure, a well-intended (perhaps) and well-publicized one (for sure), that never stood a chance to change anything.

Why? Their process was flawed. First, they didn't reckon with or *unsubscribe* publicly from Friedman's famous notion that "the social responsibility of business is to increase its profits." (In fact, the fifth bullet of their statement still included the corporation's responsibility to create "value" for its shareholders.) I am not saying that shareholders shouldn't make money, but you can't redefine something by restating its original definition.

They also never actually answered the question at hand: *What is the purpose of a corporation?* Nowhere did they articulate, write, and subscribe to (sign under) a new belief, spelled out and clear, that "the purpose of a corporation is to be an engine of well-being in society." Sorry to play English teacher here, but the result of the group's work was a written statement. The actual words are crucially important.

Further, the group made no shared commitment about how to bring their new "commitments" inside the 181 organizations the signers lead. (There was no mechanism to ensure Step 2, no formal or agreed-upon way to rewrite all the subscriptions that govern their organizations.) If there is no commitment to make changes to policies, or practices—or the very models these policies and practices help structure—then the rewriting of a collective subscription like this means nothing.

What we saw in the immediate years that followed this Purpose was record-breaking profits from America's leading corporations and the highest unemployment rates since the Great Depression. Yes, the circus hit. It was world changing and unexpected (arguably). But if this Purpose statement was meant to truly transform the purpose of a corporation, then we would have seen much different behavior as we went through the worst economic disaster in a century.

A year after issuing this statement, the Business Roundtable checked in with the 181 executives. One CEO reported this update:

> We used the purpose to guide our response to both crises [the pandemic and the social unrest sparked by racial injustice]. These actions included an unprecedented fundraising effort in support of COVID-19 relief, holding our first companywide town hall to discuss racial inequality, creating a new Chief Diversity Officer role on our executive leadership team, and rolling out a global policy that amplified our unequivocal stance against racial misconduct.

Like countless other companies throughout the country, they raised some money, held a town hall, hired a new executive, and issued *a* policy praising diversity. Are these actions "bad" or counterproductive? No. Are they going to produce transformation? Also no. Why? Because if 181 CEOs want to transform the purpose of a corporation, they have to transform what a corporation *is*—at its core. They must redesign *the very model of a modern major corporation* (can you hear the music from *The Pirates of Penzance*? Just me?), in order to serve whatever new purpose it is meant to serve. Otherwise, a purpose statement like this is a platitude. It makes a mockery of "corporate responsibility."

A close look at the word *transformation* can be helpful here. As a society seeking transformation, we're not looking for change for change's sake. We are not looking for performance. And we're certainly not looking for half measures. When we talk about personal transformation, societal transformation, or that of any circle or organization—the type of transformation that will effect a collective renewal—it is vital to understand *form*.

A corporation's form is made up of its many different arms and shapes. Its form includes everything from the physical spaces that it occupies; to the number of people it employs, sells to, involves, and engages with; to the legal and financial forms it takes on paper. *What is the business model? What is the revenue model?* Those are shapes. Those are its form. *How do the contracts, policies, and protocols in place that execute that model contribute to and, in effect, hold up the form of the company? What do the reporting structures look like? What does the "org chart" look like? How do these interior shapes affect and effect the whole? How do they affect everyone inside the circle and outside of it?*

In all of our collective circles, that examination is the same. It just looks a little different. First, what form does the circle or organization currently take? What form do we want it to take? How do we get from A to B (or even Z)? We have to examine the structures inside. This is the work of leaders. To engage, to debate, to understand, and to propose and advocate for redesign. To help our circles identify their forms and the cycles of automation that they are trapped in that are giving them their shape, in effect making them look, sound, smell, taste, and feel the way they do.

If those 181 CEOs are serious about transforming the corporation, they will look at the very *form* of a corporation—its design—and change it (the change is the *trans* part of the word transformation). Its current form is what is breeding societal illness. A business model that sends zero dollars to the federal government in taxes is not one that can ever claim it is "supporting the communities in which it works." A model that raises prices astronomically is not one "delivering value to our customers." You cannot "invest in our employees" when you lay off large swaths of them. You're not "dealing fairly and ethically with our suppliers" when you rewrite agreements that exploit them.

The question to be asked is this: What changes need to be made to the *form* of a corporation itself?

Andrew Carnegie and the early-twentieth-century industrialists understood this when they introduced the use of trusts. The concept of trusts was used by early Greeks and Romans and further developed in twelfth-century England. In a fast-changing America of the late 1800s, industrialists used them to redesign business models, transferring the stocks of many smaller companies to overhead "trusts" that could operate from coast to coast. These trusts quickly became the enemy of populist politicians like Teddy Roosevelt and Woodrow Wilson, who argued that the trust was an instrument of abuse. Modern antitrust law is the descendant of these debates and policies. Love them or loathe them (that's not my point), trusts were a new *form* for businesses to take. Carnegie and his contemporaries understood that to transform their businesses, they had to change their very form.

The same was true in Britain and France in the nineteenth-century housing market, when the cooperative housing movement began. Here in America, it was 1881 when the first "co-op" was built in New York City. The Rembrandt was built at 157 West Fifty-Seventh Street, meant to attract artists (hence its name), who were considered more open to alternate housing structures, and for whom the living style of the day—large, single-family townhomes—was (already!) unaffordable. In what became known as "canned housing," cooperatives offered a novel idea: what if, instead of owning a home, you could collectively own a building, and your share in the company that owned that building entitled you to a flat in it? The co-op model changed New York housing. Fast-forward nearly one hundred fifty years, and that form is no longer novel, but it is surely enduring. Now, co-ops remain a more affordable option, compared to renting or buying a condo. ("More affordable" in Manhattan still means they are laughably expensive.)

I offer these examples not to advocate for their *specific forms* but as testimony to the fact that to get new results, we must explore new forms. As the famous Einstein quote goes: "Insanity is doing the same thing over and over and expecting different results." The very form of the modern corporation must change if it is ever to effect societal wellness or do any of the things "The Statement on the Purpose of a Corporation" was supposed to do.

Our world is in a state of chaotic disarray. It is a mess. And good people everywhere are depressed because it all seems so unchangeable. It will take divergent thinking to transform our systems and effect collective renewal.

Here are some recommendations for how best to approach collective renewal as we help our circles reckon with reimagining their *underlying subscriptions*, their *people subscriptions*, and their *surface subscriptions*.

Call out performative change

Just as individual renewal is not about a new haircut or new clothes or a new car, collective renewal is not about a new logo or even a new committee. Circles within circles are maddening. Working groups to study the possibility of proposing a new committee to write a report on maybe one day thinking about even discussing the prospect of change—this is an exercise in insanity. Kindly call it out and propose getting to the heart of the matter. None of us has any more patience for wasting our four thousand weeks.

Come from wellness, not anger

Anger certainly has its place. But we cannot create collective renewal from a place of constant rage. I have had a lot of fun in this book using my own anger and exasperation for comic effect. The truth is that anger breeds more anger. Fury begets fury. Wrath triggers wrath. Like the saying goes: *garbage in, garbage out.* If you want to advocate for wellness, you have to come from a place of wellness. That's why it is imperative to put yourself through a process of individual renewal before you reengage with your circles.

Propose solutions

We're all exhausted by our collective bitterness. You can't lead by constantly bitching about things. Collective renewal relies on new energy, new forms, and new ideas. Taking back our time, attention, and purpose from the Big Forces means we have more minutes, focus, money, and opportunities to be creative and to seek creative solutions to the pressing problems of the day. It also means we have more love to have the hard conversations and debates. Who is writing these solutions? You. Be that person.

Stop thinking in top-down hierarchies

Yes, leadership roles are important. They help us scale renewal by giving us the chance to affect the design of the systems that run our world. But you can lead from wherever you are. Power may be concentrated at the very top, but there are endless loci of power for you to focus on. Click-up economics has trained us to think that only those at the very top matter. That is a lie. In fact, it is too much pressure for those at the top.

Expect the assholes

Every circle we participate in has assholes in it. They're there. They're not going anywhere. If we are waiting for them to walk away or magically become incredible humans, the sand will run out of our hourglass. Let's stop wasting our time fighting against them. We are only giving them more power.

Follow the money

As you engage in helping your circles analyze their forms, you will inevitably encounter some flow of cash somewhere. From our families to the church to the local Kiwanis Club to the state, every circle touches money in some form. How that money is raised, what it is used for, where it is invested, and who it compensates—these are important to the design of any circle. As you locate a circle's underlying ideas, beliefs, and notions, also locate the money. If the money is being spent and invested wisely, it will support positive acts of wellness for the circle and the greater society. If it is not, it will support acts of illness. Helping our circles unsubscribe from Big Oil, for example, is as important as helping them unsubscribe from disempowering beliefs.

Lastly, I do not want to miss the most obvious and most important step for collective renewal. We must demand change—actual progress—from our elected leaders. We must hold them to higher standards. The blending of business, entertainment, and politics is proving disastrous for our democracy. Our representatives (and their teams) are the people who write and execute mass collective subscriptions. They contract, transact, engage, promise, and execute on our behalf. Their choices affect ours. Their behavior affects ours. Their lack of dignity, care, and kindness ripples through the entire society. And so we can no longer settle for elevating the worst of us to public office. We must support our best. And when we do, we must demand that they, in turn, represent the interests of the greater We. That most certainly includes holding the Big Forces to account.

There are any number of public policy proposals that could come out of the ideas I have presented in this book. I will refrain here from including them. It is important that we call on our leaders, and the public-policy pros they employ who are trained in writing policy, to step up. Our laws are our national subscriptions. Our collective renewal relies on rewriting them. I imagine much of that policy, though, might center around this idea: *I have the right to be an engaged citizen without the consumer marketplace being constantly thrust upon me. I have a right to be a customer without being a subscriber. And I have a right to thrive outside the infinite loop.*

Conclusion
New Futures

Welcome to the 2020s. The times we find ourselves living in beg us to reevaluate who we are. They call on us to become something perhaps different than we envisioned. And that can be unsettling, unnerving. Or thrilling. It all depends on how we look at it. What is certain is that it calls on us to reevaluate our promises. And to mourn who we thought we were going to be before we can embrace and celebrate the opportunity to meet the moment and live into a different kind of destiny. The mourning doesn't mean we start from scratch. It doesn't even mean we don't get out of life what we thought we would. It may actually more closely align us with the world around us and allow us to be part of the world instead of constantly fighting for our place in it.

It is time that we make peace with this truth about our modern, digital world: *this system keeps you small because it benefits from your smallness.* Now it is time for you to be bigger. It's time for all of us to be bigger. And if being bigger is simply not what you signed up for, I hope this book offered you strategies to be happier. All I really mean by "bigger" is powerful enough to have the mad, wild, crazy *gall* to be happy in this life. Change starts inside you and inside me. It is a lot of work, but it's well worth doing.

The future will be full of more change than we can even imagine. We must become adaptable, resilient, and buoyant. To have the lives we want, we must learn how to welcome change, prepare for it, expect it, and respond immediately to it. Because of the circus and all the other massive changes that the 2020s have brought and will bring, life as we knew it will never be the same. Work will change. Careers will change. Cities will change. Transportation will change. Food will change. Our children will change.

What is constant is that humans will always seek love, trust, hope, inspiration, joy, laughter, pride, and respect. By understanding that these emotions are at the core of society, we can take comfort in their constancy while the world goes nuts around us. This is actually liberating. It calls on us to control what we can control and let the rest go. It calls on us to be present—really present—to our lives, because the future as we have envisioned it does not exist. That movie is over. Lights up. The brightness can be scary. It can also be electrifying to the spirit. That spark, that stirring—that is where all creativity begins. That is where all power originates. And it is where the bullshit ends.

Thanks!

It has been the honor of my life to write this book and to spend this time on the other side of your page. The pandemic cracked me in two. This is what was inside. These years have changed me. They have changed us. Who are we as people—and as *a* people—if we don't let them change us?

When my essay "Prepare for the Ultimate Gaslighting" circled the globe, it was accompanied by a pretty incredible photograph. That photograph was taken by a West Coast photographer named Gabriel Duarte. It shows a clear Los Angeles, free of smog, free of traffic, and free of pollution. The photo was so striking because it was reflective of the city Los Angelenos want to live in. It was reflective of a world we all want to live in. I have never believed more that that is completely possible.

As I write these final pages, I am summoned to the kitchen to polish the Easter eggs. My fiancé and I spent last night dyeing eggs the Balkan way. He's from Montenegro. Here's how it goes: You buy a pair of pantyhose from a local shop. (Yes, the clerk was confused, even here in New York City.) You pick leaves from Twenty-Second Street. (We are likely the only people in Manhattan who have ever picked leaves off the trees on Twenty-Second Street.) You wrap the eggs in the pantyhose, which hold your leaves in place on the eggs as you boil the eggs in beets and onion skins. The beets and onion skins dye the eggs, leaving beautiful images of leaves and twigs on them. When the eggs have cooled, you polish them with cooking oil. No packaging. No dyes. No spin-art machine. No fake green grass. You just arrange them in a nice bowl. You can eat them without

Googling "Can you eat dyed Easter eggs?" These Easter eggs have come to symbolize my renewal. I am decorating them with a man named Nenad. We met after I subscribed to the notion that *I am worthy of love. I want a partner who extends my joy.* When I started to look simply for joy, I found it. And kindness, I found it. And love, there it was. Love, in the end, is our only purpose. Nenad and I met as I emerged from the dark well. I put back into my life some key elements that made me healthier and happier. I found new joys. And I simply left the rest. I wish you the same.

Acknowledgments

There are few things one can create alone in the world. While I have relished my time solo at my laptop to put these words to paper, this book would not be possible without the unyielding support of so many who offered their guidance, wisdom, advice, and insights. Thank you to my fearless editor, Julianna Haubner, who understood from our first meeting what I wanted this book to be and who gave me the time, space, and flexibility to write it. Julianna, your brilliant mind, endless patience, and sharp talents have made this collaboration easy, smooth, and joyful. Thank you to David Kass, Meredith Vilarello, Lauren Wein, and Jofie Ferrari-Adler for their trust, encouragement, and partnership. Thank you to Ben Loehnen for your friendship and kind counsel. Thank you to Julie Stevenson, my literary agent at Massie & McQuilkin, for believing there was a book to be written and for shepherding this project with great care from the beginning. Julie, our first phone call renewed me. There would be no book without you. Thank you to Michelle Woo, Indrani Sen, Jon Gluck, Harris Sockel, Amy Shearn, and all those at Medium who gave me an expanded platform to continue my writing. And thank you to my friends, family, colleagues, and to all those online who read and shared my original essay. Your embrace of my work and your enthusiasm for a better society and better world have inspired me. To the critics, I say thank you, too. You have helped me think more deeply about the issues and arguments in these conversations. We get nowhere without respectful disagreement.

I want to thank Julia, Tony, and Scott, whose great talents as MFTs have helped me transform my life. Thank you to Pascal, Patty, and Alan for introducing me to the concept of transformational work. This is where it has all led twenty years later. And to Stephen, whose work has brought all my projects to a new level.

New York City is not the same without Lisa Quiroz-Garcia or Peter Wertheim. You were smart, loving, witty angels when you were here with us on this planet. You are angels now. You may not walk our streets anymore, but your presence will always be felt.

Thank you to Sarah Knight, Oliver Burkeman, Alex Wenzke, Sarah Blanchard, Eddie Joyce, Michael Clinton, Amy Shearn, and Susie Arons. Your counsel helped me navigate. Thank you to Tootsie, Marissa, and Jamie for your support. Thank you to my colleagues at Boro Five and Staten Island Academy for your partnership. Thank you to Caroline for always being my partner in rhyme. Thank you to Caren and Frank for teaching me about history and justice. And Mark for showing me how to find myself then raise my voice. Thank you to the small circle I asked to read my initial drafts, especially to Christopher Fraga, whose intellect and thoughtful notes were invaluable. My conversations with all of you about life, work, money, politics, God—they are the whole point. I send my gratitude to my friends, colleagues, and partners in all the circles of my life who were patient with me as I not only unsubscribed but then disappeared into my "writing cave" (uh, Kona Coffee Roasters on Seventh Avenue) to write a book about it all. I wrote this book for all of us who are struggling to make sense of this odd future we find ourselves living in. Know that if I have pissed you off, I have done it with great love. Thank you to Joe and David for birthing the unsubscribe icon, to Anthony and Amir for being my day-to-day sounding board, and to Steve for your brotherhood. Thank you to May for decades of support.

I save my family for last because it has been a long and tumultuous road, and I could not have weathered the storms along the way without your love. When I "run to the love," I run to you. Thank you to the entire Gambuto-DeNicolo-Santangelo-Amista-Manzella-Djelevic clan. Dom, Dom, Joe, Phil, you make me a better man.

Mom, Dad, Marisa, Dana, I share our story in many forms and ways in this book and in other projects because we have been given a life of boundless support, and so many in this world have not. If sharing helps someone else—or another family—these are stories worth telling. Mom, no one knows better what it has truly taken for me to build a life as a creative. You have never flinched, and I am eternally grateful for your faith. And to my future husband, Nenad, who came into my life as the circus turned both our worlds completely upside down, *volim te. Ti si moj najdraži.*

Resources

To learn more about how to apply these ideas to your everyday life, family, business, and to our world, visit www.juliovincent.com for downloadable resources.

Selected Bibliography

While most of this book represents my personal viewpoints on our changing society, those views have been influenced by some incredible authors and their books. I am including a short bibliography here of books that have inspired my work, as well as books that I recommend reading to further explore the wide variety of topics I have covered in this book.

Because part one of the book makes arguments about history, economics, and psychology, I have noted my references. Parts two, three, and four come primarily from my personal experiences. As such, I have opted not to cite specific sources. For all notes where a leading source was not available, I have included one or two relevant readings for you to explore.

BOOKS QUOTED, MENTIONED, OR CITED

Baker, Billy. *We Need to Hang Out: A Memoir of Making Friends.* New York: Avid Reader Press, 2022.

Baxter, Robbie Kellman. *The Forever Transaction: How to Build a Subscription Model So Compelling, Your Customers Will Never Want to Leave.* New York: McGraw Hill, 2020.

Burkeman, Oliver. *Four Thousand Weeks: Time Management for Mortals.* New York: Farrar, Straus and Giroux, 2021.

Clear, James. *Atomic Habits: An Easy & Proven Way to Build Good Habits & Break Bad Ones.* London, United Kingdom: Penguin Publishing Group, 2018.

Dunbar, Robin. *How Many Friends Does One Person Need? Dunbar's Number and Other Evolutionary Quirks.* Cambridge: Harvard University Press, 2011.

Ferriss, Timothy. *The 4-Hour Workweek.* New York: Crown Publishers, 2007.

Frankfurt, Harry G. *On Bullshit.* Princeton: Princeton University Press, 2005.

Galloway, Scott. *Adrift: America in 100 Charts.* New York: Penguin Publishing Group, 2022.

Giblin, Rebecca, and Cory Doctorow. *Chokepoint Capitalism: How Big Tech and Big Content Captured Creative Labor Markets and How We'll Win Them Back.* Boston: Beacon Press, 2022.

Graeber, David, and David Wengrow. *The Dawn of Everything: A New History of Humanity.* New York: Picador, 2023.

Immerwahr, Daniel. *How to Hide an Empire: A History of the Greater United States.* New York: Farrar, Straus and Giroux, 2019.

Klein, Ezra. *Why We're Polarized.* New York: Avid Reader Press, 2020.

Mask, Deirdre. *The Address Book: What Street Addresses Reveal About Identity, Race, Wealth, and Power.* New York: St. Martin's Publishing Group, 2020.

Maslow, A. H. *A Theory of Human Motivation.* Hoboken: Start Publishing LLC, 2013.

Nietzsche, Friedrich. *The Portable Nietzsche.* New York: Penguin Publishing Group, 1977.

Piirto, Rebecca. *Beyond Mind Games: The Marketing Power of Psychographics.* United States: American Demographics Books, 1991.

Pollan, Michael. *The Omnivore's Dilemma: A Natural History of Four Meals.* New York: Penguin Publishing Group, 2007.

Rush, A. John, et al. *Cognitive Therapy of Depression.* New York: Guilford Publications, 1979.

Ryan, Christopher. *Civilized to Death: The Price of Progress.* New York: Avid Reader Press, 2020.

Sachs, Jonah. *Winning the Story Wars: Why Those Who Tell (and Live) the Best Stories Will Rule the Future.* Cambridge: Harvard Business Review Press, 2012.

Smith, Adam. *The Wealth of Nations: Books 1–3.* London, United Kingdom: Penguin Publishing Group, 1982.

Stoller, Matt. *Goliath: The 100-Year War Between Monopoly Power and Democracy.* New York: Simon & Schuster, 2020.

Tzuo, Tien, and Gabe Weisert. *Subscribed: Why the Subscription Model Will Be Your Company's Future—and What to Do About It.* New York: Penguin Publishing Group, 2018.

Warren, Elizabeth. *Persist.* New York: Henry Holt and Company, 2021.

Yang, Andrew. *The War on Normal People: The Truth About America's Disappearing Jobs and Why Universal Basic Income Is Our Future.* New York: Hachette Books, 2018.

Zuboff, Shoshana. *The Age of Surveillance Capitalism: The Fight for a Human Future at the New Frontier of Power.* New York: Public Affairs, 2019.

ADDITIONAL BOOKS THAT INSPIRED THE CONVERSATION

Benadusi, Lorenzo. *The Enemy of the New Man: Homosexuality in Fascist Italy.* Madison: University of Wisconsin Press, 2012.

Chibber, Vivek. *Confronting Capitalism: How the World Works and How to Change It.* London, United Kingdom: Verso Books, 2022.

Evans, Dave, and Bill Burnett. *Designing Your Life: How to Build a Well-Lived, Joyful Life.* New York: Knopf Doubleday Publishing Group, 2016.

Galloway, Scott. *The Four: The Hidden DNA of Amazon, Apple, Facebook, and Google.* New York: Penguin Publishing Group, 2017.

Haidt, Jonathan, and Greg Lukianoff. *The Coddling of the American Mind: How Good Intentions and Bad Ideas Are Setting Up a Generation for Failure.* New York: Penguin Publishing Group, 2018.

Hon, Adrian. *You've Been Played: How Corporations, Governments, and Schools Use Games to Control Us All.* New York: Basic Books, 2022.

Isenberg, Nancy. *White Trash: The 400-Year Untold History of Class in America.* New York: Penguin Publishing Group, 2016.

Knight, Sarah. *The Life-Changing Magic of Not Giving a F*ck.* London, United Kingdom: Quercus, 2015.

Kondo, Marie. *The Life-Changing Magic of Tidying Up: The Japanese Art of Decluttering and Organizing.* Berkeley: Clarkson Potter/Ten Speed, 2014.

Manson, Mark. *The Subtle Art of Not Giving a F*ck: A Counterintuitive Approach to Living a Good Life.* New York: HarperCollins, 2016.

McKee, Robert. *Story: Style, Structure, Substance, and the Principles of Screenwriting.* London, United Kingdom: HarperCollins, 2010.

McKee, Steve. *Power Branding: Leveraging the Success of the World's Best Brands.* New York: St. Martin's Publishing Group, 2014.

Millburn, Joshua Fields, and Ryan Nicodemus. *Love People, Use Things: Because the Opposite Never Works.* New York: Celadon Books, 2021.

Nichols, Tom. *The Death of Expertise: The Campaign Against Established Knowledge and Why it Matters.* Oxford, United Kingdom: Oxford University Press, 2017.

O'Neil, Cathy. *Weapons of Math Destruction: How Big Data Increases Inequality and Threatens Democracy.* New York: Crown, 2016.

O'Rourke, Beto. *We've Got to Try: How the Fight for Voting Rights Makes Everything Else Possible.* New York: Flatiron Books, 2022.

Piketty, Thomas. *Capital in the Twenty-First Century.* Cambridge: Harvard University Press, 2017.

Primack, Brian A. *You Are What You Click: How Being Selective, Positive, and Creative Can Transform Your Social Media Experience.* San Francisco: Chronicle Books LLC, 2021.

Scheinbaum, Angeline Close. *The Dark Side of Social Media: A Consumer Psychology Perspective.* London, United Kingdom: Taylor & Francis, 2017.

Schuster, Tara. *Buy Yourself the F*cking Lilies: And Other Rituals to Fix Your Life, from Someone Who's Been There.* New York: Dial Press, 2020.

Sebestyen, Victor. *1946: The Making of the Modern World.* New York: Knopf Doubleday Publishing Group, 2016.

Sincero, Jen. *You Are a Badass: How to Stop Doubting Your Greatness and Start Living an Awesome Life.* Philadelphia: Running Press, 2013.

Notes

INTRODUCTION: RELENTLESS

xxvi   *The relentlessness is, of course, driven*: J. Horowitz, R. Igielnik, and R. Kochhar, "Most Americans Say There Is Too Much Economic Inequality in the US, But Fewer Than Half Call It a Priority," "Section 1: Trends in Income and Wealth Inequality," Pew Research Center, 2020, https://www.pewresearch.org/social-trends/2020/01/09/trends-in-income-and-wealth-inequality/.

xxvi   *The caffeinated go-go-go benefits*: R. Kochhar and S. Sechopoulos, "How the American Middle Class Has Changed in the Past Five Decades," Pew Research Center, 2022, https://www.pewresearch.org/fact-tank/2022/04/20/how-the-american-middle-class-has-changed-in-the-past-five-decades/.

xxvii   *In the United States, our levels*: Marissa Sharif, Cassie Mogilner, and Hal Hershfield, "The Effects of Being Time Poor and Time Rich on Life Satisfaction," SSRN, 2018, https://ssrn.com/abstract=3285436 or http://dx.doi.org/10.2139/ssrn.3285436.

xxvii   *We love to tout*: One could point to multiple sets of data to prove this out, but one overall "rating" or "ranking" comes from *U.S. News & World Report*, which now lists the United States of America number 21 in "Quality of Life," *U.S. News & World Report*, 2022, https://www.usnews.com/news/best-countries/rankings/quality-of-life.

xxvii   *We may have an Alexa*: C. Berger, "The Executive-Worker Pay Gap Keeps Getting Bigger as CEOs Rake In an Average $27.8 Million a Year," *Fortune*, October 7, 2022, https://fortune.com/2022/10/07/ceo-worker-pay-gap-wealth-inequality-pandemic/.

xxvii   *Our communities and our country*: It's worth looking at levels pre-pandemic and post-pandemic. In 2018, *NBC News* reported that "Major depression on the rise among everyone, new data shows" in a report (https://www.nbcnews.com/health/health-news/major-depression-rise-among-everyone-new-data-shows-n873146). That report cited Blue Cross Blue Shield data, which came "from 41 million health records and counts people who got a diagnosis of major depression." The pandemic certainly made it all worse. During the pandemic, the *New York Times* cited a CDC survey in its report, "Young Adults Report Rising Levels of Anxiety and Depression in Pandemic: A new CDC survey indicates that young people, as well as Blacks and Latinos of all ages, are showing signs of deteriorating mental health and some are resorting to substance abuse." J. Hoffman, *New York Times*, August 13, 2020, updated October 5, 2021, https://www.nytimes.com/2020/08/13/health/Covid-mental-health-anxiety.html.

xxvii *a nationwide drug epidemic*: While many press outlets reported this, I am referring to the announcement by the United States Department of Justice entitled "Justice Department Announces Global Resolution of Criminal and Civil Investigations with Opioid Manufacturer Purdue Pharma and Civil Settlement with Members of the Sackler Family," October 21, 2020, https://www.justice.gov/opa/pr/justice-department-announces-global-resolution-criminal-and-civil-investigations-opioid.

xxviii *Private life is dead*: Here I am referring to the 2022 Supreme Court decision *Dobbs v. Jackson Women's Health Organization*, that ultimately invalidated a citizen's constitutional protections for fundamental-decision privacy, https://www.supremecourt.gov/opinions/21pdf/19-1392_6j37.pdf. You can also read more about the implication of *Dobbs* on privacy at https://www.wired.com/story/scotus-dobbs-roe-privacy-abortion/.

xxviii *Our cable bill is rising*: This has been reported across the country, but this is a good resource for understanding the business practices employed by the major cable providers: https://www.washingtonpost.com/technology/2021/07/13/internet-cable-bills/.

xxviii *The price of a cocktail*: H. Wee, "Some Americans Can't Afford to Buy Homes in Their Hometown," CNBC, February 23, 2016, https://www.cnbc.com/2016/02/22/some-americans-cant-afford-to-buy-homes-in-their-hometown.html. Worth exploring too is Emily Badger's September 25, 2022, report for the *New York Times*, "Whatever Happened to the Starter Home? The Economics of the Housing Market, and the Local Rules That Shape It, Have Squeezed Out Entry-Level Homes," https://www.nytimes.com/2022/09/25/upshot/starter-home-prices.html.

xxix *There are three hundred shootings*: NBC News Chicago, "2021 Ends as Chicago's Deadliest Year in a Quarter Century," January 1, 2022, https://www.nbcchicago.com/news/local/2021-ends-as-chicagos-deadliest-year-in-a-quarter-century/2719307/.

xxix *38 million people live below*: J. Creamer, E. Shrider, K. Burns, and F. Chen, "Poverty in the United States: 2021," United States Census Bureau, September 13, 2022, https://www.census.gov/library/publications/2022/demo/p60-277.html.

ONE: A HORSE ON SPEED

3   *That is, after all*: D. Mask, *The Address Book* (New York: St. Martin's Press, 2020).

4   *Flash forward two hundred fifty years*: D. Immerwahr, *How to Hide an Empire: A History of the Greater United States* (New York: Macmillan, 2019).

8   *What we tend to gloss over*: While many authors make this argument, perhaps one of the most comprehensive explorations comes from M. Stoller, *Goliath: The 100-Year War Between Monopoly Power and Democracy* (New York: Simon & Schuster, 2020).

8   *Less than a week after*: You can read a full transcript of that speech online at: https://transcripts.cnn.com/show/se/date/2001-09-16/segment/03.

9   *Three weeks later, President George W. Bush*: You can read a full transcript of that speech online in the White House archives at: https://georgewbush -whitehouse.archives.gov/news/releases/2001/10/20011011-7.html.

10 *In fact, economists now pin*: S. Lohr, "Economists Pin More Blame on Tech for Rising Inequality," *New York Times*, January 11, 2022, updated January 20, 2022, https://www.nytimes.com/2022/01/11/technology /income-inequality-technology.html.

12 *In May of that year*: Patrick Kelley, associate administrator, Office of Capital Access, testified at a Senate Small Business Committee hearing on August 2, 2022. Video and searchable transcript of his testimony: https:// www.c-span.org/video/?522119-1/covid-19-economic-injury-disaster -loans.

12 *And on the other side*: J. Lee and L. Jacobson, "Why Americans Are Drowning in Debt," CNBC Report, August 27, 2022, https://www.cnbc.com /video/2022/08/27/why-americans-are-drowning-in-debt.html.

15 *A man named Sylvan Goldman*: S. Meacham, "Oklahoma City Inventor of Shopping Cart a Symbol of Local Innovation," *Oklahoman*, January 17, 2018, https://www.oklahoman.com/story/news/2018/01/17 /oklahoma-city-inventor-of-shopping-cart-a-symbol-of-local-innova tion/60549084007/.

18 *The ladder we are all meant*: The numbers in this paragraph all represent the wealth of the wealthiest individual for the year listed, as listed and cited individually on Wikipedia.

18 *Manigault was only £33,000 richer*: While there are multiple sources for Mr. Manigault's wealth, I am referring to his entry in the *South Carolina Encyclopedia*, which states: "According to his 1774 probate inventory, Manigault left an estate valued at £32,737.8 sterling." That encyclopedia

cites multiple sources. See: https://www.scencyclopedia.org/sce/entries
/manigault-peter/.

20 *When the more progressive*: This refers to Andrew Yang's term, discussed as
"human capitalism" or "human-centered capitalism" in A. Yang, *The War
on Normal People: The Truth About America's Disappearing Jobs and Why
Universal Basic Income Is Our Future* (New York: Hachette Books, 2019).

20 *We can lie to ourselves*: This statistic comes from S. Mamedova and E. Paw-
lowski, "A Description of US Adults Who Are Not Digitally Literate,"
a May 2018 report from the US Department of Education, "Figure 1:
Digital Literacy Rates. Percentage Distribution of Digital Literacy Status
Among US Adults Ages 16–65: 2012," US Department of Education,
National Center for Education Statistics, Organization for Economic
Cooperation and Development (OECD), Program for the International
Assessment of Adult Competencies (PIAAC), 2012, https://nces.ed.gov
/pubs2018/2018161.pdf.

22 *Wells Fargo now services*: While there are multiple sources of these customer numbers available online, my numbers come from https://www
.statista.com.

22 *In many industries, only*: While there are multiple sources that illustrate
market share in each industry, a good overall source for understanding
the consolidation of industrial giants is the White House, "Fact Sheet:
Executive Order on Promoting Competition in the American Economy,"
July 9, 2021, https://www.whitehouse.gov/briefing-room/statements
-releases/2021/07/09/fact-sheet-executive-order-on-promoting-competi
tion-in-the-american-economy/.

TWO: THE INFINITE LOOP

26 *As the story goes*: The story of the founding of Netflix has been told many
times in multiple forums, but I first read it from J. Scipioni, " 'Anyone'
Could Have Built Netflix, According to Its Co-founder," CNBC, September 18, 2019, https://www.cnbc.com/2019/09/18/co-founder-marc
-randolph-anyone-could-do-start-up-like-netflix.html.

27 *The average US consumer*: Yahoo Finance, "Average US Consumer Now Has
5 Retail Subscriptions," November 26, 2021, https://finance.yahoo.com
/news/average-us-consumer-now-5-090001666.html. Additional numbers
in this paragraph come from S. O'Brien, "Consumers Spend an Average
$133 More Each Month on Subscriptions Than They Realize, Study Shows,"
CNBC Report, June 2022, https://www.cnbc.com/2022/06/02/consumers
-spend-133-more-monthly-on-subscriptions-than-they-realize.html.

30   *The subscription model emerged*: T. Tzuo and G. Weisert, *Subscribed: Why the Subscription Model Will Be Your Company's Future—and What to Do About It* (New York: Portfolio, 2018).

30   *and* The Forever Transaction: R. Baxter, *The Forever Transaction: How to Build a Subscription Model So Compelling, Your Customers Will Never Want to Leave* (New York: McGraw Hill, 2020).

THREE: ONE BIG COLLABORATION

41   *As of this writing*: L. Ceci, "Number of Apps Available in Leading App Stores Q3 2022," Statista, November 8, 2022, https://www.statista.com /statistics/276623/number-of-apps-available-in-leading-app-stores/. Additional numbers in this paragraph come from two reports that cite their own references: https://www.zippia.com/advice/mobile-app-indus try-statistics/ and https://buildfire.com/app-statistics/.

45   *In her book*: S. Zuboff, *The Age of Surveillance Capitalism: The Fight for a Human Future at the New Frontier of Power* (New York: PublicAffair, 2019).

48   *We learned even before the circus*: A. Sherter, "Nearly 40% of Americans Can't Cover a Surprise $400 Expense," CBS News, May 2019. This is based on this Federal Reserve report: https://www.federalreserve.gov/pub lications/files/2018-report-economic-well-being-us-households-201905 .pdf.

49   *Instead, they got bonuses*: While this was widely reported, here is one source that reported the earnings of the CEO of Lehman Brothers: B. Ross and A. Gomstyn, "Lehman Brothers Boss Defends $484 Million in Salary, Bonus: Fuld Becomes Poster Boy for Wall Street Greed at Heated Con gressional Hearing," ABC News, October 6, 2008, https://abcnews.go .com/Blotter/story?id=5965360&page=1. Bonuses to CEOs continued during the pandemic, even as workers were laid off. See A. Campbell, "CEOs Got Bonuses While Workers Struggled During the Pandemic," Center for Public Integrity, August 20, 2021, https://publicintegrity.org /inside-publici/newsletters/watchdog-newsletter/ceo-pay-workers-strug gled-pandemic/.

49   *In turn, the banks*: S. Cowley, "Despite Billions in Fees, Banks Predict Meager Profits on P.P.P. Loans," *New York Times*, October 1, 2020, https:// www.nytimes.com/2020/10/01/business/ppp-loans-bank-profits.html.

49   *The top four—JPMorgan Chase*: This calculation comes from a Sep tember 8, 2022, Bankrate report by Matthew Goldberg, https://www .bankrate.com/banking/biggest-banks-in-america/.

49 *According to the FDIC*: H. Johnson, "The National Average Savings Interest Rate Is Near Zero: Here's How You Can Earn Much More," *Time*, July 5, 2022, https://time.com/nextadvisor/banking/savings/average-interest-rate-savings-accounts/.

50 *In 1990, it was closer*: F. Coppola, Report for American Express, February 1, 2022, https://www.americanexpress.com/en-us/credit-cards/credit-intel/average-savings-account-interest/. Article sources are cited.

50 *JPMorgan Chase made*: This number comes directly from the "net income" reported on the company's "2021 Annual Report," https://www.jpmorganchase.com/content/dam/jpmc/jpmorgan-chase-and-co/investor-relations/documents/annualreport-2021.pdf. Bloomberg reported its CEO's salary here: https://www.bloomberg.com/news/articles/2022-01-20/jpmorgan-raises-ceo-dimon-s-pay-10-to-34-5-million-for-2021.

50 *Consumers paid $11 billion*: M. Walsh, "Banks Took $11 Billion in Overdraft Fees in 2019," *New York Times*, June 3, 2020, https://www.nytimes.com/2020/06/03/business/banks-overdraft-fees.html. The *Times* cited research by the Center for Responsible Lending.

50 *down from $17 billion in 2018*: These numbers have been widely reported, but here is one source: M. Leonhardt, "Cutting Overdraft Fees Could Save Americans $17 Billion a Year—But Banks Are Slow to Make Changes," *Fortune*, May 16, 2022, https://fortune.com/2022/05/16/cutting-overdraft-fees-could-save-americans-17-billion-a-year/ and at https://www.forbes.com/advisor/personal-finance/how-to-prevent-overdraft-fees/.

51 *This is commonly referred to*: This scheme, also known as the Four Corners Model, originally evolved in the 1990s. One clear and basic explanation can be found at https://www.clearhaus.com/blog/a-quick-guide-to-payments-in-e-commerce-four-party-scheme/.

53 *In her book* How to Do Nothing: J. Odell, *How to Do Nothing: Resisting the Attention Economy* (New York: Melville House Books, 2019).

55 *Frances Haugen*: You can read the full testimony to the United States Senate Committee on Commerce, Science and Transportation here: https://www.commerce.senate.gov/services/files/FC8A558E-824E-4914-BEDB-3A7B1190BD49.

56 *In their book* Chokepoint Capitalism: C. Doctorow and R. Giblin, *Chokepoint Capitalism: How Big Tech and Big Content Captured Creative Labor Markets and How We'll Win Them Back* (New York: Beacon Press, 2022).

57 *The Big Brands now*: E. Klein, *Why We're Polarized* (New York: Avid Reader Press, 2020).

59 *In one of my all-time favorite books*: J. Sachs, *Winning the Story Wars: Why*

Those Who Tell—and Live—the Best Stories Will Rule the Future (Cambridge, MA: Harvard Business Review Press, 2012).

FOUR: THE HEART OF IT ALL

62 *But let's remember that*: Numbers on American stockholding come from R. Frank, "The Wealthiest 10% of Americans Own a Record 89% of All US Stocks," CNBC Report, October 18, 2021. For a fuller picture of our country's gross inequality, visit www.inequality.org. Inequality.org is a project of the Institute for Policy Studies.

67 *In his brilliant, pocket-sized*: H. Frankfurt, *On Bullshit* (Princeton, NJ: Princeton University Press, 2005).

69 *There is a reason*: You can find the announcement online at https://www.merriam-webster.com/words-at-play/word-of-the-year.

FIVE: THE PEOPLE PROBLEM

77 *In his book* Four Thousand Weeks: O. Burkeman, *Four Thousand Weeks: Time Management for Mortals* (New York: Farrar, Straus and Giroux, 2021).

80 *During the 2016 Democratic primary*: Links to the white paper on Secretary Buttigieg's website have changed since his campaign, but an online copy of the white paper can be found at https://img1.wsimg.com/blobby/go/cbd42df5-83a8-43c3-a3f8-bc695c99bac5/downloads/Pete%20Buttigieg%20MH-SA%20Plan.pdf?ver=1568040281093.

81 *In 2017, the former US Surgeon General*: V. Murthy, "Work and the Loneliness Epidemic: Reducing Isolation at Work Is Good for Business," *Harvard Business Review*, September 26, 2017, https://hbr.org/2017/09/work-and-the-loneliness-epidemic.

85 *In his book* Civilized to Death: C. Ryan, *Civilized to Death: The Price of Progress* (New York: Avid Reader Press, 2020).

86 *In 2022, Timothy Snyder*: https://podcasts.apple.com/au/podcast/timothy-snyder-on-the-myths-that-blinded-the-west/id1548604447?i=100055
4066715.

87 *Author James Clear*: J. Clear, *Atomic Habits: An Easy & Proven Way to Build Good Habits & Break Bad Ones* (New York: Avery, 2018).

90 *According to psychologist Abraham Maslow's hierarchy*: The original paper was published by Maslow in 1943. Abraham H. Maslow, "A Theory of Human Motivation," *Psychological Review* 50, no. 4 (July 1943).

About the Author

JULIO VINCENT GAMBUTO is the author of the viral essay "Prepare for the Ultimate Gaslighting," which started a worldwide conversation, reaching more than twenty-one million readers in ninety-eight countries. A moviemaker who has written, directed, and produced film and television content for the *New Yorker*, Nickelodeon, PBS, E! Entertainment, and Samuel Goldwyn Films, Julio graduated from Harvard University and earned his MFA from the USC School of Cinematic Arts, where he was an Annenberg Fellow. He lives in New York City with his fiancé. Learn more at www.juliovincent.com.

It finally got quiet.

Please Unsubscribe, Thanks!

Julio Vincent Gambuto

This reading group guide for Please Unsubscribe, Thanks! *includes an introduction, discussion questions, and ideas for enhancing your book club. The suggested questions are intended to help your reading group find new and interesting angles and topics for your discussion. We hope that these ideas will enrich your conversation and increase your enjoyment of the book.*

Introduction

When the pandemic brought the world to a standstill, author Julio Vincent Gambuto realized a powerful truth: in the pre-pandemic world, Americans were exhausted, lonely, unhappy, wildly over-worked and overbooked, drowning in sea of constantly being on the go and needing to buy more, more, more. But when that pressure disappeared, people rediscovered what was important to them—and for perhaps the first time in a long time, they were being honest. Honest about what they wanted, what they believed in. Honest about the problems they were facing within their families, friend groups, workplaces, towns, and society overall. That honesty, he noticed, had the potential to make the ground shift. Now, in *Please Unsubscribe, Thanks!*, Gambuto gives us a radical blueprint for the ways we can take a deep breath, renew and commit to a life that we really want, individually and collectively, from unsubscribing to emails and automated subscriptions to reevaluating the presence of people and ideas and habits that no longer serve us or make us happy.

Topics & Questions for Discussion

1. *Please Unsubscribe, Thanks!* begins in 2020, when the world was brought to a standstill due to the coronavirus pandemic, a period during which many people were forced to sit still, reevaluate, and rebuild.

   What was your experience during those months? Immediately after? Did you step back from certain aspects of your life, or question your habits or outlooks? Did you feel stress? Did you feel relief? What did you learn about yourself? What did you feel you wanted to change in your life and/or in that of your family?

2. In this book, Gambuto takes us through the process of "unsubscribing" from the various commitments, relationships, and ideas that keep us and our lives on autopilot and that block us from sources of true satisfaction—but acknowledges that it's not easy. In fact, it may take a while, or be a practice that you have to return to from time to time.

   What makes you nervous about unsubscription? What anxieties or fears does the idea provoke? What doubts do you have? How easy or difficult do you think it would be to do this? Are there certain ideas that are easier and more doable for you?

3. The idea of modern life being "relentless" appears frequently throughout *Please Unsubscribe, Thanks!* and becomes one of the main reasons why Gambuto feels compelled to make a change in his life.

   What in your life feels relentless? It can be as simple as the number of email newsletters in your inbox, or the amount you are expected to travel for work, or the numerous daily demands of having a family.

4. Gambuto was inspired to write his *Medium* piece, "Prepare for the Ultimate Gaslighting" after sensing an emerging narrative of "going back to normal"—but, he thought, what is "normal"? What is "normal" to you? Think about (and list, if you'd like) what you consider to be the "normal" responsibilities you have and/or expectations to which you are held. What does "normal" life feels and looks like to you?

   Now, consider that list. Which responsibilities or expectations did you create? Which ones were put upon you? By whom? Which are carried out with joy? Which out of obligation? How do these different categories make you feel, and how do you approach them? If you could get rid of any of the expectations or responsibilities you have on those lists, which would they be?

5. In the opening chapter of the book, Gambuto explains that the American idea of "the pursuit of happiness" is central to our modern struggles with finding balance and getting ourselves off autopilot, because our idea of "happiness" changes as we participate more and more in capitalism and consumerism.

Think about what your idea of "happiness" was at different stages of your life, and what it is now. Has it changed? Have different or new factors been introduced? And what larger forces may have influenced that vision? Where do you get your ideas about what constitutes happiness?

6. Another big theme in *Please Unsubscribe, Thanks!* is our relationship with technology, and how individual interactions add up to influence balances of power. We live in an age, the author says, of "click-up economics," a process in which our spending is accelerated and our needs are immediately met, but at the cost of putting disproportionate power in the hands of those governing those systems.

Consider your relationship with technology—what it might offer you and how it might improve your life. Then, consider what power and information you may be giving away through those interactions. Do you agree that there is a larger issue at play, or that it is just the price of living in a modern information age?

7. "The Big Forces"—Big Tech, Big Banks, Big Brands, Big Media, and the Big Parties, which interacts with all of them—are the entities we fight against when we decide to unsubscribe. They rely on our automated behaviors and subscriptions to survive and grow, ultimately keeping us in loops that don't serve us, or make us happy.

Which big force, in your opinion, is the most problematic, or holds the most outsized influence, in today's world? What are some ways that we can take power back?

8. How we define and sustain relationships, Gambuto argues in this book, has also been impacted by the language and outlooks

of the Big Forces. Dating and marriage is an "investment"; people online are "brands" that we follow; colleagues become "work spouses" who know personal details of our home lives. These blurred lines and misapplied definitions have turned human bonding into its own kind of subscription, with terms and conditions of commitment—and it usually means we are spending time and energy on the wrong people.

Turn to page 132 in your book, where there is a diagram of "The Dartboard." Organize your various interpersonal relationships by the categories it outlines, as they exist now, and organize the rings to reflect their level of importance and influence in your life. Then, create a second dartboard, with the ideal distribution and categorization of those same relationships. What are the similarities between the two? The differences?

9. Our subscriptions within a work environment is a huge part of *Please Unsubscribe, Thanks!*—and certainly, all of our daily lives. Work is likely the most difficult space to unsubscribe in, because (unless we are a manager or boss or business owner) we don't always have power as an individual, and work is a financial necessity for many.

What options laid out by Gambuto in the work chapter felt helpful and realistic? What are ways that you can adjust your relationship to your job (if that is something you would like to do without going to extremes? And at what point do you think an extreme might be necessary?

10. Gambuto argues that ideas, notions, personal philosophies, and beliefs are also all subscriptions, and they, perhaps more than anything else, shape our experience as we move through the world. In chapter twelve, Gambuto introduces the "sticky

story," a narrative that stays with you and becomes a central part of your outlook, and the author encourages a repositioning of those stories to understand which might be helpful and which might be harmful.

What is your stickiest story? How has it motivated you, helped you, formed you—or maybe held you back? And what subtle or significant changes can you make to that narrative to make sure it's serving you well?

11. "The Dark Well" is the period after the unsubscribe, a time of transition and realignment when everything settles in. Whether or not you have embarked upon your unsubscription process yet, or reached the Dark Well, what seems to you like it would be the hardest thing to lose and/or sit without? What could you replace it with? How might you best cope with not having it?

12. There is great opportunity for individual renewal in "The Great Unsubscribe," but Gambuto explains that, if everyone came together in that experience, we could create collective change as well. What do you think we are most in need of as a family, school, work, local, national, global community, and how do you think unsubscribing could help?

13. If you have gone through a process of unsubscription: How do you feel now? What were the hardest parts, and what surprised you as being perhaps a little bit easier to let go of? If you haven't embarked on the journey quite yet, what are you hoping to accomplish?

Enhance Your Book Club

1. In the spirit of *Please Unsubscribe, Thanks!* commit to being fully present during your book club meeting and discussion. Put everyone's phones in a bowl or in a stack on a table on the other side of the room (ringers can be on, if someone needs to be reachable), and don't touch them until everyone is ready to go home.

2. Have an "unsubscribe" portion of your gathering. Before everyone leaves, retrieve your phones or devices and, together, unsubscribe from any email distribution lists or social media accounts that no longer serve you—and celebrate that first step!

3. Use your book club as an accountability group. After you read and discuss *Please Unsubscribe, Thanks!,* continue to discuss the impact of unsubscribing or reprioritizing your commitments, and share with your fellow members how these decisions have impacted your life. Inspire one another to do more, and support one another if things get difficult.